U.S. Naval History Sources in the United States

U.S. Naval History Sources in the United States

Compiled and Edited by
Dean C. Allard
Martha L. Crawley
Mary W. Edmison

GOVERNMENT REPRINTS PRESS
Washington, D.C.

© Ross & Perry, Inc. 2001 All rights reserved.

No claim to U.S. government work contained throughout this book.

Protected under the Berne Convention. Published 2001

Printed in The United States of America
Ross & Perry, Inc. Publishers
717 Second St., N.E., Suite 200
Washington, D.C. 20002
Telephone (202) 675-8300
Facsimile (202) 675-8400
info@RossPerry.com

SAN 253-8555

Government Reprints Press Edition 2001

Government Reprints Press is an Imprint of Ross & Perry, Inc.

Previously printed as "U.S. Naval History Sources in the United States" by the Naval History Division, Department of Navy.

Library of Congress Control Number: 2001094682

http://www.GPOreprints.com

ISBN 1-931641-99-4

⊚ The paper used in this publication meets the requirements for permanence established by the American National Standard for Information Sciences "Permanence of Paper for Printed Library Materials" (ANSI Z39.48-1984).

All rights reserved. No copyrighted part of this publication may be reproduced, stored in a retrieval system, or transmitted, in any form or by any means, electronic, photocopying, recording, or otherwise, without the prior written permission of the publisher.

Contents

	Page
INTRODUCTION BY DIRECTOR OF NAVAL HISTORY	v
EDITORIAL NOTE	vii
REPOSITORIES BY STATES	
Alabama	1
California	2
Colorado	12
Connecticut	13
Delaware	19
District of Columbia	22
Florida	69
Georgia	72
Hawaii	75
Illinois	76
Indiana	80
Iowa	82
Kansas	83
Louisiana	85
Maine	87
Maryland	89
Massachusetts	101
Michigan	113
Minnesota	117
Mississippi	119
Missouri	120
Nebraska	122
New Hampshire	123
New Jersey	125
New York	130
North Carolina	147
Ohio	158

	Page
Oklahoma	163
Oregon	164
Pennsylvania	165
Rhode Island	178
South Carolina	183
Tennessee	185
Texas	187
Utah	190
Vermont	190
Virginia	191
Washington	198
West Virginia	201
Wisconsin	202
Wyoming	205
INDEX	207

Introduction

This publication seeks to aid students of naval history by identifying manuscript, archival, and other special collections deposited in more than 250 American archives and libraries. Most of these materials are the private papers of officers, men, and civilian officials of the U.S. Navy. In addition, listings are included for the personal paper collections of the chairmen of Congressional naval committees and other individuals with a significant interest in naval affairs, the records of a number of business firms that acted as naval contractors, and official records of the U.S. Navy. When information was available for private and official documents relating to other uniformed maritime services of the United States, or foreign navies closely associated with our nation's history, entries for these documents also were included.

The starting point for the present compilation was *U.S. Naval History Sources in the Washington Area and Suggested Research Subjects*, a 1970 publication of the Naval History Division. In updating that work's coverage and expanding its scope to include repositories throughout the United States, the editors consulted accession notes appearing in scholarly journals, individual manuscript catalogs, and such overall references as the *National Union Catalog of Manuscript Collections* (Library of Congress and other publishers, 1959–   ); *Directory of Archives and Manuscript Repositories in the United States* (National Historical Publications and Records Commission, 1978); Philip M. Hamer, ed., *A Guide to Archives and Manuscripts in the United States* (Yale University Press, 1961); and William Matthews, *American Diaries in Manuscript, 1580–1954: A Descriptive Bibliography* (University of Georgia Press, 1974). The information obtained from these sources then was forwarded to the appropriate repository with the request that the data be reviewed for accuracy and completeness. We greatly appreciate the generous responses received from these organizations.

In addition to the repository staffs, the Naval History Division is indebted to a number of other individuals who contributed to the preparation of this Guide. Vice Admiral Walter S. DeLany, USN (Ret.), President of the Naval Historical Foundation, and his staff; Mr. Richard A. Baker and the staff of the Senate Historical Office; Professor K. Jack Bauer of the Rensselaer Polytechnic Institute; Mr. Al Christman of the Naval Weapons Center, China Lake, California; and the staff of the National Union Catalog of Manuscripts in the Library of Congress provided valuable references to several general categories of sources. Within the Navy's historical office, Miss Barbara Lynch and Mr. John Vajda of the Navy Department Library, Ms. Nina F. Statum and Mr. Edward J. Marolda of the Operational Archives, and Mrs. Agnes F. Hoover of the Curator Branch, offered excellent advice and assistance. The index was prepared by Ms. Mary Palmer of Arlington, Virginia.

Although every effort has been devoted to making the compilation as complete and accurate as possible, it is inevitable that omissions and errors will appear in a work of this scope. Reports of such discrepancies will be appreciated so that they can be included in future editions.

It is evident from this Guide that the sources of naval history are extremely rich. They also are widely distributed throughout the United States. The editors and I hope that this publication will encourage and facilitate research in the many dimensions of U.S. naval history that deserve further study.

April 1979

JOHN D. H. KANE, JR.
Rear Admiral, USN (Ret.)
Director of Naval History

Editorial Note

Individual entries in this publication include the title of a collection or group and, whenever possible, an indication of the dates and volume of the material. Some personal diaries, ship logs, and other individual manuscripts have been identified; but, when collections of these items are very extensive, or if specific references are not available, only general descriptions are provided. Citations also are provided for published guides providing more detailed descriptive data on individual collections. Scholars intending to use these documents are urged to consult such catalogs and to correspond directly with the appropriate repository concerning hours of operation, services available, and possible access restrictions.

All officers and men listed in this volume are members of the Regular Navy unless otherwise indicated by such designations as USNR (U.S. Naval Reserve), USNRF (U.S. Naval Reserve Force), CSN (Confederate States Navy), USMC (U.S. Marine Corps), USCG (U.S. Coast Guard), or RN (Royal Navy). Most ships are commissioned U.S. naval vessels (USS) but in some instances reference is made to Confederate (CSS), Coast Guard (USCG), or British (HMS) units.

Rear Admiral Alfred Thayer Mahan, naval officer and historian of the influence of seapower

ALABAMA

	Dates	Volume
Alabama Department of Archives and History 624 Washington Avenue Montgomery, AL 36130		
Senator Charles Tait, Chairman of the Senate Naval Affairs Committee, 1814–18	1768–1874	1,000 items
Auburn University Archives Auburn, AL 36830		
General Franklin A. Hart, USMC	1916–54	1,500 items
General Holland M. Smith, USMC	1904–67	432 items
Brigadier General Joseph Lester Stewart, USMC	1938–65	3,000 items
Mobile Public Library Mobile, AL 36602		
Hunley Collection (relates to the Confederate submarine *Hunley*; includes material on later vessels named for *Hunley*)	1861–1969	900 items

CALIFORNIA

	Dates	Volume
California Historical Society 2090 Jackson Street San Francisco, CA 94109		
Senator George C. Perkins, Chairman of the Senate Committee on Naval Affairs, 1909–13	1878–1920	2 ft.
Rear Admiral John D. Sloat		
Federal Archives and Records Center **Archives Branch** 24000 Avila Road Laguna Niguel, CA 92677		
United States Coast Guard Unit Logs (RG 26)	1970–75	ca. 4 ft.
Federal Archives and Records Center **Archives Branch** 1000 Commodore Drive San Bruno, CA 94066		
Records of the Government of American Samoa	1900–66	163 ft.
Records of the Office of the Territories, Government of Guam	1946–76	1 ft.
Henry E. Huntington Library San Marino, CA 91108		
Lieutenant William Henry Allen	1800–38	92 items
Albert Douglas Beach, Darien Exploring Expedition	1870–71	1 vol.
Sir Francis Beaufort, RN	1765–1953	2,143 items

California

	Dates	Volume
Lieutenant James L. Blair	1845–79	165 items
Lawrence F. Bower, collector (includes naval documents of the War of 1812 and the Civil War)	1802–1904	63 items
Admiral Charles Rene Dominique Gochet Destouches, French Navy	1754–1804	117 items
Thomas Haines Dudley (includes documents on blockade running in the Civil War)	1843–1959	4,717 items
Robert Saunders Dundas, First Lord of the Admiralty	1812–14	42 items
William Eaton, naval agent	1792–1829	555 items
Admiral David Glasgow Farragut	1863–80	102 items
Gustavus Vasa Fox, Assistant Secretary of the Navy, 1861–66	1861–82	109 items
James Edward Glazier (includes material on hospital ships)	1861–1922	174 items
Admiral Earl Richard Howe, RN	1776–99	408 items
Charles Thomas Harbeck, collector (includes material relating to the U.S. Navy)	1732–1915	539 items
Admiral Earl Richard Howe, RN	1776–99	408 items
Rear Admiral Thornton Alexander Jenkins	1846–92	59 items
Commander Matthew Fontaine Maury, Union and Confederate naval officer (in Maury Family Collection)	1755–1900	165 items
Admiral Horatio Nelson, RN	1777–1805	280 items
Captain John B. Nicolson	1819–38	4 items, incl. 1 vol.
USS *Olympia*	1895–99	275 items
John Henry Hobart Peshine (U.S. naval and Army officer, Military Attache at Madrid)	1849–1903	800 items
Sir George Pocock, RN	1733–93	1,170 items
Rear Admiral Charles Henry Poor	1855–70	4 items, incl. 2 vols.
Admiral David Dixon Porter	1861–66	750 items
Purser Rodman McCauley Price	1842–90	256 items
Admiral Cloudisley Shovell, RN (in the Shovell-Rooke Papers)	1690–1705	85 items
Spence-Lowell Collection (includes material relating to Purser Keith Spence, the U.S. Navy, and the Tripolitan War)	1740–1958	321 items
Captain Thomas Truxtun	1795–1817	13 items
U.S. Naval Office, San Francisco	1851–58	1 vol.

U.S. Naval History Sources

	Dates	Volume
U.S. Navy, Official Correspondence	1853–84	1 vol.
Gideon Welles, Secretary of the Navy, 1861–69	1846–1902	600 items
Commander Selim Edwin Woodworth, USNR	1834–1947	1,600 items

Guide: *Guide to American Historical Manuscripts in the Huntington Library.* San Marino, Calif.: Huntington Library Publications, 1979.

**Hoover Institution
on War, Revolution, and Peace
Stanford, CA 94305**

	Dates	Volume
Captain Lester Armour, USNR	1942–43	1 box
Bailey-Ryan Collection (restricted collection; research materials of historians Thomas A. Bailey and Captain Paul B. Ryan, USN (Ret.), in preparation of their book *The Lusitania Disaster*)	1973–75	11 boxes
Vice Admiral Wilder D. Baker	1914–75	4½ boxes, 10 items

Three outstanding leaders of World War II—Admirals Nimitz, King, and Spruance—on board cruiser Indianapolis *at Saipan, July 1944*

California

	Dates	*Volume*
Rear Admiral Robert W. Berry	1906–69	3½ boxes
Vice Admiral Thomas H. Binford	1940–67	½ box
Louis H. Bolander, naval bibliographer	1928–29	1 box
Commander Lloyd M. Bucher	1970–75	68 boxes, 1 item
Vice Admiral Elliott Buckmaster	1947–48	55 photographs
Lieutenant General John R. Chaisson, USMC	1940–75	17 boxes
Captain Church A. Chappel	1925–53	1 box
Admiral Charles M. Cooke, Jr.	1920–64	35 boxes, 2 envelopes
Rear Admiral Benton C. Decker	1914–21	1 box
Rear Admiral Dwight Dickinson, Jr.	1918, 1928–29	½ box
Vice Admiral Clarence E. Ekstrom	1943–62	1 box, 36 envelopes, 12 items
Brigadier General Edward H. Forney, USMC	1950–64	2 ft., 2 vols.
Rear Admiral Wayne Neal Gamet	1918–20, 1939–40	1 folder
Vice Admiral Hugh H. Goodwin	n.d.	1 folder
Vice Admiral Elton W. Grenfell	1926–69	11½ boxes, 5 binders
Rear Admiral Harry A. Guthrie	n.d.	1 folder
Emmett A. Hoskins (account of naval service)	1917–19	1 folder
Vice Admiral Ralph E. Jennings	1918–66	5 boxes, 9 envelopes, 4 items
Admiral Charles T. Joy	1951–52	3 vols., ½ box
Captain Tracy B. Kittredge, USNR	1910–57	51 boxes
Lieutenant General Victor H. Krulak, USMC	1958–77	1 box
Captain Joseph U. Lademan, Jr.	1942–69	½ box
Admiral Charles A. Lockwood, Jr.	1924–63	1 box
Vice Admiral Victor D. Long	1925–59	1 envelope
Commander Harold F. Lynn	1943–45	1 box, 5 items
Vice Admiral Milton E. Miles	1923–58	9 boxes
Admiral Ben Moreell (oral history)		1 item
Robert W. Moreno (collection of photographs showing Pacific operations)	ca. 1942–45	180 items
Rear Admiral Arthur G. Robinson	1913–68	½ box

U.S. Naval History Sources

	Dates	Volume
Quartermaster 1st Class Maurice G. Rosenwald	1917–19	1 vol.
General Harry Schmidt, USMC	1909–64	3 boxes
General David M. Shoup, USMC	1927–71	20 ft.
Admiral Raymond A. Spruance	1937–63	1 box
Captain Edward J. Steichen, USNR	1942–45	72 items
Admiral Harry C. Stevenson	1939–45	1 envelope, 7 items

Commodore Dudley W. Knox, naval officer, historian, and Director of the Office of Naval Records and Library, 1921–1946

	Dates	Volume
Robert B. Stinnett, naval photographer	1944–45	515 photographs
Gilchrist B. Stockton (includes material on the establishment of the Jacksonville Naval Air Base)	1911–59	11 boxes
Ellery C. Stowell (includes material on Declaration of London, 1909)	1909–11	1 box
Commander Richard A. Stratton (restricted collection)	1967–73	14 boxes
Admiral Lewis L. Strauss (includes oral history interview)	1918, 1945, n.d.	1 box
Rear Admiral Paul H. Talbot (photocopy of diary)	ca. 1941–42	1 box
Rear Admiral Robert A. Theobald	1908–59	12 boxes
U.S. Navy Headquarters, Commander in Chief, U.S. Pacific Fleet and Pacific Ocean Areas (Advance Headquarters, Guam)	1945	226 items
U.S. Navy, Office of Naval Intelligence (history of Solomon Islands Campaign 1942–43)	1943–44	½ box
U.S. Navy, Office of the Chief of Naval Operations (Cross Cultural Survey Staff at Yale University)	ca. 1942	2 file cabinets
U.S. Navy Training Division (includes World War II training posters)	ca. 1942–45	770 items
Rear Admiral Clifford E. Van Hook	1909–47	1 box
Admiral Alexander H. Van Keuren	1903–46	8 boxes
R. E. Vining (naval photographs)	ca. 1942–45	
Vice Admiral Charles E. Weakley	1945–72	4 boxes
Rear Admiral Charles J. Whiting	1925–69	9 boxes, 1 item

Other naval documents are filed under various U.S. Navy headings.

Naval Facilities Engineering Command Archives
U.S. Naval Construction Battalion Center
Port Hueneme, CA 93041

Admiral Ben Moreell	1874–1969	3,500 items
U.S. Naval Construction Force (Seabee) Records	1942–77	
U.S. Navy Civil Engineer Corps Records	1942–77	
U.S. Naval Facilities Engineering Command Records (formerly Bureau of Yards and Docks)	1942–77	

U.S. Naval History Sources

	Dates	Volume

Naval Ocean Systems Center
San Diego, CA 92152

This organization was created through the 1977 merger of the Naval Undersea Center and the Naval Electronics Laboratory Center. Its Public Affairs office has extensive documentation on technical history, while administrative aspects appear in command histories. Files are available of the Center's newspaper, which is indexed.

Naval Postgraduate School
Dudley Knox Library
Monterey, CA 93940

	Dates	Volume
Captain Christopher A. Buckley Collection (manuscript and photographic materials)	ca. 1890–1920	ca. 400 items

Naval Training Center
Historical Museum
San Diego, CA 92133

	Dates	Volume
Captain Edward Simpson ("forwarding book" kept during cruise of USS *Omaha*)	1877	1 vol.

Naval Weapons Center
Technical Library
China Lake, CA 93555

The Naval Ordnance Test Station established in 1943 at China Lake was designated a Center in 1967. Later it absorbed the Naval Ordnance Laboratory, Corona, California. A collection of Archival and Reference Documents grew out of research for the two published volumes of the Center's history, 1943–48. Included are copies of early correspondence, historical summaries, biographical data, clippings, photographs, project summaries, chronologies, and informal project histories.

Also available is an extensive collection of transcribed taped interviews, which includes interviews with people who played key roles in the establishment and operation of the Center. In addition to the NWC interviews there is a collection of interviews about Rear Admiral W. S. Parsons and his role in research and development. Unpublished manuscript histories include "Salt Wells Pilot Plant Story, 1945–1954," by K. H. Robinson, July 1954; "Technical History of the U.S. Naval Ordnance Test Station, 1943–1953," December 1975; and "Anthology of World War II Unpublished Manuscript Histories," a compilation of unpublished writings on the early years of the Naval Ordnance Test Station from June 1943 through 1945.

Navy Personnel Research and Development Center
San Diego, CA 92152

This Center was created in 1973 through the merger of two personnel research laboratories established in the early 1950s. Two looseleaf binders entitled, "Historical Background Data for Personnel R & D Laboratory, San Diego, Calif., and Personnel R & D Laboratory, Washington, D.C.," and "History of NPRDC and Predecessor Laboratories for Use in the History of Navy Laboratories" contain select historical records dating from 1956 to 1972. Included are memoranda regarding organizational and mission changes, the philosophy of personnel research, and administrative problems.

Oakland Public Library
125 14th Street
Oakland, CA 94612

	Dates	Volume
U.S. Coast Guard Cutter *Bear*	1889–1932	15 ft.

Stanford University Libraries
Stanford, CA 94305

	Dates	Volume
American Explorers and Adventurers (includes material relating to Surgeon Elisha Kent Kane and John Paul Jones)	1785–1855	125 items
Harwood Family (includes papers relating to Rear Admiral Andrew Allen Harwood)	1767–1969	555 items
Curtis Dwight Wilbur, Secretary of the Navy, 1924–29	1924–30	ca. 350 items

Guide: Stanford University Library, Division of Special Collections, Manuscripts Department. *Cataloged Manuscripts.* Stanford, Cal.: The Library, 1970.

University of California, Berkeley
Bancroft Library
Berkeley, CA 94720

	Dates	Volume
Rear Admiral Theodorus Bailey	1846–48	1 vol.
Lieutenant Edward F. Beale	ca. 1888	1 item

	Dates	Volume
Midshipman John Cramer (journal of a voyage on board USS *Franklin*)	1821–22	1 item
Rear Admiral George Foster Emmons (excerpts from journal maintained in USS *Ossipee*)	1867	1 item
Ensign George C. Foulk (includes material relating to duty as naval agent and Charge d'Affaires, U.S. Legation, Korea, 1877)	ca. 1876–89	460 items
William McKendree Gwin, Chairman of Senate Committee on Naval Affairs, 1851–55	1857–85	100 items
Thomas Oliver Larkin, naval agent	1822–56	36 vols., 181 folders
Captain Thomas MacDonough	1810	1 item
William H. Meyers, gunner on board USS *Cyane*	1841–44	2 vols., portfolio of 13 items
Acting Ensign William Nelson (in Batchelder-Nelson family papers)	1835–1956	2 boxes, 1 portfolio
Lieutenant William A. Parker (log book kept on board USS *Cyane*)	1842–44	1 item
Rear Admiral Charles F. Pond	1876–1929	4 cartons
Purser Rodman McCauley Price	1843–92	2 boxes
Benjamin Schreiber (journals kept on board USS *Marietta*, 1898–99, and USS *Iris*, 1914)	1898–99, 1914	2 vols.
Paymaster General James H. Watmough	1844–55	1 letterbook, 6 items
John Wilson, naval agent	1840–97	4 boxes
Medical Director William M. Wood (includes log kept while fleet surgeon of the Pacific Squadron, on board USS *Portsmouth*)	1844–45	1 vol.

Guide: Morgan, Dale L., and George P. Hammond, eds. *A Guide to the Manuscript Collections of the Bancroft Library*. Berkeley: University of California Press, 1963.

University of California, Los Angeles
Special Collections
University Research Library
Los Angeles, CA 90024

	Dates	Volume
Rear Admiral Daniel Ammen	1836–98	2 ft.
Brevet Major Archibald H. Gillespie, USMC	1845–60	900 items
Ensign Thomas C. Lancey	1846–85	4 ft.
Purser Rodman McCauley Price	1847–84	145 items

California

	Dates	*Volume*
Gideon Welles, Secretary of the Navy, 1861–69	1830–66	91 items
John B. Wirtz (journal kept on board USS *Lancaster*)	1859–62	

University of California, San Diego
The University Library
La Jolla, CA 92037

Captain Harry L. Pence	1902–45	

University of Southern California
University Library
University Park
Los Angeles, CA 90007

Admiral William Harrison Standley	1892–1958	25 ft.

Vallejo Naval and Historic Museum
Research and Accessions Division
734 Marin St.
Vallejo, CA 94590

The museum holds documents dating from 1800 concerning the Mare Island Naval Shipyard and relating to the U.S. Navy on the west coast.

COLORADO

	Dates	Volume
State Historical Society of Colorado Colorado Heritage Center 1300 Broadway Denver, CO 80203		
Paymaster Dominick B. Batione (in Benecia Batione Papers)	1860–90	
Acting Ensign Charles H. Danforth	1861–62	50 items

1864 capture of Confederate flagship Tennessee *(right) at Mobile Bay by forces under the command of Admiral Farragut*

CONNECTICUT

	Dates	Volume
Connecticut Historical Society Collections 1 Elizabeth Street Hartford, CT 06105		
Acting Paymaster Sherman W. Adams (also Secretary of the Naval Veterans Association of Connecticut)	1832–1901	1 box
American Revolution Manuscripts (includes letters, journals, logs, muster rolls, and other documents relating to naval affairs)	1765–91	1,140 items
Albert L. Butler, collector (includes several letters to Secretaries of the Navy)		55 items
Samuel Colt, naval inventor	1830–61	3,500 items
Silas Deane (includes naval material)	1740–1842	3 ft.
Gideon Welles, Secretary of the Navy, 1861–69	1820–78	1,500 items
Connecticut State Library 231 Capitol Avenue Hartford, CT 06115		
Jacob B. Gurley Collection of Naval Manuscripts	1734–82	17 items
Charles A. Hart (diary maintained on board USS *Sonoma*)	1863	1 item
Assistant Paymaster John M. Pearl, CSN	1863–65	600 items
Shipbuilding and Naval Records of the Connecticut Committee of the Pay Table	1775–84	2 ft.
Isaac Toucey, Secretary of the Navy, 1857–61	1831–70, 1831–49	97 items, 1 vol.

U.S. Naval History Sources

	Dates	Volume
Litchfield Historical Society **Litchfield, CT 06759**		
Holdings Concerning Ships (includes items for USS *Constitution*, USS *Washington*, privateers, and other ships located throughout several collections)	1772–1847	41 items
Mystic Seaport **G. W. Blunt White Library** **Mystic, CT 06355**		
Paymaster Frank H. Arms	1862–63	1 vol.
Captain James Barron	1833–43	72 items, 19 letters
Acting Master John W. Bentley (served as prize master)	1858–66	23 items
Acting Master Oliver Colburn	1842–90	34 items
Cox and Stevens Company, naval architectural firm (includes ship plans)	1941–45	
USS *John Adams*	1802–03, 1832–33	journal, 29 items
Naval logbook and journal collection		
Newman Family Papers (includes papers of Commander William D. Newman, Lieutenant William B. Newman, and Lieutenant L. Howard Newman)	1835–96	120 items
Captain Oliver H. Perry (account book maintained in USS *Revenge*)	1810	1 item
William M. C. Philbrick, naval architect	ca. 1895	35 items
Captain Charles W. Pickering (journal maintained in USS *Kearsarge*)	1862–64	1 item
Charles A. Poole (journals of cruises in USS *Kearsarge*)	1861–64	4 vols.
Rear Admiral Oscar F. Stanton	1850–1900	204 items
Captain Silas Talbot	1767–1867	3,000 items
William Wainwright (journals maintained in USS *Kearsarge*)	1861–64	3 vols.

Connecticut

	Dates	Volume

New Haven Colony Historical Society
114 Whitney Avenue
New Haven, CT 06510

	Dates	Volume
David Bushnell, naval inventor (in Ezra Stiles Papers)	1787	
Lieutenant Henry Eld	ca. 1831–47	3 boxes, 1 item
Rear Admiral Andrew Hull Foote	1837–63	150 items
Commodore Timothy Hunt (in the Maritime Collection)	1828–61	2 boxes
Jared Ingersoll, Sr., lawyer and Judge of the Court of Vice-Admiralty in the Middle Colonies (in Ingersoll Family Papers)	ca. 1769	
Captain Robert Townsend (in the Maritime Collection)	1803–71	1 box

New London County Historical Society
11 Blinman St.
New London, CT 06320

	Dates	Volume
Continental Ship *Alfred*	1775	3 items
Midshipman Charles Bulkeley	1775–76	1 item
Captain Dudley Saltonstall	1779–83	
Nathaniel Shaw, Continental naval agent for Connecticut (in Nathaniel and Thomas Shaw Letters and Papers)	1776–83	
Continental Ship *Trumbull*	1777–78	7 items

Submarine Force Library and Museum
Box 700
Naval Submarine Base New London
Groton, CT 06340

	Dates	Volume
Admiral James Fife, Jr.	ca. 1920–70	1 file drawer
John P. Holland, submarine inventor and engineer (in the Morris Collection; binders of papers, letters, photographs, and other items)	1876–1914	10 vols.
Simon Lake, submarine inventor (includes records of his Lake Torpedo Boat Company)		1 drawer

U.S. Naval History Sources

	Dates	Volume
Vice Admiral Emory S. Land	1915–16	1 vol.
World War II Submarine Patrol Reports (copies of originals in Naval Historical Center)	1942–45	

Trinity College
Watkinson Library
Hartford, CT 06106

	Dates	Volume
Goodwin Family (includes material relating to Lieutenant John R. Madison)	1814–69	150 items
Captain William Leverreth Hudson	1842	1 journal

U.S. Coast Guard Academy Library
New London, CT 06320

	Dates	Volume
Revenue Cutter Service (includes ship logs)	1789–1946	300 items
USS *Tucker* (quartermaster log)	1933	1 vol.

Yale University
Manuscripts and Archives
Sterling Memorial Library
New Haven, CT 06520

	Dates	Volume
Aerial Coast Patrol Unit No. 1, U.S. Navy (Yale aviation unit)	1917–19	
Hanson Baldwin (midshipman in U.S. Navy and military affairs reporter)		
Lieutenant James L. Blair (journal kept on board USS *Vincennes* during the U.S. Exploring Expedition)	1841–42	1 vol.
Captain George M. Colvocoresses	1840	1 vol.
Captain David Conner		
James Fenimore Cooper (American novelist and midshipman in the U.S. Navy)		2,000 items
Sir Thomas Duckworth, RN	1793–1812	
Lieutenant Henry Eld, Jr.	1832–51	2 vols., 100 items
Rear Admiral George Foster Emmons	1836–50	11 vols., 4,000 items
Surgeon Amos Evans (vol. 2 of prescription book from USS *Constitution*; vol. 1 in University of Michigan's William L. Clements Library)	1812–13	1 vol.

Connecticut

Lieutenant David S. Ingalls, USNRF, shooting down a German observation balloon, 1918. Ingalls, a former member of the Yale aviation unit, also destroyed four enemy aircraft during World War I

	Dates	Volume
Surgeon Silas Holmes	1831–42	3 vols.
Hooker Family Papers (includes Commander Edward Hooker)	1777–1919	24 boxes
Commodore Samuel Lockwood	1822–85	1 ft.
Commander Chauncey McKinley Louttit, USNR (psychologist, educator, and naval officer in World War II)	1917–56	25,000 items
Royal Navy (logbooks)	1808–39	69 vols.
Nathaniel Shaw (Revolutionary War naval agent for Connecticut and the Continental Congress)	1753–95	32 vols., 29 boxes
Surgeon Benajah Ticknor	1818–52	2 ft.

U.S. Naval History Sources

	Dates	Volume
Midshipman Joseph A. Underwood (journal kept in USS *Relief* and *Vincennes* during the U.S. Exploring Expedition)	1838–40	1 vol.
Williams Family (includes Samuel Wells Williams who accompanied Matthew C. Perry on his mission to open Japan)	1824–1939	3,100 items

DELAWARE

	Dates	Volume
Eleutherian Mills Historical Library **Greenville, DE 19807**		
Harry Fletcher Brown, Chief Chemist of the Torpedo Station, Newport, R.I.	1893–1900	22 vols.
Rear Admiral John Adolphus Bernard Dahlgren	1847–70	66 items
Rear Admiral Samuel Francis DuPont	1806–88	ca. 49,000 items
Harvey Steel Company (naval contractor)	1796–1913	400 items
Alexander McKinley (diary kept while private secretary to Rear Admiral David G. Farragut)	1864	1 vol.
U.S. Navy Department (accounts and correspondence with the U.S. War and Navy Departments)		
USS *North Carolina*	1824–27	16 items
Commander Irvine Shubrick	1817–81	445 items

Guide: Riggs, John Beverley. *A Guide to the Manuscripts in the Elutherian Mills Historical Library.* Greenville, Del.: Elutherian Mills Historical Library, 1970.

Historical Society of Delaware
505 Market Street Mall
Wilmington, DE 19801

	Dates	Volume
Commodore John Prichet Gillis	1847–71	200 items, 30 vols.
Colonel James Hemphill Jones, USMC (accompanied Matthew Perry on his voyage to Japan)	1821–80	30 items
Captain Thomas Macdonough	1783–1825	9 items
Lieutenant William L. Martine	ca. 1850	3 items

U.S. Naval History Sources

	Dates	Volume
Naval Papers	18th and 19th centuries	27 items
Thomas M. Rodney, Secretary to Legation, Buenos Aires (on the voyage of the USS *Congress* to Buenos Aires in 1823)	1800–74	1 vol.
Captain William M. Walker	ca. 1863	1 vol.

Winterthur Museum
The Joseph Downs Manuscript and
Microfilm Collection
Wilmington, DE 19735

Estate of Captain John Barry, Philadelphia	1803	inventory
USS *Chesapeake* (journal kept by Midshipman Francis Nichols)	Dec. 1812–Mar. 1813	1 journal
USS *Constellation* (notebook of L.B. Messenger)	1873	1 notebook

Commodore John Barry, a prominent naval leader of the American Revolution and during the Quasi War with France

DISTRICT OF COLUMBIA

American National Red Cross
Archives
National Headquarters
Washington, DC 20006

Records relating to the U.S. Navy, Coast Guard, and Marine Corps are interfiled with material from other agencies in the Red Cross Archives's Record Groups 4 and 5. They consist primarily of documents dating from 1946 to the present. Among other topics represented are Red Cross aid to naval personnel and families, prisoner of war relief, Red Cross chapters and other activities at naval hospitals and installations, use of naval radio facilities, Red Cross services to the Coast Guard and Marine Corps, and services to military retirees and veterans. Pre-1946 Red Cross records are located in the National Archives.

Aviation History Unit
Office of the Deputy Chief of Naval
   Operations (Air)
Building 146
Washington Navy Yard
Washington, DC 20374

In addition to the records of this office held by the Naval Historical Center, the Aviation Unit retains yearly histories submitted on a regular basis by naval aviation commands from mid-1957 through the present. From 1953 to mid-1957 no requirement existed for the submission of historical data by air units. The Aviation Unit also keeps a collection of documents pertaining to naval aviation during World War I and materials related to the development of naval aviation from 1911 to World War II.

District of Columbia

	Dates	*Volume*
The Catholic University of America **Department of Archives and Manuscripts** **Washington, DC 20064**		
Dioscesan War Councils, activities at ports of embarkation (in records of the National Catholic War Council, now U.S. Catholic Conference)	1917–19	
Correspondence with War and Navy Department Commissions on Training Camp Activities (in records of the National Catholic War Council, now U.S. Catholic Conference)	1917–19	7 folders
U.S. Navy Pay Officers School (narrative reports in the annual reports of the Rector, *Catholic University Bulletin*)	1917–19	
Georgetown University Library **Special Collections Division** **37th and O Sts., N.W.** **Washington, DC 20057**		
Purser Joseph H. Causten	1805–1920	1 in.
Captain Stephen Decatur (letters received concerning the capture of HMS *Macedonian*)	1812–45	1 vol.
William Oswald Dundas, Confederate soldier and sailor (includes correspondence with Lieutenant James Edward Calhoun, USN)	1839–1920	3 in.
Captain Miles P. DuVal, Captain of the Port of the Pacific Terminal of the Panama Canal, 1941–44 (restricted collection; in addition, the library holds other papers on the Panama Canal)	1930–78	11 ft.
Rear Admiral Jackson McElmell	1854–1908	3 in.
Navy Neutrality Board (in the papers of James Brown Scott)	1914–17	ca. 2 ft.
Captain John Rodgers	1813–15	1 in.
Pay Director Adolph Eugene Watson	1820–67	1 in.

Library of Congress
Manuscript Division
2nd and Independence Ave., S.E.
Washington, DC 20540

The Manuscript Division's extraordinarily rich collections include many groups in U.S. naval history, in addition to extensive transcripts obtained from foreign repositories. Checklists and, in some instances card indexes, exist for individual collections. Information on the Manuscript Division's overall holdings is contained in Philip M. Hamer, ed., *A Guide to Archives and Manuscripts in the United States* (New Haven: Yale University Press, 1961), U.S. Library of Congress, *The National Union Catalogue of Manuscript Collections* (1959—   ), and in annual reports of accessions appearing in the *Quarterly Journal of the Library of Congress*. A specialized guide is Richard B. Bickel, comp., *Manuscripts on Microfilm: A Checklist of the Holdings in the Manuscript Division* (Washington: Library of Congress, 1975). Supplementing these materials are a number of collections in other divisions of the Library of Congress, including the Prints and Photographs Division, Geography and Map Division, the Rare Book Division, and the Newspaper Reading Room.

The Naval Historical Foundation has deposited in the Library of Congress its extensive collection of naval officer papers which are described separately in this guide. The list that follows includes the Library of Congress's own holdings of manuscripts.

	Dates	Volume
Assistant Surgeon Samuel W. Abbott	1861—80	1 vol.
Surgeon Augustus Alvey Adee (in Adee Family Papers)	1825—44	
Passed Assistant Engineer William A. H. Allen	1863—84	14 items
Lieutenant William Henry Allen	1793—1841	6 items
Andrew Doria (journal of cruise, Captain Nicholas Biddle, Commanding; in transcripts from British archives)	1776	1 vol.
Anglo-Dutch War, 1780—84	1780—83	1 journal
Bancroft-Bliss Papers (includes George Bancroft, Secretary of the Navy, 1845—46)	1788—1928	5,800 items
Captain Joshua Barney	1759—1818	4 items
Captain John Barry	1770—1801	55 items
Commander William Bartlett (papers relating to prizes and captures)	1775—76	136 items
Bayard Family Papers (includes material on Senator Richard Henry Bayard, Chairman of the Senate Committee on Naval Affairs, 1843—45)	1797—1855	1,400 items

District of Columbia

	Dates	Volume
Admiral William S. Benson	1791–1941	14,000 items
Captain James Biddle	1825–32	1 box
Lieutenant W. H. Bixby	1882–86	1 box
Charles J. Bonaparte, Secretary of the Navy, 1905–06	1790–1921	80,000 items
Vice Admiral Joel T. Boone	1905–70	24,000 items
Paymaster General John Bradford	1776–82	1 box
Rear Admiral Mark L. Bristol	1887–1939	40,000 items
Daniel Dodge Brodhead, naval agent	1821–53	1,300 items
Midshipman Horatio Nelson Cady	1823–31	1 vol.
William E. Chandler, Secretary of the Navy, 1882–85	1863–1917	25,000 items
William Conant Church, founder of the *The Army and Navy Journal*	1862–1924	350 items
Seaman Joseph G. Clark	ca. 1838–41	1 journal
Rear Admiral Sir George Cockburn, RN	1788–1847	4,400 items
Confederate States of America Records (official and semi-official records of the Confederate Government, including the Departments of State, Justice, Treasury, Navy, War and the Post Office; the correspondence of cabinet officers, leading officials, and of diplomatic and consular missions; and financial records and pardons)	1861–65	18,500 items
Captain David Conner	1817–47	400 items
Chief Engineer William H. Cushman	ca. 1855–65	24 items
Rear Admiral John A. Dahlgren	1824–89	10,000 items
Captain Richard Dale	1776–1802	168 items, 5 vols.
Josephus Daniels, Secretary of the Navy, 1913–21	1806–1948	931 boxes
Midshipman Joseph S. Day		8 items
Decatur House Papers (in Beale Family Papers; includes papers of Captain Stephen Decatur and architect Benjamin Latrobe's sketches of Decatur House)	1801–1957	8 ft.
Admiral George Dewey	1820–1919	25,000 items
Commander Silas Duncan	1812–13	1 vol.
Commodore Henry Eagle (log kept on board USS *Santee*)	1861–62	2 vols.
Master John James Edon (in Peter Force Collection; concerns *Apollon*)	1821	1 item

25

Admiral David G. Farragut, the famed Civil War hero, depicted in a Matthew Brady photograph

District of Columbia

	Dates	Volume
General Merritt A. Edson, USMC	1906–55	69 boxes
Lieutenant Henry Eld	1831–49	150 items
George Fielding Eliot, journalist and military analyst (includes correspondence with Admiral Arleigh A. Burke and other naval officers)	1939–71	5,000 items
Chaplain Jared L. Elliott	1838–42	325 items
Assistant Engineer Harry S. Elseffer	1874–86	80 items
John Ericsson, naval inventor	1821–89	10 boxes
Lieutenant Alessandro Fabbri, USNR	1917–22	1,000 items
Admiral David G. Farragut	1810–69	12 items
Surgeon Charles T. Fahs	1858–59	1 diary
Senator John Fairfield, Chairman of the Senate Committee on Naval Affairs, 1845–47	1828–67	2,000 items
Rear Admiral Andrew Hull Foote	1838–63	800 items
Peter Force Collection (contains many documents relating to the American Revolution, including naval documents in addition to those listed here)		
Forton Prison, England (journals maintained by American seaman)	1777–79	2 items
Foxardo Affair (relates to raid by David Porter against pirate base in Foxardo, Puerto Rico)	1824	1 item
Robert Fulton, naval inventor	1809–14	1 box
Captain David Geisinger (journal kept on board USS *Wasp*)	1814–15	1 vol.
Privateer *General Sullivan* (minutes of Proprietors, Portsmouth, N.H.)	1777–80	1 box
John H. Glenn, Jr., Marine Corps officer and astronaut		90,000 items
Rear Admiral Louis M. Goldsborough	1817–74	8,000 items
Great Britain, Admiralty (transcripts)	ca. 1689–1917	41,400 items
Lieutenant Alexander W. Habersham (in Habersham Family Papers)	ca. 1861	
Acting Master Isaac Hallock	1858–60	200 items
Lieutenant Thomas S. Hamersly	1821–24	1 vol.
Midshipman Thomas J. Harris	1824–27	2 vols.
Second Assistant Engineer Edward L. Hewitt	1864	1 vol.
Rear Admiral Richmond Pearson Hobson	1890–1937	121 boxes
Chaplain Roswell Randall Hoes	1895–1912	700 items
Captain Isaac Hull		14 items

U.S. Naval History Sources

	Dates	Volume
William Henry Hunt, Secretary of the Navy, 1881–82	1881–82	500 items (microfilm)
Lieutenant George Hurst	1825–26	1 journal
International Naval Conference, London (in U.S. Navy Miscellany)	1909	
Passed Midshipman Alonzo C. Jackson	1841–46	2 journals
Captain John Paul Jones (additional items in other collections)	1775–89	4 boxes
Lieutenant Horace Scudder Klyce	1911–33	4,800 items
Franklin Knox, Secretary of the Navy, 1940–44	1898–1954	13 boxes, 7 vols.
USS *Lackawanna*	1873–77	1 box
Vice Admiral Emory Scott Land	1901–72	5,700 items
Fleet Admiral William D. Leahy	1893–1959	27 items
General John A. LeJeune, USMC	1882–1942	5,500 items
Captain John Lenthall	1843	1 vol.
Charles Lever (journal kept on board USS *Release*)	1855	1 vol.
Captain Uriah P. Levy	1842–57	1 box
Lieutenant William S. Lovell	1850–55	1 vol.
Lieutenant Commander Charles Oscar Maas, USNR	1917–25	1 box
Rear Admiral Alfred Thayer Mahan	1824–1914	1,000 items
Senator Willie Person Mangum, Chairman of the Senate Committee on Naval Affairs, 1841–43	1771–1906	5,000 items
Glenn L. Martin, aviation industrialist	1910–55	55,000 items
Commander Matthew Fontaine Maury, Union and Confederate naval officer	1825–1927	14,000 items
Captain Thomas MacDonough	1815–25	150 items
Admiral Lynde D. McCormick	1909–59	3,600 items
Henry and Robert Dundas, 1st and 2nd Viscount Melville, First Lords of the Admiralty, 1804–05 and ca. 1812	1661–1829	100 items
George von Lengerke Meyer, Secretary of the Navy, 1909–13	1901–17	50 items
Miscellaneous Manuscripts Collection (contains many documents relating to ships and naval officers in addition to those listed)		
Acting Ensign Benjamin Mitchell	1861–65	1 vol.
Admiral Marc Andrew Mitscher	1910–52	900 items
William H. Moody, Secretary of the Navy, 1902–04	1879–1916	3,000 items

District of Columbia

	Dates	Volume
Morse Family Collection (includes material on naval officers, including Commander P. C. Wederstrandt)	1806–65	75 items
Simon Newcomb, astronomer, U.S. Naval Observatory	1854–1936	46,000 items
USS *Ontario*	1817–19	1 vol.
Joseph B. Osborn, Civil War sailor and soldier	1862–65	584 items
Palmer-Loper Papers (includes Master Nathaniel Brown Palmer and other seagoing members of the family)	1767–1900	4,000 items
Titian Ramsay Peale, naturalist on Wilkes Expedition	1819–42	6 journals
Commodore Matthew C. Perry	1838–1933	200 items
Lieutenant Raymond H. Perry	1812–14	1 box
Admiral David Dixon Porter	1790–1899	7,000 items
Commodore Edward Preble	1680–1809	5,000 items
Master Samuel Chester Reid	1807–60	33 items
Remey Family Papers (restricted collection; includes material on Rear Admiral George C. Remey)	1855–1932	1,225 items
Senator William C. Rives, Chairman of the Senate Committee on Naval Affairs, 1836–39	1674–1939	50,400 items
Edmund Roberts (journals)	1804, 1805, 1832–34	3 vols.
Lydia S. M. Robinson, Secretary of Department 6, Navy League of the United States, Philadelphia, Pa.	1914–36	13,500 items
Rodgers Family Papers (includes papers of Commodore John Rodgers and other naval members of the family)	1740–1957	11,150 items
Theodore Roosevelt, Assistant Secretary of the Navy, 1897–98, and President (additional material in other collections)	1870–1940	1,148 containers
Commander John Loyall Saunders	1844–47	350 items
Professor Thomas J. J. See, naval astronomer and mathematician	1887–1960	30,000 items
Commander George L. Selden (in Peter Force Collection; journals kept on board USS *Fairfield*)	1828–30	1 box
Lieutenant Robert R. Selden	1843–54	3 vols.
Commander Raphael Semmes, Union and Confederate naval officer	1848–58	1 vol.

U.S. Naval History Sources

	Dates	Volume
Captain James Sever	1794–1801	310 items
Acting Volunteer Lieutenant William F. Shankland	1862	1 vol.
Shaw Manuscripts (in Peter Force Collection; chiefly relates to privateering and naval prisoners; includes Thomas Shaw, Commissary for Prisoners, New London)	1775–82	1 vol.
Robert Smith, Secretary of the Navy, 1801–09	1800–15	11 items
Samuel Lewis Southard, Secretary of the Navy, 1823–29	1809–48	120 items
Rear Admiral Charles Stillman Sperry	1862–1912	2,300 items
Lieutenant John Glendy Sproston	1854	1 box
Benjamin Stoddert, Secretary of the Navy, 1798–1801	1784–1812	40 items
Midshipman Charles C. B. Thompson (journal kept on board USS *Franklin*)	1806	1 vol.
Purser Herman Thorne	1813–16	1 box
Benjamin Franklin Tracy, Secretary of the Navy, 1889–93	1870–1924	13,000 items
Surgeon Samuel Russel Trevett, Jr.	1811–21	letterbook
Captain Thomas Truxtun	1795–1820	158 items
Captain Samuel Tucker	1777–81	½ ft.
Merle Tuve (restricted collection; includes material on the development of the VT fuze in World War II)	1916–72	145,000 items
U.S. Navy Miscellany		250 items
U.S. Navy—Prizes and Captures	1776–81	11 items
Assistant Surgeon Ransford E. Van Gieson	1856–78	350 items
Rear Admiral Edward Vernon, RN, and Admiral Charles Wager, RN (in Peter Force Collection)	1654–1773	4 ft.
Alan T. Waterman (includes material as official in Office of Naval Research, 1946–51)	1918–67	22 ft.
Gideon Welles, Secretary of the Navy, 1861–69	1777–1911	15,000 items
William Whitney, Secretary of the Navy, 1885–89	1757–1904	20,000 items
Curtis Dwight Wilbur, Secretary of the Navy, 1924–29	1924–29	700 items
Rear Admiral Charles Wilkes	1607–1959	6,500 items
Representative Henry A. Wise, Chairman of the House Committee on Naval Affairs, 1842–43	1836–58	350 items
Levi Woodbury, Secretary of the Navy, 1831–34	1638–1899	19,350 items
Vice Admiral Clark Howell Woodward	1926–50	1,100 items

District of Columbia

	Dates	Volume
Lieutenant Alexander S. Wotherspoon (in Wotherspoon Family Papers)	1917–18	
Admiral Harry E. Yarnell	1936–39	3,500 items

Marine Corps History and Museums Division
Marine Corps Historical Center
Building 58
Washington Navy Yard
Washington, DC 20374

The History and Museums Division maintains a library, a historical archives, a reference section, personal papers, and oral history, military music, art, and photographic collections. Additionally, it operates the Marine Corps Museum with its extensive collection of artifacts.

The Library contains approximately 24,000 volumes concentrating on military and naval history, Marine Corps history, and amphibious warfare.

The Archives Section has cognizance over Marine Corps operational records, which include approximately 4,000 cubic feet of plans, command diaries, command chronologies, and after-action reports. Also included are trip reports by former Commandants and Assistant Commandants, records from the annual General Officer Symposium, and certain board reports. Records dating from 1798–1914 have been accessioned by the National Archives, while materials from 1914–64 have been transferred to the Washington National Records Center, Suitland, Maryland, for temporary storage.

The Reference Section of the Division has collected a large body of material on Marine Corps topics and has divided it into subject, biographical, geographical, and unit files. These files cover the entire span of Marine Corps history and include reports, documents, newspaper and magazine clippings, histories, and photographs. Of special interest are the biographical files on over 5,000 Marines. In addition, this section maintains microfilm copies of muster rolls and unit diaries for the war periods between 1798 and 1865 and for all years between 1893 and 1964.

The Oral History Collection includes transcripts of extended interviews with more than 200 prominent, retired Marines. In addition, a collection relating largely to Vietnam operations has sound tapes of approximately 6,500 interviews with active duty Marines conducted by Marine field historians. Transcripts are not available for this group of oral interviews.

The Personal Papers Collection, which is described in Charles A. Wood's *Marine Corps Personal Papers Collection Catalog* (Washington, D.C.: Marine Corps History and Museums Div., USMC, 1974), has over 600 collections open for scholarly research. Among the most important are:

Corporal Water A. Bronson (1870–73)
Colonel John L. Broome (1848–88)

Brigadier General Wilburt S. Brown (1919–53)
Major General Smedley D. Butler (1898–1936)
General Clifton B. Cates (1917–54)
General Leonard F. Chapman, Jr. (1935–71)
Brigadier General Henry C. Cochrane (1842–1913)
Colonel Thomas Y. Field (1847–89)
Sergeant Frank J. Flandera (1895–1900)
General Ben H. Fuller (1885–1934)
General Roy S. Geiger (1907–47)
General Wallace M. Greene, Jr. (1930–67)
Lieutenant General Field Harris (1917–53)
Major General William P. T. Hill (1917–55)
General Thomas Holcomb (1940–44)
Major General Louis M. Little (1899–1942)
General Keith B. McCutcheon (1937–71)
Colonel Samuel Miller (1814–56)

A Marine full dress drill at the Marine Barracks, Mare Island Naval Shipyard, 1907

District of Columbia

Major General Joseph H. Pendleton (1878–1924)
Brigadier General George C. Reid (1898–1930)
General Holland M. Smith (1909–46)
Lieutenant General Julian C. Smith (1909–46)
Colonel McLane Tilton (1861–1914)
Major Levi Twiggs (1834–50)
Private Oscar C. Upham (1898–1902)
Lieutenant Colonel Harold H. Utley (1907–44)
Major General Clayton B. Vogel (1904–46)
Major General Littleton W. T. Waller (1880–1920)
Lieutenant General Walter W. Wensinger (1917–56)
Lieutenant General Louis E. Woods (1917–51)
Master Sergeant Paul Woyshner (1901–30)

The Military Music Collection is especially strong in two areas, the works of John Philip Sousa and the history of the U.S. Marine Band, the "President's Own." The collection contains thousands of musical scores both printed and manuscript, including Sousa originals.

The Art Collection contains approximately 6,200 sketches, paintings, prints, posters, and sculptures relating especially to Marine Corps service in the Vietnam War.

The Still Photographic Archives has over 500,000 negatives and transparencies depicting the history of the Marine Corps from World War II to the present. Approximately 16,000 photographs of the period prior to World War II have been transferred to the National Archives.

The Marine Corps Museum is located on the first floor of the Historical Center. Its exhibits illustrate through the use of uniforms, weapons, and other military equipage, graphics, contemporary art, and documents, a chronological review of the Marine Corps's role in American history. In addition changing displays of Marine Corps art and topical exhibits of martial artifacts are presented in a separate gallery.

The Motion Picture and Television Archives of the Marine Corps, which come under the general cognizance of the Historical Center, are physically located in Building 2013, Marine Corps Development and Education Command, Quantico, Virginia. More than 6,000,000 feet of film footage dating from 1912 is available. (See also the James Carson Breckenridge Library and the Marine Corps Aviation Museum, also in Quantico, Va.)

National Aeronautics and Space Administration
History Office Archives
300 7th Street, S.W.
Washington, DC 20546

	Dates	*Volume*
Records, papers of individual officials, interviews, press clippings, publications, and other	1825–1979	ca. 900 ft.

documents relating to all aspects of the space program, including the activities of naval personnel assigned to NASA, naval space recovery forces, and scientific and technical cooperation between NASA and the Navy.

Guide: Roland, Alex. *A Guide to Research in NASA History*. Washington, D.C.: NASA Headquarters, 1977.

National Society of the Daughters of the American Revolution
1776 D Street, N.W.
Washington, DC 20006

The DAR Library is rich in publications relating to early American genealogy. The Library is open to DAR members free of charge, and to non-members for a fee of $1.00. The *Patriot Index* (Washington: The Society, 1966) and its supplements published in 1969, 1973, and 1976 list thousands of names with origins in the American Revolutionary period, including many naval officers and men.

The DAR Americana Collection in the Office of the Historian General contains about 5,500 early American manuscripts dating from colonial times to about 1830. Included are documents relating to Captain Elisha Hinman of the Continental Navy.

Naval Historical Center
Washington Navy Yard
9th and M Streets, S.E.
Washington, DC 20374

The Naval Historical Center originated in 1800 when the Navy Department Library was established at the direction of President John Adams. In 1881, the librarians began to collect and edit for publication the naval records of the Civil War. That portion of the library's staff engaged in this work soon became known as the Naval War Records Office and, collectively with the library, was designated the Office of Naval Records and Library. After a series of organizational changes, including the addition of historical writing, museum, and curatorial functions, the Navy's central historical organization became known as the Naval History Division in 1952. In 1971, the Division became a component of the newly established Naval Historical Center.

In connection with its various programs, the Center maintains extensive research collections. Many of these are described in published bibliographies and catalogs that are identified, together with the organization's other titles, in *Naval Historical*

District of Columbia

Uniformed and civilian personnel in a Navy Department office, Washington, D.C., 1919

Publications in Print (Washington: GPO, 1979). This pamphlet, which is updated periodically, will be provided to interested researchers upon request.

The holdings and activities of the several branches of the Center, all of which are located in the Washington Navy Yard, are described below.

Curator Branch

The Curator Branch performs curatorial functions for most Navy owned historical properties. Its holdings of museum objects, including paintings and prints, number over 115,000. These materials are made available on a loan basis to naval commands, Department of Defense activities, and to museums and other organizations eligible to receive such properties.

The Curator's Photographic Section holds more than 150,000 historic still photographs which span the entire period of U.S. Naval history. Its collections are the principal American pictorial resource on naval history through World War I and provide a valuable supplement to the holdings of the National Archives and Naval Photographic Center for subsequent years. Its special collections include more than 3,000 contemporary illustrations on the American Revolution gathered in connection with the *Naval Documents of the American Revolution* project, and modest historic motion picture assets. Reproductions of artworks and photographs in the Curator Branch collections are available to other Government agencies and to the general public for publication, display, and other uses. Limited research services can be provided by the staff. Facilities are maintained for visiting researchers.

Historical Research Branch

This Branch provides a broad historical research, writing, and editing capability. It holds an extensive collection of approximately 1,000 microfilm reels (including newspapers) plus thousands of photocopies of naval and maritime documents of the American Revolution gathered from public archives, libraries, historical societies, and private collections in this country and abroad. A selection of these documents is published or will appear in subsequent volumes of the ongoing series *Naval Documents of the American Revolution* which is a major publication of the Branch. The entire collection, bringing together for the first time primary material from many areas and repositories, is available for research. Finding aids have been developed for the American Revolution documents and for the results of the Branch's research in the War of 1812, the Civil War, and other areas of naval history.

Navy Department Library

The Navy Department Library contains 140,000 volumes. Subject matter concentrations include naval history, naval biography and autobiography, exploration, and naval science and technology. The Library is very rich in naval periodicals, many of which exist in long series. The Library's open shelf system increases its attractiveness as a research institution for students of naval history.

The Library's publications include *United States Naval History: A Bibliography* (Washington: GPO, 1972) and *The War at Sea: France and the American Revolution: A Bibliography* (Washington: GPO, 1976). A number of manuscipt bibliographies on special subjects, prepared by the Library's staff, are also available.

Special collections include approximately 5,000 rare books, some of them unique, dating from the 16th through the 20th century. This collection includes many narratives of voyages of the 18th and 19th centuries. Most of the works are in English, although there is a scattering of foreign language works. Among the holdings are various British naval pamphlets from 1690 to 1877; the volumes of the *Naval Chronicle* from 1799 to 1817; and the *Navy Registers* beginning in 1813. Some of the early *Navy Registers* were collected by Rear Admiral George Preble who added marginal notes, newspaper clippings, and photographs. There are also a number of marine dictionaries and many volumes dealing with uniforms, naval signals, navigation, and naval tactics.

The Library maintains the Office of Naval Records and Library collection, consisting of about 1,000 historic manuscripts, most of which date from the 19th century. These manuscripts are filed in alphabetical order by main entry. Subject cataloging of this material currently is underway. Additionally, the Library has a collection of graduate theses and dissertations in naval history, and a valuable group of approximately 300 unpublished administrative histories of major World War II naval commands. The administrative histories are available in microfilm form for inter-library loan. They are described in William C. Heimdahl and Edward J. Marolda, comps., *Guide to United States Naval Administrative Histories of World War II* (Washington: Naval History Division, 1976). Additional special collections include microfilms of naval documents and records dealing with naval operations during the War of 1812, approximately 3,000 maps and charts relating to the naval aspects of the American Revolution, and microfilms of many of the naval records in the National Archives. Small groups of the latter reels can be forwarded to scholars through inter-library loan channels.

The Navy Department Librarian, who also acts as the Coordinator of Navy Department Libraries, can supply general information on the various naval technical libraries and suggest those institutions that are likely to hold materials in particular subject areas. A union list of books held by naval libraries in the Washington area is maintained in the Navy Department Library and a similar catalog for periodicals is under preparation. Arrangement should be made directly with specific technical libraries to consult their materials. Such repositories are maintained by the Systems Commands of the Navy, the Office of Naval Research, Naval Research Laboratory, and other major commands in the Washington vicinity.

Navy Memorial Museum

This organization is the Navy's central historical museum. It has over 30,000 square feet of indoor display area plus an outdoor park of almost equal size. The museum's displays depict the Navy's wartime operations, weapons, and leaders, as well as the service's peacetime contributions in such fields as aeronautics, diplomacy, electronics, exploration, humanitarian service, marine engineering, medicine, navigation, oceanography, and space flight. The museum's centerpiece is a fighting top from frigate *Constitution*. More than 5,000 other artifacts are displayed, including models of notable warships, memorabilia from the men who served in them, and naval art. The outdoor display contains many large naval artifacts.

Operational Archives

This organization maintains a select group of manuscripts, records, and historical documents that support the programs of the Naval Historical Center and provide

U.S. Naval History Sources

The Navy Memorial Museum, Washington Navy Yard

information required by the Navy and other governmental agencies. Many of these resources also are available for scholarly and public use.

The bulk of the Branch's holdings date since 1939. In terms of subject matter, they relate to naval operations, policy and strategy, the history of specific commands, and officer biography. Among the materials are operational reports and plans, selected series of records from the Office of the Chief of Naval Operations and other commands, histories of naval activities, individual officer papers, groups of naval radio messages, oral history transcripts, and non-record materials relating to the German, Japanese, and British navies. A small early records collection includes a few pre-World War II personal paper collections and a historical reference file that is notable for its biographical coverage of 19th century naval officers.

The Operational Archives prepares guides to sources, edits and publishes volumes on modern naval history, and is writing the multi-volume *United States Navy and the Vietnam Conflict* (Washington: GPO, 1976–   ). Among the published guides to the Branch's holdings is *World War II Histories and Historical Reports in the U.S. Naval History Division* (Washington: Naval History Division, 1973).

The list of manuscripts and records appearing below represents the declassified and unclassified collections of the Operational Archives as of 1979. It is updated periodically to reflect the declassification of additional groups and transfers to other repositories. Researchers interested in these resources may obtain the most recent list by writing to the Operational Archives.

Records Organized by the Operational Archives

	Dates	Volume
Action and Operational Reports of Naval Commands	ca. 1941–53	1,200 ft.
War Diaries of Naval Commands	1941–53	900 ft.
Strategic and Operational Planning Documents	1939–50	270 ft.
Submarine Patrol Reports	1941–50	72 ft.
Miscellaneous Record Material and Publications (including histories, interviews, manuals, intelligence summaries, and Fleet organizational documents)	1939–50	570 ft.
Selected Records on the Navy's Role in the Atomic Energy Program	1939–45	4 ft.
Records Relating to the Asiatic Fleet and Asiatic Defense Campaign	1933–44	2 ft.
Records Relating to the Loss of Amelia Earhart Putnam	1937–70	4 ft.
Documents from the Files of Naval Operating Commands	1941–63	42 ft.

U.S. Naval History Sources

	Dates	Volume
China Repository (documents on the Navy in China)	ca. 1920–present	1 ft.

Records of Naval Commands and Offices

	Dates	Volume
Central Security-Classified Records of the Offices of the Secretary of the Navy/Chief of Naval Operations	1940–47	1,250 ft.
Records of the Immediate Offices of the Chief of Naval Operations/Commander in Chief, U.S. Fleet	1942–50	25 ft.
Records of the Aviation History Unit, Office of the Chief of Naval Operations (histories of aviation units, 1943–52; and office files of Deputy Chiefs of Naval Operations for Air, 1943–63)	1943–63	183 ft.
Records of the War Plans (later Strategic Plans) Division, Office of the Chief of Naval Operations	1917–55	150 ft.
Records of the Base Maintenance Division, Office of the Chief of Naval Operations (includes histories of overseas bases)	1939–57	20 ft.
Records of the Logistics Plans Division, Office of the Chief of Naval Operations	1941–46	18 ft.
Records of the Awards Branch, Administration Division, Office of the Chief of Naval Operations	1919–45	20 ft.
Source Material Collected for Historical Projects associated with the Naval History Division, Office of the Chief of Naval Operations (including office files of Samuel E. Morison in connection with the writing of *History of United States Naval Operations in World War II*)	1934–70	150 ft.
Records of the Naval Transportation Service Division, Office of the Chief of Naval Operations	1939–49	5 ft.
Records of the Organization Research and Policy Division, Office of the Chief of Naval Operations	1947–49	90 ft.
Records of the Civil Affairs/Military Government	1939–45	50 ft.

District of Columbia

	Dates	Volume
Branch, Office of the Chief of Naval Operations		
Records of the Submarine Warfare Division, Office of the Chief of Naval Operations	1915–52	10 ft.
Records of the Top Secret Control Office, Office of the Chief of Naval Operations	1944–50	51 ft.
Records of the Central Division, Office of the Chief of Naval Operations	1941–43	1 ft.
Records of the Politico-Military Affairs Division, Office of the Chief of Naval Operations	1944–50	20 ft.
Records of the Fleet Operations Division, Office of the Chief of Naval Operations	1944–50	18 ft.
Records of the Movement Report Center, Office of the Chief of Naval Operations (microfiche file of ship movements)	1942–60	10 ft.
Logs of the Security Watch Officer and Duty Officer, Office of the Chief of Naval Operations	1939–57	3 ft.
Records of the Ship Material Readiness Division, Office of the Chief of Naval Operations	1942–63	1 ft.
Central Classified Records of the Commander in Chief, U.S. Fleet	1942–45	850 ft.
Records of the Tenth Fleet, Office of the Commander in Chief, U.S. Fleet	1941–46	349 ft.
Records of the Operations Division, Office of the Commander in Chief, U.S. Fleet	1941–45	10 ft.
Records of the New Weapons, Research, and Development Section, Office of the Commander in Chief, U.S. Fleet	1943–45	8 ft.
Records of the Top Secret Control Office, Office of the Commander in Chief, U.S. Fleet	1944–45	15 ft.
Records of Naval Forces, Europe	1938–46	16 ft.
Records of U.S. Naval Group, China	1942–46	44 ft.
Records of Seventh Fleet	1942–44	3 ft.
Records of Amphibious Force, U.S. Atlantic Fleet	1941–44	3 ft.
Records of Naval Forces, Northwest African Waters	1942–43	2 ft.
Records of U.S. Naval Forces, Marianas	1945–46	4 ft.
Records of Submarines, Seventh Fleet	1942–43	3 ft.
Records of Service Force, U.S. Atlantic Fleet	1939–44	5 ft.
Records of U.S. Naval Air Station, Bermuda	1942–45	4 ft.

U.S. Naval History Sources

Massed waves of landing craft, supported by larger naval units, during the invasion of Iwo Jima, 1945

	Dates	*Volume*
Records of the Navy Secretariat, Joint Army-Navy Board	1903–47	13 ft.
Records of the General Board of the Navy	1901–51	231 ft.
Records of the Navy Section, U.S. Strategic Bombing Survey	1940–47	27 ft.
Records of the World War II Battle Evaluation Group, Naval War College	1933–52	9 ft.
Records of the Strength Statistics and Casualty Branches, and of the Assistant Chief for Women, Bureau of Naval Personnel	1939–72	140 ft.
Records of the Officer Biographies Branch, Office of Naval Information	1941–74	465 ft.

District of Columbia

	Dates	Volume
Statistical Records of the Operations Evaluation Group	1941–45	22 ft.
Reports and Related Records of the U.S. Naval Technical Mission to Europe	1945–47	28 ft.
Registered Publications Library, U.S. Naval Station, Washington, D.C.	1904–45	50 ft.
Applied Physics Laboratory, Johns Hopkins University (records relating to the development of the VT fuze)	1942–56	2 ft.

Records from Foreign Sources

	Dates	Volume
Previously Classified Publications of the British Navy	1914–45	78 ft.
Translated Records of the German Navy, Essays by German Officers, and Related Studies	1922–45	98 ft.
Microfilmed Records of the Imperial Japanese Navy, Related Translations, and Studies	1939–45	117 ft.

Immediate Office Files and Other Records of Individuals

	Dates	Volume
Admiral Oscar C. Badger	1948–58	1 ft.
Admiral Daniel E. Barbey	1942–69	21 ft.
Admiral Richard E. Byrd	1941–45	8 ft.
Rear Admiral Louis Dreller	1929–59	5 ft.
Vice Admiral Calvin T. Durgin	1942–51	2 ft.
Captain Miles P. Duval	1943–49	7 ft.
Rear Admiral Robert A. J. English	1939–46	6 ft.
Admiral Aubrey W. Fitch	1943–44	3 ft.
Secretary of the Navy James V. Forrestal (includes photocopy of diary, 1944–49)	1934–51	2 ft.
Admiral Thomas C. Hart	1899–1956	2 ft.
Admiral Harry W. Hill	1942–50	8 ft.
Fleet Admiral Ernest J. King	1941–46	8 ft.
Admiral Alan G. Kirk	1937–45	16 ft.
Captain Tracy B. Kittredge	1941–50	5 ft.
Secretary of the Navy Frank Knox	1940–44	3 ft.
Fleet Admiral William D. Leahy	1938–59	9 ft.
Rear Admiral Mitchell D. Matthews	1928–77	2 ft.
Vice Admiral Charles B. Momsen	1927–53	2 ft.
Fleet Admiral Chester W. Nimitz	1901–67	70 ft.

U.S. Naval History Sources

	Dates	Volume
Vice Admiral Ralph A. Ofstie	1942–55	9 ft.
Admiral William V. Pratt	1885–1957	8 ft.
Captain William D. Puleston	1840–1945	2 ft.
Admiral Dewitt C. Ramsey	1912–57	4 ft.
Admiral Forrest P. Sherman	1947–51	4 ft.
Admiral Raymond A. Spruance	1926–68	2 ft.
Admiral R. Kelly Turner	1939–61	7 ft.
Vice Admiral Homer N. Wallin	1941–46	3 ft.
Admiral Harry E. Yarnell	1897–1960	10 ft.
Fragmentary Collections of Naval Officer Papers	1919–76	ca. 8 ft.
Oral Histories of Naval Officers and Officials (including oral history projects of the U.S. Naval Institute and Columbia University)	1960–78	14 ft.

U.S. Naval Message Files

Chart Room, Commander in Chief, U.S. Fleet	1940–46	70 ft.
Convoy and Routing Section, Office of the Commander in Chief, U.S. Fleet (microfilm)	1941–45	4 ft.
Commander in Chief, Southwest Pacific Area	1942–44	2 ft.
Commander in Chief, Atlantic and Atlantic Fleet	1940–46	76 ft.
Commander in Chief, U.S. Pacific Fleet (microfilm)	1941–45	10 ft.
Commander, U.S. Third Fleet	1943–45	3 ft.
Commander, U.S. Naval Forces, Northwest African Waters	1943	2 ft.
Commander Task Force 122 (Western Naval Task Force, Normandy Landings)	1944	2 ft.
Commander, Third Amphibious Force	1944–45	1 ft.
Commander, Cruiser Division Seven	1943–44	5 ft.
Commander, Submarines, U.S. Pacific Fleet	1942–45	7 ft.
Commander, Submarines, Western and Eastern Australia	1943–45	4 ft.
Commander, Submarine Squadron Fifty	1942–43	1 ft.
USS *Marblehead*	1941–42	2 ft.
Commanding General, U.S. Army Command, South Pacific	1942–44	1 ft.
Collected Messages on Operations in the Southwest Pacific	1941–42	2 ft.

Early Records Collection

	Dates	Volume
Historical Reference (Z) Files (including ZB-Biography; ZC-Ships; ZE-Places; ZO-Operations; ZV-Miscellaneous)	1775–1975	140 ft.
Papers of Lieutenant Ambrose C. Cramer (includes manuscript history of U.S. Naval Aviation in France)	1917–19	½ ft.
Papers of Admiral of the Navy George Dewey	1893–1917	4 ft.
Diaries of Captain Glenn F. Howell	1905–71	30 ft.
Papers of Acting Assistant Paymaster Joseph H. Jenkins	1862–65	1 ft.
Diaries and Papers of Rear Admiral Spencer S. Wood	1882–1940	4 ft.
Papers of Lieutenant Commander Phillip W. Yeatman	1917–18	1 ft.

Ships' History Branch

Over 14,000 individual source folders, containing historical reports, press clippings, and correspondence, are available for research in this office. These files document the careers of most of the ships which have seen commissioned service in the Navy from the American Revolution to the present time. Card files contain some information on smaller ships and craft. Approximately 2,000 mimeographed histories of individual ships are available for official distribution and public sale. The Branch's major publication is the *Dictionary of American Naval Fighting Ships,* which contains histories of most commissioned ships of the Continental and United States Navies as well as appendices containing such material as tabulated data on naval ships by type; classification of naval ships and craft; naval aircraft; and Confederate forces afloat.

Special collections include comprehensive files detailing the naming of naval ships since World War I and the designation of their sponsors. Published information on earlier ship sponsors is also available. The Branch has reference files on historic ship memorials and nautical museums, as well as files and compiled bibliographies of published works on the history and evolution of naval ships and on other naval and nautical subjects of general interest.

U.S. Naval History Sources

Naval Historical Foundation
Building 220, Room 218
Washington Navy Yard
Washington, DC 20374

The Naval Historical Foundation is a private, nonprofit organization devoted to the preservation of American naval and maritime history and tradition. In addition to collecting naval manuscripts, the Foundation publishes historical booklets and operates the Truxtun-Decatur Naval Museum, which is located one block north of the White House at 1610 H Street, N.W. The museum's exhibits are changed periodically. Also to be found in the museum are other special holdings, including the Ferdinand Eberstadt Collection consisting of 1,200 naval and maritime engravings, etchings, and lithographs dating from the 16th to the 20th Centuries.

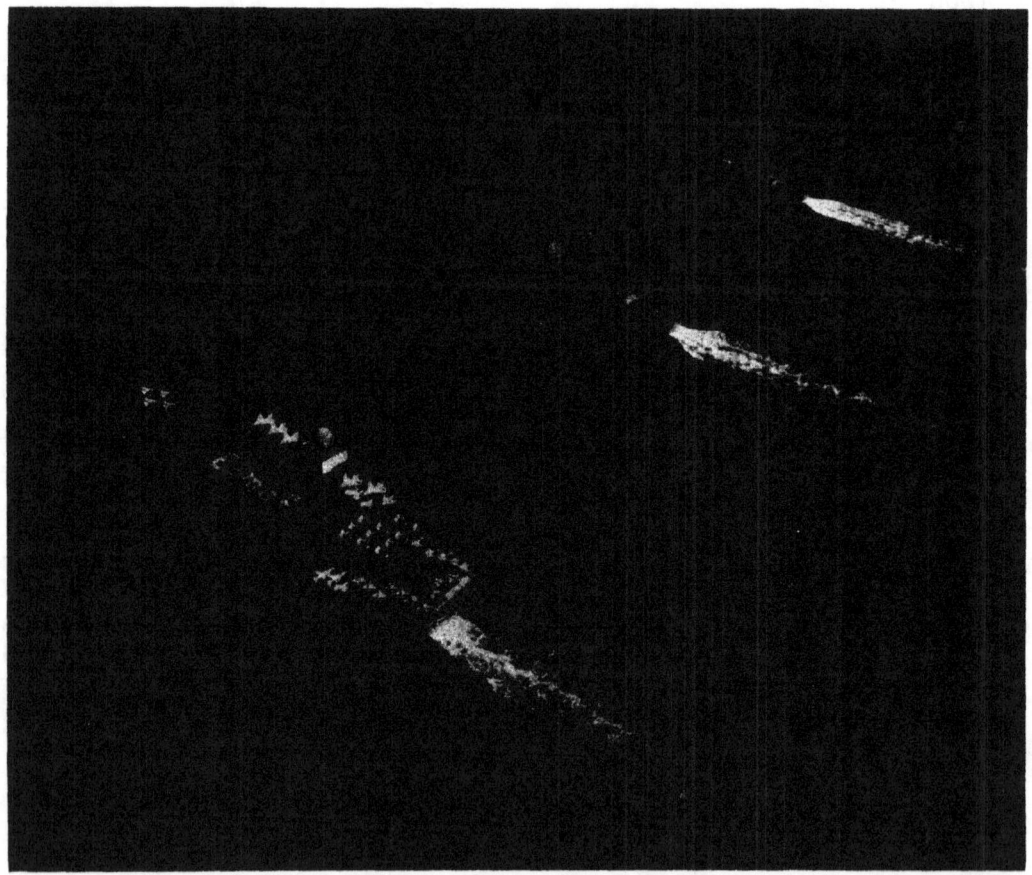

A task group of nuclear-powered ships in the Mediterranean, 1964. From bottom to top: carrier Enterprise, *cruiser* Long Beach, *and frigate* Bainbridge

District of Columbia

The Foundation's collections of private papers represent the largest single group of such material in the United States. Most of these are deposited in the Manuscript Division of the Library of Congress and are described in more detail in *Naval Historical Foundation Manuscript Collection: A Catalog* (Washington: Library of Congress, 1974). Many of these collections are further described in registers available from the Manuscript Division. As indicated below, some papers also are retained in the Foundation's own repository in the Washington Navy Yard. Access to these papers may be arranged by appointment by contacting the Foundation's Secretary in advance of a planned visit.

Collections Of Naval Historical Foundation Papers In The Library Of Congress

	Dates	*Volume*
Commander Edward B. Babbitt	1822–1919	1½ ft.
Commodore William Bainbridge	1804–28	8 items
Rear Admiral Harry A. Baldridge	1902–47	100 items
Commodore James Barron	1831–49	½ ft.
Purser John A. Bates	1849–53	1 vol.
Commodore Richard W. Bates	1780–1865	18 items
Rear Admiral Lester A. Beardslee	1850–1900	128 items
Rear Admiral George E. Belknap	1857–1903	1,400 items
Rear Admiral Reginald R. Belknap	1784–1929	7,100 items
Rear Admiral Henry H. Bell	1866	1 item
John H. Bellamy, wood carver	1941	7 items
Captain Frank M. Bennett	1893–1902	200 items
Rear Admiral Luther G. Billings	1865–1900	12 items
Commander Donald C. Bingham	1835–1932	100 items
Lieutenant Commander Charles F. Blake	1862–64	1 journal
Admiral Claude C. Bloch	1926–44	1,400 items
Rear Admiral Charles Boarman	1838–58	1 vol.
Vice Admiral Harold G. Bowen	1931–65	400 items
Rear Admiral Frank Braisted	1884–1914	25 items
Breck Family (family members include Ensign Edward Breck, 1674–1713; Richard Axtell who served in USS *Yantic*, 1874; Joseph Berry, shipmaster, 1828–65; and John Breck, merchant, 1705–61)	1780–1949	10 items
Joseph L. Brent, Confederate Army Officer	1863	2 items
Rear Admiral Mark L. Bristol	1913–18	100 items
Medical Director John M. Browne	1853–78	10 items
Browning Family (includes the correspondence of	1824–1917	900 items

U.S. Naval History Sources

	Dates	Volume
Lieutenant Robert L. Browning (1803–50) and journal relating to voyages of USS *Vincennes, Ohio,* and *Congress*)		
Rear Admiral Willard H. Brownson	1894–1931	49 items
Otway Burns, shipbuilder and privateer	1813	1 item
Commander Edmund Byrne	1825–50	33 items
Rear Admiral John L. Callan	1907–56	4,000 items
Commander Alfred B. Canaga	1872–1928	9 items
Admiral William B. Caperton	1873–1937	700 items
Commander James W. Carlin	1889	1 item
Passed Assistant Surgeon Dudley N. Carpenter	1897–1901	17 items
Rear Admiral Samuel P. Carter	1882	1 item
Midshipman Clarence Cary, CSN	1905, 1926	1 item
Rear Admiral Silas Casey	1771–1941	300 items
Captain Washington I. Chambers	1871–1943	12,000 items
Chaplain Philander Chase	1818–19	1 journal
Rear Admiral Colby M. Chester	1913–28	300 items
Commander Greenleaf Cilley	1847–67	1 item
William Bell Clark, naval historian	1770–1950	170 items
Captain Alexander Claxton	1832–41	11 items
Alexander F. I. Cochrane, RN	1814	2 items
Commander Albert M. Cohen	1904–55	200 items
Rear Admiral Edmund R. Colhoun	1839–88	1,200 items
Passed Assistant Surgeon Daniel B. Conrad	1855–64	2 diaries
USS *Constitution*	1802–1955	45 items
Rear Admiral George A. Converse	1895–1908	250 items
Lieutenant John A. Cook	1812–31	8 items
Rear Admiral Harold D. Cooke	1918–45	2 items
Rear Admiral Charles S. Cotton	1860–1921	600 items
Joseph P. Couthouy, scientist	1842	3 items
Allyn J. Crosby, historian	1794–1940	61 items
Leonard F. Cushing, naval architect	1794–1959	3,600 items
John B. Dabney, U.S. Consul	1814	1 item
Rear Admiral John A. Dahlgren	1843–70	75 items
Ensign Herbert L. Danforth	1942–72	7 items
Captain Stephen Decatur (includes log kept on board USS *Philadelphia*)	1800–01	3 items
Lieutenant Edwin J. DeHaven	1843–54	15 items
Commodore Robert G. Denig	1885–87	13 items
Captain John H. Dent	1803–10	1 vol.
Admiral of the Navy George Dewey	1890–1943	14 items
Admiral Francis W. Dickins	1788–1905	8 items

District of Columbia

	Dates	Volume
Captain Roscoe F. Dillen	1925–27	45 items
Captain Edward J. Dorn	1868–1936	1,000 items
Edward Lee Dorsett, collector	1814–1926	150 items
Rear Admiral Leonard James Dow	1945–67	2,500 items
Commodore Bladen Dulany	1817–55	500 items
Commodore William W. Dungan	1862–97	11 items
Rear Admiral William H. Emory	1877–1948	2,100 items
Rear Admiral Robley D. Evans	1901–50	5 items
Admiral David G. Farragut	1816–69	400 items
Acting Master Walter E. H. Fentress (history of Navy Yard, Portsmouth, N.H.)	1876	1 item
Commodore Thomas S. Fillebrown	1861	1 item
USS *Flirt*	1841–42	1 journal
Lieutenant George C. Foulk	1872–1950	300 items
Josiah Fox, naval constructor	1795–1845	15 items
Rear Admiral William F. Fullam	1877–1919	3,850 items
Rear Admiral Julius A. Furer	1910–62	2,800 items
Greene C. Furman, lawyer	1862–1954	3 items
Rear Admiral Joseph P. Fyffe	1892	1 item
Lieutenant Benjamin S. Gantt	1834–51	6 items
Obed Gardner, master mariner	1841	1 item
Captain Charles C. Gill	1916–35	3 items
Lieutenant Commander Simon P. Gillett	1858–76	12 items
Commodore James H. Gillis	1854–87	5 items
Admiral Albert Gleaves	1803–1946	6,000 items
Gove Family	1848–1911	7 items
Acting Ensign John W. Grattan	1862–1937	300 items
Rear Admiral Joseph F. Green	1828–1960	60 items
Chief Engineer Albert S. Greene	1853–96	300 items
Vice Admiral John W. Greenslade	1937–57	1,400 items
Captain Virgil C. Griffin, Jr.	1916–46	33 items
Captain John Gwinn	1815–64	900 items
Fleet Admiral William F. Halsey	1907–59	22,000 items
Rear Admiral Purnell F. Harrington	1861–85	100 items
Midshipman George W. Harrison	1839–44	39 items
John Porter Hatch, Army Officer	1866	1 item
Rear Admiral Stanford C. Hooper	1899–1955	14,000 items
Admiral Frederick J. Horne	1908–67	1,000 items
Medical Director Gustavus R. B. Horner	1826–1911	4,900 items
USS *Independence*	1815	1 item
Admiral Royal R. Ingersoll	1864–1931	40 items
Commodore Philip C. Johnson	1861	6 items

U.S. Naval History Sources

Fleet Admiral Ernest J. King, Chief of Naval Operations and Commander in Chief, United States Fleet, during World War II

	Dates	Volume
Admiral Hilary P. Jones	1889–1937	2,400 items
Captain John Paul Jones	1785	1 item
Lieutenant P. A. J. P. Jones	1805–13	15 items
Midshipman Charles C. Julian	1897–99	1 diary
Captain Louis A. Kaiser	1899–1901	1 diary
Thomas Kearny, lawyer	1931–36	3 items
Lieutenant Commander Edward N. Kellogg and Captain Edward S. Kellogg	1859–1937	500 items
Rear Admiral Lewis A. Kimberly	1889–96	50 items
Rear Admiral Husband E. Kimmel	1954–55	200 items
Fleet Admiral Ernest J. King	1908–66	10,000 items
Commander Louis A. Kingsley	1866–68	2 items
Admiral Alan G. Kirk	1919–61	125 items

	Dates	Volume
Rear Admiral Herbert B. Knowles	1941–45	1,500 items
Commodore Dudley W. Knox	1865–1950	6,500 items
Chief Electrician Richard W. Konter	1920	1 item
Rear Admiral Samuel P. Lee	1860–69	19,000 items
Captain John C. Leonard	1887–1920	300 items
HMS *Linnet*	1814	12 items
Charles G. Little, naval aviator	1917–57	78 items
Admiral Charles A. Lockwood	1904–67	7,600 items
Rear Admiral John Lowe	1860–1945	600 items
Rear Admiral Stephen B. Luce	1799–1938	8,000 items
Captain Edward P. Lull	1867–79	1 vol.
Rear Admiral Alfred T. Mahan	1861–1913	5 items
USS *Malvern*	1863	1 vol.
Manila Bay Society	1901–33	300 items
Captain Charles C. Marsh	1898–1917	28 items
Rear Admiral William A. Marshall	1876–1906	100 items
Rear Admiral John Marston	1850–62	250 items
Surgeon Arthur Matthewson	1861–65	9 items
Lieutenant John Mayrant, Revolutionary War naval officer	1926–27	4 items
Chief Engineer Robert W. McCleery	1859–63	3 items
Vice Admiral Newton A. McCully	1917–27	4 items
Rear Admiral Samuel McGowan	1883–1943	2,000 items
Commander Charles McGregor	1868–87	2 items
Captain Frederick V. McNair	1916–22	700 items
Rear Admiral Charles B. McVay	1896–1950	900 items
Lieutenant John F. Meigs	1914–40	1,500 items
Rear Admiral George W. Melville	1871–1911	125 items
Vice Admiral Aaron S. Merrill	1925–63	600 items
Medical Director John S. Messersmith	1837–54	3 items
Captain Cyrus R. Miller	1918	2 items
Lieutenant Edward Moale, Jr.	1887–89	1 journal
James M. Morgan, CSN	n.d.	1 item
John O. Morse, whaler captain	1829–35	142 items
Captain D. J. Munro, RN (in Harold D. Cooke Collection)	1940–45	2 in.
Captain Henry C. Mustin	1886–1924	2,400 items
Admiral Horatio Nelson, RN	1801	1 item
Evan Nepean, Clerk, British Admiralty	1803	2 items
Rear Admiral Reginald F. Nicholson	1873–1939	20 items
Commodore Sommerville Nicholson	1839–81	70 items
Lieutenant Henry C. Nields	1867	1 item

U.S. Naval History Sources

	Dates	Volume
Nonsuch (privateer)	1812	1 logbook
Rear Admiral Charles F. O'Neil	1833–1927	5,500 items
Luis de Onis, Spanish Minister to U.S.	1812	1 item
Rear Admiral William S. Parsons	1943–53	1,500 items
Commodore Daniel T. Patterson	1802–1904	1,750 items
Charles O. Paullin, naval historian	1931	4 items
Landsman William Pelham	1864	1 item
Charlemagne Massena Peralte, Haitian guerilla leader	1919	1 item
Captain George H. Perkins	1857–1936	500 items
Commodore Matthew C. Perry	1839–1931	10 items
Commodore Oliver H. Perry	1845	4 items
Rear Admiral George T. Pettengill	1863–1937	7 items
Rear Admiral Richard H. Phillips	1917–58	600 items
Lieutenant Lloyd Phoenix	1921–27	2 items
Medical Director Ninian Pinkney	1830–78	900 items
Captain Edwin T. Pollock	1898–1939	18 items
Pook Family	1937	5 items
Porter Family (chiefly of Captain David Porter and Admiral David D. Porter)	1811–81	600 items
Mary Edith Powel, naval biographer	1747–1922	32,000 items
Admiral William V. Pratt	1862–1963	200 items
Admiral William Radford	1847–90	53 items
Commander Charles W. Rae	1870–71	1 journal
Chaplain Edward K. Rawson	n.d.	1 item
William L. Reid	1852	14 items
Rear Admiral George C. Remey	1902–35	1 item
Rear Admiral William Reynolds	1877–80	2 items
Captain Holden C. Richardson	1844–1946	3,600 items
Commodore Charles G. Ridgely	1815–26	4 items
Captain Frank E. Ridgely	1898–1924	150 items
Arthur S. Riggs, naval officer and author	1929–52	900 items
Major General William E. Riley, USMC	1941–48	800 items
Rodgers Family (includes Captain John Rodgers, 1773–1838, Rear Admiral John Rodgers, 1812–1882, and Admiral William L. Rodgers)	1788–1944	15,500 items
Lieutenant William T. Rodgers	1813–17	6 items
Rear Admiral Francis A. Roe	1842–1901	500 items
Vice Admiral Stephen C. Rowan	1826–90	4 items
Major General John H. Russell, USMC	1861–75	18 items
Commander George P. Ryan	1860–1952	75 items
Captain Nathan Sargent	1866–1957	2,700 items

District of Columbia

	Dates	Volume
Captain Horace B. Sawyer	1812–1950	900 items
Captain Cornelius M. Schoonmaker	1833–1931	1,400 items
Rear Admiral Thomas O. Selfridge, Sr.	1809–1927	750 items
Rear Admiral Thomas O. Selfridge, Jr.	1852–1927	1,900 items
Admiral David F. Sellers	1860–1949	6,500 items
Commodore Alexander A. Semmes	1869–71	2 items
Vice Admiral John F. Shafroth	1926–45	1,800 items
Captain John Shaw	1798–1895	1,200 items
General William T. Sherman, U.S. Army	1887	1 item
Rear Admiral Robert W. Shufeldt	1836–1910	15,000 items
Rear Admiral Montgomery Sicard	1800–1948	1,200 items
Captain Clayton M. Simmers	1830–1921	6 items
Admiral William S. Sims	1856–1951	43,000 items
Pay Director Daniel A. Smith	1863–1905	38 items
Captain Stuart F. Smith	1860–1951	300 items
Rear Admiral Elliot Snow	1790–1942	9,450 items
Captain Robert T. Spence	1822–23	1 item
Rear Admiral Charles S. Sperry	1899	2 items
Admiral William H. Standley	1895–1963	2,500 items
Commodore Daniel S. Stellwagen	1814–27	4 items
Stevens Family (includes papers of Captain Thomas Holdup Stevens, Rear Admiral Thomas Holdup Stevens II, and Rear Admiral Thomas Holdup Stevens III)	1810–1952	35 items
Rear Admiral Charles Stewart	1850–65	15 items
Lieutenant David R. Stewart	1834	35 items
Major George Stillman, Revolutionary War Army officer	1775–1803	54 items
Admiral Joseph Strauss	1881–1922	25 items
USS *Susquehanna*	1853–65	3 items
Captain Powers Symington	1916–57	38 items
Paymaster John F. Tarbell	1876–77	1 journal
Admiral Edward D. Taussig	1867–1900	33 items
Vice Admiral Joseph K. Taussig	1921	1 item
Rear Admiral Henry C. Taylor	1862–1904	300 items
Admiral Montgomery M. Taylor	1890–1936	1,200 items
Lieutenant Colville Terret	1850–59	6 items
Rear Admiral Henry K. Thatcher	1866	1 item
Rear Admiral Charles M. Thomas	1907–08	80 items
Purser Gardner Thomas	1815–32	11 items
Captain Thomas Tingey (includes log of USS *Ganges*, 1797)	1795–1827	55 items

U.S. Naval History Sources

	Dates	Volume
Captain Thomas Truxtun	1796–1885	13 items
Rear Admiral Thomas Turner	1834–35	27 items
USS *President Lincoln* Club	1918–68	500 items
U.S. Naval Observatory	1833–1900	10,000 items
U.S. Naval War College	1884–1914	27 items
United States Navy	1899–1933	6 items
U.S. Navy Department	1840–63	10 items
U.S. Navy Submarines	1936	10 items
U.S. Navy Yard, Charlestown, Mass.	1801–05	14 items
Midshipman Guysbert B. Vroom	1791–99	1 vol.
Wainwright Family (includes Commander Richard Wainwright and Rear Admiral Richard Wainwright)	1842–1941	18 items
Rear Admiral John G. Walker	1873–1903	1,750 items
Rear Admiral John C. Watson	1845–1960	1,500 items
Commander Harrie Webster	1889–1913	50 items
Rear Admiral Roger Welles	1884–1926	2,100 items
Tom Henderson Wells, naval officer and naval historian	ca. 1950s	1,500 items
Lieutenant George P. Welsh	1771–1851	7 items
Commander George S. Welsh	1879–80	2 items
Rear Admiral William H. Whiting	1731–1952	500 items
Vice Admiral Theodore S. Wilkinson	1942–45	200 items
Charles E. Williams, naval engineer	1904–16	11 items
Rear Admiral Henry Williams	1896–98	20 items
Captain John C. Wilson	1898	1 item
Lieutenant Commander Samuel L. Wilson	1862–1939	22 items
Lieutenant Francis Winslow	1834–37	1 journal
Captain John A. Winslow	1864–88	10 items
Captain Henry A. Wise	1850–69	90 items
Wood Family (includes Chief Engineer William W. Wood and Colonel Thomas Newton Wood, USMC)	1836–1906	28 items
Commodore Selim E. Woodworth	1851–65	4 items
Rear Admiral John L. Worden	1861–98	65 items
Commander Edward M. Yard	1828–81	2 items

Collections In The Naval Historical Foundation Repository
Building 210, Washington Navy Yard

Hanson W. Baldwin, journalist and naval officer	1924–75	2 ft.
Rear Admiral Albert S. Barker	1883–1905	

District of Columbia

	Dates	*Volume*
Captain John S. Barleon	1939–42	8 ft.
Commander Guy Barnes	1909–45	1 letterbook
Rear Admiral Reginald R. Belknap	1919–26	2 ft.
Rear Admiral Harold M. Bemis	1904–46	1 ft.
Captain Victor F. Blakeslee	1940–44	1 ft.
Admiral William H. P. Blandy	1943–47	2 ft.
Captain George P. Blow	1898–1918	9 items
Vice Admiral Harold G. Bowen	1946–57	4 ft.
Admiral Arleigh A. Burke	1930–70	8 ft.
Captain John Cadwaleder (journal kept on board USS *Enterprise*)	1835	1 vol.
Captain John L. Cecil	1939–47	1 ft.
Captain Isaac Chauncey (in Redman Collection)	1830	2 items

Admiral Arleigh A. Burke, Chief of Naval Operations, 1955–1961, and famed World War II commander

	Dates	Volume
Captain George Warren Clark, USNR	1918	20 items
Rear Admiral Richardson Clover	1880	1 journal
Rear Admiral Hutch I. Cone	1898	1 journal
USS *Constitution*	1819	1 item
Rear Admiral Charles S. Cotton (log of USS *Minnesota*)	1861	1 item
Captain Paul C. Crosley	1910	3 vols.
Captain Damon E. Cummings	1914–64	2 ft.
Admiral William De Rohan (Sicilian Navy)	1871–79	12 items
Commander Grattan C. Dichman	1913–24	2 ft.
Lieutenant Commander Herbert O. Dunn (journal kept on board USS *Hartford*)	1877	1 vol.
Captain Lucius C. Dunn	1909–51	4 ft.
Lieutenant Samuel S. Elbert	1934	5 items
Seaman Edward Elliott	1867–87	2 items
Commander Theodore Ellyson	1912–20	1 ft.
Eugene Ely, aviator	1911	2 vols.
Admiral David G. Farragut	1834–59	2 items
Captain Glover T. Ferguson (includes correspondence with Gideon Welles, Secretary of the Navy, 1861–69, and Admiral David G. Farragut)	1861–65	13 items
Admiral Albert Gleaves	1897	1 item
Commander Walton Goodwin (journal kept on board USS *Quinnebaug*)	1867	1 item
Vice Admiral John W. Greenslade	1900–46	2 ft.
Captain Harry W. Greer	1939–64	1 ft.
Captain Paul C. Grening	1925–50	1 ft.
Lieutenant Commander Reynold T. Hall	1881	1 vol.
Dr. C. M. Hamisch, collector	1846–62	10 items
Robert Johnson Hare-Powel, naval officer	1914–43	26 items
Commander J. N. Hemphill (journal kept on board USS *Winnipec*)	1865	1 items
Admiral H. K. Hewitt	1907–50	6 ft.
Chief Hospitalman George F. Holland	1897–1902	53 items
Rear Admiral William L. Howard	1880–90	1 items
Captain Isaac Hull	1864–70	10 items
Admiral Raymond P. Hunter	1812, 1903–21	4 items
USS *Independence* (general orders)	1815	
Admiral Royal R. Ingersoll (includes material on the Great White Fleet)	1907–08	1 folder

	Dates	Volume
USS *Iroquois*	1889–90	2 items
Chief Engineer James B. Kimball	1856–61	1 vol.
Captain Earl H. Kincaid	1894–1946	1 ft.
Captain Porter King, CSA	1861	9 items
Senator Henry C. Lodge	1912	1 item
Rear Admiral John Lowe	1838	1 item
USS *Macedonian*	1818–20, 1864	1 logbook
USS *Maine*	1908	2 items
Midshipman Anson G. McCook	1842	4 items
Rear Admiral Samuel McGowan	1908–20	2 ft.
Captain Frederick V. McNair	1919–20	1 ft.
Captain Robert T. Merrill (includes material on the Merchant Marine)	1950–58	1 ft.
Admiral George D. Murray	1915–49	1 ft.
Captain Henry C. Mustin (includes log kept on board USS *Samar*)	1892–1920	2 ft.
Captain Harry W. Need (material concerning Navy's search for Amelia Earhart)	1937	2 items
Captain E. G. Oberlin	1919–41	3 folders
Captain Frederick L. Oliver (includes log of USS *Salt Lake City*)	1930–31	2 items
Rear Admiral Charles O'Neil	1914	1 diary
Captain Philip R. Osborn (material on USS *Olympia*)	1902	4 items
Rear Admiral Hugo Osterhaus (includes journals kept on board USS *Baltimore, Enterprise*)	1886–96	5 items
Midshipman Joseph Parrish (journal kept on board USS *Mississippi*)	1842	1 item
Commander George H. Perkins	1864, 1892–96	3 items
Rear Admirals Thomas S. Phelps and John Rodgers (letter book)	1877	1 item
USS *President Lincoln* Club	1917–18	1 ft.
Captain H. G. Purcell	1915	1 vol.
Rear Admiral Frederick G. Pyne	1901–44	1 ft.
Queenstown Association (World War I naval operations)	1917–27	1 ft.
Rear Admiral Albert C. Read	1917–46	7 items
Captain Holden C. Richardson	1900–46	2 ft.
Rear Admiral Thomas H. Robbins, Jr.	1919–63	1 ft.
Rear Admiral John Rodgers	1851–52	1 folder

	Dates	Volume
Vice Admiral Harry E. Sanders	1924–56	1 ft.
USS *Saratoga*	1934	20 items
Rear Admiral Frederick Schley	1847–90	1 journal
Rear Admiral Thomas O. Selfridge, Sr. (copy of journal kept on board USS *Mississippi*)	1861–62	1 item
Vice Admiral Alexander Sharp, Jr.	1905–38	50 items
USS *Siboney*	1918–19	78 items
Rear Admiral Montgomery Sicard	1869	1 items
Admiral William S. Sims	1891	1 item
Seaman George P. Slayback, Jr.	1917–18	1 vol.
Admiral William H. Standley	1890–1940	12 items
Commander Raymond Stone	1919–36	5 ft.
Rear Admiral Joseph Strauss	1920–22	1 ft.
Rear Admiral George W. Sumner	1862	1 item
Rear Admiral Charles Thomas	1876–1900	2 ft.
Lieutenant Lewin W. Thomas	1915–20	20 items
Rear Admiral Richard Wainwright	1880–1900	3 items
Lieutenant Commander Pendleton G. Watmough (log kept on board USS *Kansas*)	1864	1 item
Rear Admiral Adolphus E. Watson	1915–45	1 ft.
Commander George S. Welsh	1875, 1882, 1879–80	4 journals
Charles W. Whistler (logs kept on board USS *Constitution* and *Independence*)	1848–52	2 items
Admiral Theodore S. Wilkinson	1914	50 items
Commander Francis Winslow (letterbook from service on board USS *Water Witch*)	1861–62	1 item

Naval Photographic Center
Washington, DC 20374

The Still Photo Library of this Center has a very large indexed collection dating from 1 July 1958. Earlier material has been deposited in the National Archives as part of Record Group 80. Sixty-three million feet of stock film dating from 1958 and about 45 million feet of edited film dating from about 1940 are retained in the Motion Picture Library. Access requirements and information on still photography can be obtained from the Commanding Officer, U.S. Naval Photographic Center, U.S. Naval Station, Washington, D.C. 20374. Motion picture inquiries should be directed to the Chief of Information (OI-220), Department of the Navy, Washington, D.C. 20350.

District of Columbia

Naval Research Laboratory Library
4555 Overlook Ave., S.W.
Washington, DC 20375

The Naval Research Laboratory Library maintains a small but important collection of published and manuscript works related to the history of the Laboratory from its founding in 1923 to the present. In addition, the Library holds a relatively complete set of papers and documents written by NRL scientists. Archival records of the institution up to 1942 are in Record Group 19 in the National Archives, and after 1942 in the Washington National Records Center. Prior arrangements should be made with NRL for access to materials in its custody or in the Records Center.

Smithsonian Institution
Washington, DC 20560

Archives
1000 Jefferson Drive, S.W.

The Smithsonian's Archives holds the official records of the Institution and personal papers of many former Secretaries, as well as the papers of several exploring expeditions led by the Navy or in which naval officers were closely involved. Included are papers of the United States Exploring Expedition of 1838–42, commanded by Lieutenant Charles Wilkes; the North Pacific Exploring Expedition, 1853–56; and the *Polaris* Expedition, 1871–73. Also included are papers of various naval officers and scientists whose work reflects the Navy's support and participation in scientific activities of the nineteenth and twentieth centuries.

Guide: Smithsonian Archives. *Guide to the Smithsonian Archives.* Washington, D.C.: Smithsonian Institution Press, 1978.

Archives of American Art
Washington Center
FA-PG Building
8th and F Streets, N.W.
Washington, DC 20390

	Dates	*Volume*
Louis Bouche (includes material on his service in the Navy during World War I as a camouflage artist)	1933–73	2 reels of microfilm
Vernon Howe Bailey, artist (includes drawings of U.S. Navy ships, submarines, naval stations,	1932–50	600 items

U.S. Naval History Sources

	Dates	Volume
aviation, and other topics, as well as Marine Corps training scenes)		
Lieutenant Commander Griffith Baily Coale, USNR (muralist and marine painter who served as a naval artist in World War II)	1926–45	3,000 items (also on 6 reels of microfilm)
Ensign Joseph Hirsch (includes photographs of his war and naval works)	1932–70	2 reels of microfilm
U.S. Shipping Board, Emergency Fleet Corporation, National Service Section (material on ship poster competition)	1918	6 reels of microfilm

Guide: Archives of American Art. *Checklist of the Collection.* 2nd ed., rev. Washington, D.C.: the Archives, 1977.

National Air and Space Museum Library
10th and Independence Ave., N.W.

The Museum's outstanding collection of military aircraft, other relics, and photographs includes much material of interest to the naval air historian. Of particular note is the Library's collection of microfilmed record cards for stricken naval aircraft, 1911–65 (incomplete), filed by serial number only, and active record cards, 1966–73 (also incomplete). The Admiral Dewitt Clinton Ramsey Room contains biographical files which include information on naval aerospace personalities, and a photographic collection which includes material on naval aircraft and airships.

National Museum of History and Technology
14th St. and Constitution Ave., N.W.

Division of Naval History, **Room 4020**

	Dates	Volume
Assistant Engineer James M. Adams	ca. 1847–68	less than 1 ft.
Howard I. Chapelle, marine architect and historian	ca. 1920s–70s	ca. 38 ft.
Collected Materials on Naval History (includes journals of naval and marine officers and flight logs of Vice Admiral Frank D. Wagner and Rear Admiral William A. Moffett)	18th–20th c.	65 ft.
Division of Naval History Biographical Reference File		10 ft.

District of Columbia

	Dates	Volume
Division of Naval History Naval Ship History Reference Collection		16½ ft.
Division of Naval History Ship Photographs		2 ft.
Assistant Purser Thomas C. Dudley (papers chiefly concerning his service on Perry's mission to Japan)	ca. 1847–64	1 ft.
Henry P. Fleischman, seaman on board USS *Chesapeake*	1813	less than 1 ft.
Captain Simon P. Fullinwider, Chief of the Mine Section, Bureau of Ordnance, 1917–18	1917–19	1 ft.
Rear Admiral W. R. Furlong (relates to the history of U.S. flags)	1954–70	4½ ft.
John A. Griswold, manufacturer and congressman (material concerns his role in the building of USS *Monitor*)	ca. 1861–75, 1884–90, 1901–12	1 ft.
Charles Francis Hall, explorer (includes material on the *Polaris* expedition to the North Pole)	1860–64	2 ft.
Hyde Windlass Company (naval contractor)	ca. 1900–50	6 ft.
Japanese Print Collection (prints and bills made in Japan during Perry's visit)	1853–54	27 items
Engineer Absalom Kirby	1864–1911	less than 1 ft.
Rear Admiral Benjamin P. Lamberton	ca. 1834–1917	2 ft.
Lighthouse and Buoy Drawings	ca. 1850s–1930s	6 ft.
Lieutenant Commander Theodorus Bailey Myers Mason	ca. 1864–1901, 1909, 1912	1 ft.
Engineer William H. Nauman	1881–1903, 1923–25, 1930	less than 1 ft.
Naval Ordnance Drawings	18th–20th c.	10 ft.
Matthew C. Perry Journals (copies of journals kept on mission to Japan, 1853–54; originals located in the National Archives)	1852–54	less than 1 ft.
Albert F. Schroek, member of John Philip Sousa's United States Marine Band	ca. 1929–39, 1958	less than 1 ft.
Ship Drawings and Plans	19th–20th c.	ca. 137 ft.

U.S. Naval History Sources

	Dates	Volume
Major William B. Slack, USMC, Quartermaster of the Marine Corps	ca. 1847–60, 1880	less than 1 ft.
Michael Sofranoff, USMC, Marine Corps photographer	ca. 1940–53	1 ft.
Speiden Family Papers (includes material on Purser William Speiden's service on the United States Exploring Expedition and on his son Edgar Speiden, who also served in the Navy)	ca. 1822–94, 1904, n.d.	1 ft.
United States Coast Guard Photographs	ca. 1920–50s	15 ft.
USS *Tecumseh*	1862–64, 1967–70	2 ft.
Captain Philip Van Horn Weems	ca. 1927–70	3 ft.

Division of Political History, Room 4109

Gustavus Vasa Fox, Assistant Secretary of the Navy, 1861–66	1866–72	1 ft.

Division of Transportation, Maritime Section
Room 5008

This Division exhibits the National Watercraft Collection which deals principally with merchant shipping, and the Chapelle Collection of plans dating from the War of 1812 to the present. There are over 200 rigged models and about 400 builder's half-models among its holdings, in addition to thousands of ship plans, drawings, and photographs dating from early times to the present. The bulk of ship models, however, dates from the War of 1812. Specific collections relating to naval history are:

Howard I. Chapelle, marine architect and historian	1920s–70s	ca. 98 ft.
John W. Griffith, naval architect	1832, 1848–80	2 ft.
Marine Transportation History Collection (includes materials on U.S. Navy ships)	19th–20th c.	172 ft.

Guide: Smithsonian Institution. National Museum of History and Technology. *Guide to Manuscript Collections in the National Museum of History and Technology, 1978.* Washington, D.C.: Smithsonian Institution Press, 1978.

District of Columbia

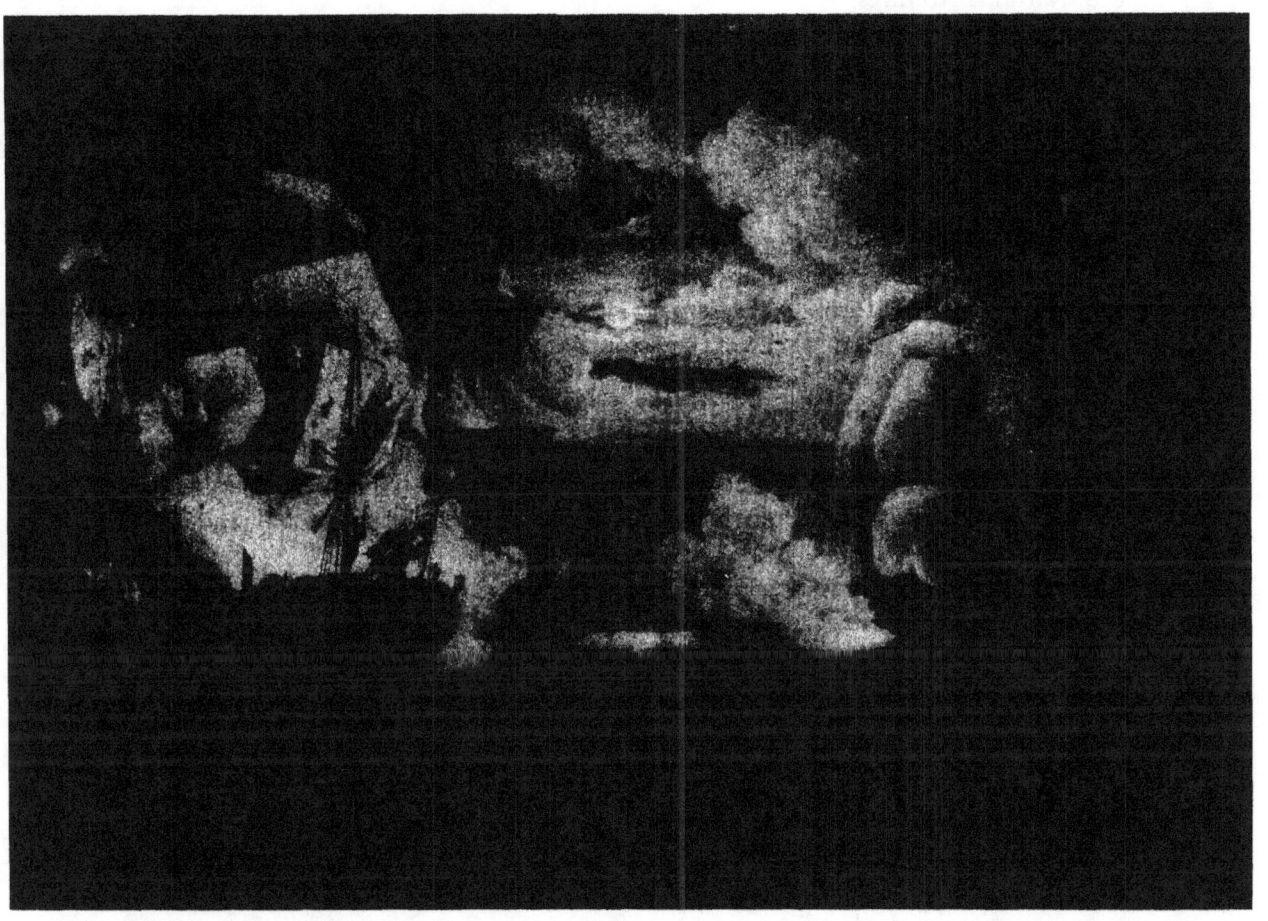

The classic action between Bon Homme Richard *and HMS* Serapis *off Flamborough Head, England, 1779*

Society of the Cincinnati
Anderson House Library and Museum
2118 Massachusetts Ave., N.W.
Washington, DC 20008

The Library, specializing in the American Revolution and early American history, holds a small map and manuscript collection, including naval documents from the Revolutionary War. The Museum has specialized displays, including exhibits relating to the Navy's role in the American Revolution and in other periods of early American history.

U.S. Naval History Sources

U.S. National Archives
8th St. and Pennsylvania Avenue, N.W.
Washington, DC 20408

The National Archives is the central repository for official records of the United States that have permanent historical or administrative value. In addition to textual materials, the agency holds cartographic and pictorial collections. It also has groups of private papers and collections of records from foreign countries.

The Navy and Old Army Branch is the primary organization within the National Archives responsible for naval materials. However, a number of naval record groups also are in the General Archives Division (physically located in the Washington National Records Center, Suitland, Md.). In addition, the Modern Military Branch has records of joint commands in which the Navy participated and collections of seized enemy documents. Technical and scientific records, including some generated by the Navy, are in the Center for Polar and Scientific Archives. Finally, naval photographic and cartographic materials are in separate Audiovisual and Cartographic Divisions.

Outside the Washington area, the National Archives operates a number of regional Federal Archives and Records Centers, including a specialized repository for military and civilian service records in St. Louis, Missouri, known as the National Personnel Records Center. Some naval records have been accessioned by Archives Branches established in most of these Centers, as indicated separately in this *Guide*. However, a greater volume of naval documentation in the records center continues to be under the control of the command or office that originally deposited the files. It is not possible to list these voluminous and often transitory holdings. Those that have permanent historical value will be accessioned at a later date by the National Archives and reported in that agency's publications.

The National Archives prepares a number of catalogs that provide detailed information on the agency's holdings. An overall source is *Guide to the National Archives of the United States* (Washington: GPO, 1974), but published or unpublished finding aids describing the content of individual record groups also are available in most instances. *Prologue,* a quarterly journal of the National Archives, lists new accessions. Scholars also will be interested in the *Catalog of National Archives Microfilm Publications* (Washington: Government Printing Office, 1974) which tabulates the extensive microfilm publications available for purchase.

Further details on specific records and finding aids may be obtained from the publications cited above or through direct correspondence with the National Archives. The list of record groups that follows is intended to provide only a general summary of the voluminous and complex holdings of that organization.

Naval Records in the National Archives

Record Group	Title	Dates	Volume
19	Records of the Bureau of Ships	1795–1949	17,198 ft.
24	Records of the Bureau of Naval Personnel	1789–1956	15,443 ft.
37	Records of the Hydrographic Office	1837–1974	2,142 ft.
38	Records of the Office of the Chief of Naval Operations	1882–1968	3,726 ft.
45	Naval Records Collection of the Office of Naval Records and Library	1775–1927	2,966 ft.
52	Records of the Bureau of Medicine and Surgery	1812–1951	1,331 ft.
71	Records of the Bureau of Yards and Docks	1820–1946	4,868 ft.
72	Records of the Bureau of Aeronautics	1911–46	8,010 ft.
74	Records of the Bureau of Ordnance	1818–1946	7,980 ft.
78	Records of the Naval Observatory	1840–1943	538 ft.
80	General Records of the Department of the Navy	1804–1965	12,112 ft.
125	Records of the Office of the Judge Advocate General	1799–1943	2,687 ft.
127	Records of the United States Marine Corps	1798–1971	2,288 ft.
143	Records of the Bureau of Supplies and Accounts	1885–1946	3,909 ft.
181	Records of Naval Districts and Shore Establishments	1783–1962	8,754 ft.
298	Records of the Office of Naval Research	1941–70	41 ft.
313	Records of Naval Operating Forces	1864–1974	18,642 ft.
405	Records of the United States Naval Academy	1836–1950	397 ft.
428	Records of the Department of the Navy	1947–50	4 ft.

Other Groups in the National Archives Containing Records Related to the Navy

Record Group	Title	Dates	Volume
23	Records of the Coast and Geodetic Survey	1806–1965	3,238 ft.
26	Records of the United States Coast Guard	1789–1975	10,828 ft.
32	Records of the United States Shipping Board	1914–38	6,502 ft.
43	Records of International Conferences, Commissions, and Expositions	1825–1968	1,358 ft.
46	Records of the United States Senate	1789–1974	14,050 ft.
59	General Records of the Department of State	1764–1974	23,247 ft.
93	War Department Collection of Revolutionary War Records	1775–98	820 ft.

U.S. Naval History Sources

Record Group	Title	Dates	Volume
117	Records of the American Battle Monuments Commission	1920–65	184 ft.
126	Records of the Office of Territories	1878–1953	753 ft.
128	Records of Joint Committees of Congress	1799–1972	632 ft.
178	Records of the United States Maritime Commission	1917–50	6,487 ft.
218	Records of the United States Joint Chiefs of Staff	1942–53	32 ft.
225	Records of Joint Army and Navy Boards and Committees	1903–47	148 ft.
227	Records of the Office of Scientific Research and Development	1939–47	3,004 ft.
233	Records of United States House of Representatives	1789–1974	17,201 ft.
238	National Archives Collection of World War II War Crimes Records	1900–50	1,620 ft.
242	National Archives Collection of Foreign Records Seized	1679–1954	5,001 ft.
243	Records of the United States Strategic Bombing Survey	1928–47	977 ft.
248	Records of the War Shipping Administration	1941–50	280 ft.
254	Records of the Shipbuilding Stabilization Committee	1940–47	53 ft.
260	Records of United States Occupation Headquarters, World War II	1942–71	11,070 ft.
267	Records of the Supreme Court of the United States (Revolutionary War Prize Cases)	1776–87	6 ft.
330	Records of the Office of the Secretary of Defense	1940–65	2,931 ft.
331	Records of Allied Operational and Occupational Authorities, World War II	1938–54	17,948 ft.
332	Records of United States Theaters of War, World War II	1939–50	529 ft.
333	Records of International Military Agencies	1941–57	153 ft.
334	Records of Interservice Agencies	1916–58	706 ft.
349	Records of Joint Commands	1942–56	245 ft.
357	Records of the Maritime Administration	1950–62	62 ft.
358	Records of the Federal Maritime Commission	1950–57	6 ft.

District of Columbia

Record Group	Title	Dates	Volume
360	Records of the Continental and Confederation Congresses and the Constitutional Convention	1774–89	312 ft.
374	Records of the Defense Atomic Support Agency	1943–71	456 ft.
401	National Archives Gift Collection of Materials Relating to Polar Regions	1750–1974	991 ft.

U.S. Naval Observatory Library
34th Street and Massachusetts Ave., N.W.
Washington, DC 20390

The Naval Observatory Library has a collection of approximately 75,000 books and journals chiefly on astronomy, but also including the fields of mathematics, physics, geophysics, and navigation. There are complete sets of publications from other observatories dating from the 19th century, periodicals in the subject field dating from the 17th century, and a collection of about 800 rare books on astronomy published between 1482 and 1800.

Although most of the archival materials for the Naval Observatory are in Record Group 78 of the National Archives, some remain in the Library. Included are lists of instruments purchased in the late 19th and early 20th centuries, scrapbooks of newspaper clippings about the Observatory, observing books for different telescopes from the 1870s through the early 1900s, a small historical photographic collection, and some William Harkness (1837–1903) correspondence and scientific papers in 4 manuscript volumes. Also in the Library are approximately 160 boxes of working papers and manuscripts for various scientific projects undertaken at the Observatory, 1870–1950. There are 8 metal boxes of materials from the 1874 Transit of Venus expeditions to the following stations: Kerguelen Island; Hobart and Campbelltown, Tasmania; Queenstown, New Zealand; Chatham Island (Pacific); Vladivostok, Siberia; Peking, China; and Nagasaki, Japan.

U.S. Navy, Bureau of Medicine and Surgery
Office of Public Affairs and *US Navy Medicine*
Building 4, Room 4005
Washington, DC 20372

	Dates	Volume
Biographical File of naval medical officers	ca. 1890s–1970s	4 file drawers

	Dates	Volume
Medical Inspector Edward M. Blackwell (in biographical file; includes diaries kept on board USS *Castine* and other naval ships)	ca. 1898–1923	4 vols.
Captain Frank L. Pleadwell, medical officer and historian	ca. 1913–47	8 items

FLORIDA

Florida State Archives
Tallahassee, FL 32301

	Dates	*Volume*
Hudson Manuscript Collection (includes documents concerning naval ordnance, naval activities at Pensacola, Florida, and French-American maritime problems)	ca. 1720–90	3 reels of microfilm

Florida State University Library
Tallahassee, FL 32306

Admiral Richard Henry Leigh	1870–1944	1,697 items
William S. Rosasco (papers relating to commercial activities in Pensacola and West Florida involving naval stores)	1880, 1916–63	4,656 items

Lakeland Public Library
100 Lake Morton Drive
Lakeland, FL 33801

Senator Park Trammell, Chairman of the Senate Naval Affairs Committee, 1933–36	1911–36	microfilm

Naval Aviation Museum
U.S. Naval Air Station
Pensacola, FL 32508

Flight Logs of Naval and Marine Corps Aviation Units	1940–71	1,500 ft.
Rear Admiral T. J. Hamilton		

U.S. Naval History Sources

Naval Coastal Systems Center
Panama City, FL 32407

This Center, which began in World War II as the Navy Mine Warfare Test Station on Solomons Island, Md., developed as the U.S. Navy Mine Countermeasures Station, the U.S. Navy Mine Defense Laboratory, and in 1972, the Naval Coastal Systems Laboratory. Designated a Center in 1978, the activity's Public Affairs Office holds miscellaneous historical collections of correspondence, clippings, newsletters, vital statistics, and annual reports. Also located here is an untitled manuscript on the history of the Mine Defense Laboratory.

The University of Florida
P. K. Yonge Library of Florida History
Gainesville, FL 32601

	Dates	*Volume*
Senator Park Trammell, Chairman of Senate Naval Affairs Committee, 1933–36	1932–36	20 boxes (also on 3 reels of microfilm)

The nuclear-powered aircraft carrier Dwight D. Eisenhower, *1978*

	Dates	Volume
Senator David Levy Yulee, Chairman of Senate Naval Affairs Committee, 1847–51	1841–86	10,000 pieces (19 reels of microfilm)

Guide: *Dictionary Catalog of the P. K. Yonge Library of Florida History, University of Florida, Gainesville.* Boston: G. K. Hall, 1977.

University of West Florida
John C. Pace Library
Pensacola, FL 32504

	Dates	Volume
Fernando Moreno Blount (includes material relating to U.S. Naval installations in the Pensacola area)	1726–1926	6,784 items
C. J. Heinberg (notebooks and documents relating to the Naval Live Oak Reservation, Santa Rosa County, Florida)		
Chief Surgeon Isaac Hulse	1799–1915	886 items
HMS *Mentor* (logbook)	1781	1 vol.
Pensacola Navy Yard (in Keep Family Papers)	1826–30	
Yonge Family Papers (includes various documents relating to the Naval Live Oak Reservation and affairs at the Pennsacola Navy Yard)	1850–80	
Youd Papers (memorandum books of Naval Inspector, U.S. Naval Station, Pensacola)	1902–03	

GEORGIA

Atlanta Federal Archives and Records Center
Archives Branch
1557 St. Joseph Ave.
East Point, GA 30344

	Dates	Volume
Cecil Field, Florida, U.S. Naval Air Station (Station log books)	1953–56	1 ft.
Glynco, Georgia, U.S. Naval Air Station (Station log books)	1952–54, 1957–59	2 ft.
Key West, Florida, U.S. Naval Air Station (Station log books)	1950–57	8 ft.
Sanford, Florida, U.S. Naval Air Station (Station log books)	1951–57	2 ft.
Sixth Naval District, Charleston, South Carolina (administration and correspondence files from the Commandant and the Industrial Manager of the Sixth Naval District and the Charleston Naval Shipyard)	1954–57, 1940–57	204 ft.
Records of Naval Air Stations in Florida and Georgia	1950–59	13 ft.

Emory University Library
Atlanta, GA 30322

	Dates	Volume
Edwin R. Benedict, sailor	1864–65	1 microfilm reel
First Assistant Engineer William Param Brooks, CSN	1861–69	24 items
Charleston Harbor Defense Papers	1861–69	140 items
Confederate States of America, Navy Secret Service (cypher used during the Civil War)	1861–65	2 items
Mate Frederic E. Davis	1860–63	69 items

Enlisted women (yeoman "F"s) standing inspection at Washington, D.C., 1918

	Dates	Volume
Commander William McBlair, Union and Confederate naval officer (in Virginia Myers McBlair Papers)	1861–62	48 letters
Savannah Squadron of the Confederate Navy		600 items
Henry Frederick Willink (includes documents relating to the building of Confederate ironclads)	1861–65	36 items

Georgia Department of Archives and History
Archives Branch
Atlanta, GA 30304

	Dates	Volume
Adjutant General's Office, Georgia Navy	1861–64	1 vol.
Register of Commissioned Officers for the Georgia Navy and Army	1861–64	1 vol.

Georgia Historical Society
501 Whitaker Street
Savannah, GA 31401

	Dates	Volume
Chief Engineer William P. Brooks, CSN	1861–69	
Confederate States Navy Papers (includes papers of Assistant Paymaster Charles Lucian Jones, CSN)	1863–65	632 items
Confederate States Army and Navy Surgeons Association	1874–89	13 items
Lieutenant Henry Gilliam (in William Jones Papers)	1809–17	

University of Georgia Libraries
Athens, GA 30602

George Francis Burleigh Baber (journal of cruises in USS *John Adams, Dale,* and *Germantown*)	1850–53	
Captain Joy Bright Hancock	1918–72	2,529 items
Commander Edith Langdale Stallings	1943–62	152 items

HAWAII

Bernice Pauahi Bishop Museum
P. O. Box 6037
Honolulu, HI 96818

	Dates	*Volume*
Pacific Scientific Information Center (includes limited naval and Coast Guard materials dealing with the Pacific area)	1935–41	140 drawers of maps, 70,000 aerial photographs, and 130 drawers of notes and publications

Guide: *Bishop Museum Library Catalog.* Boston: G. K. Hall, 1968.

Hawaii State Archives
Iolani Palace Grounds
Honolulu, HI 96813

Ensign Victor Steuart Kaleoaloha Houston (includes letters, 1877–79, from his father, Captain Edwin Samuel Houston)	1877–1940	21 ft.

University of Hawaii Library
Hawaiian Collection
Honolulu, HI 96822

Hawaii (includes journal of Lieutenant Theodorus B. M. Mason while serving in USS *Pensacola*; and journal (1794–95) maintained in HMS *Chatham* by Lieutenant Peter Puget, RN)	1786–1883	1 ft.

ILLINOIS

Federal Archives and Records Center
Archives Branch
7358 South Pulaski Road
Chicago, IL 60629

	Dates	Volume
Naval Ordnance Plant, Louisville, Kentucky (drawings of naval ordnance)	1915–65	1,500 ft.
U.S. Coast Guard Stations on the Great Lakes (log books)	1853–1972	14 ft.

Chicago Historical Society
Clark Street at North Avenue
Chicago, IL 60614

Captain Joseph Bainbridge (journal kept on board USS *Frolic*)	1814	1 vol.
Claude A. Barnett, founder of Associated Negro Press (includes materials on naval personnel)	1919–64	
William Dolan, USMC (diary maintained in USS *San Jacinto*)	1861–64	1 item
Charles F. Gunther, collector (includes extensive correspondence of naval officers and officials, logs, and other documents relating to naval affairs from the era of the American Revolution through the Civil War)	ca. 1775–1865	
Waldo Healy, seaman	1898–99	7 items
James E. Henneberry (journal kept on board USS *Essex*)	1861–64	1 item
Rear Admiral Lewis Ashfield Kimberly	1847–91	ca. 50 items
Lieutenant James Laning	1861–91	ca. 175 items
Naval Order of the United States	1895–1929	8 folders
Captain Joseph P. Sanford	1832–69	16 items

	Dates	Volume
Purser Francis B. Stockton (includes diary, 1832–34)	1832–49	5 vols.

Many additional documents of naval interest appear in other collections.

Illinois State Historical Library
Old State Capitol
Springfield, IL 62706

	Dates	Volume
Charles J. Braden, sailor	1902–08	224 items
Rear Admiral John A. B. Dahlgren (in Abraham Lincoln Papers)	ca. 1861–65	
Admiral David G. Farragut (in Christopher C. Augur Papers)		ca. 3 items
Rear Admiral Andrew H. Foote (in Wallace-Dickey Papers; additional material in Abraham Lincoln Papers)	ca. 1861–62	
Gustavus Vasa Fox, Assistant Secretary of the Navy, 1861–66 (additional material in Abraham Lincoln Papers)	1865	1 item
Rear Admiral Alfred V. Jannotta, USNR	ca. 1922–60	ca. 15 ft.
Lieutenant Louis Kempff	1860–62	7 items
Rear Admiral Harris Laning (autobiography)	n.d.	1 microfilm reel
Admiral David D. Porter (additional materials in Christopher C. Augur, Nathaniel P. Banks, John A. McClernand, and Lewis B. Parsons Papers)	1862	1 item
Acting First Assistant Engineer James L. Smith	1864	1 item
Gideon Welles, Secretary of the Navy, 1861–69 (additional material in Abraham Lincoln, John A. McClernand, and Lewis B. Parsons Papers)	1860–61	27 items
Captain Henry Augustus Wise	1862–63	3 items

Newberry Library
60 West Walton Place
Chicago, IL 60610

Rear Admiral John Adolphus Bernard Dahlgren	1858–70	1 box

U.S. Naval History Sources

University of Chicago
Joseph Regenstein Library
1100 East 57th Street
Chicago, IL 60637

	Dates	*Volume*
Samuel King Alison, nuclear physicist (includes correspondence with the Office of Naval Research)	1945–52	1,100 items
Sir John Duckworth, RN	1808–12	70 items
Marcel Schein, physicist and educator (includes proposals for research projects presented to the Office of Naval Research)	1946–60	1 ft.
U.S. Shipbuilding Labor Adjustment Board	1918	6 vols.

Gideon Welles, Secretary of the Navy, 1861–1869

(transcripts of hearings relating to labor, hours, wages in shipyards, shipbuilding plants, and private shipyard construction for the Navy)

University of Illinois at Urbana-Champaign
University Archives
Urbana, IL 61801

	Dates	Volume
Biological Computer Laboratory Contract and Conference File (includes material on contracts with the Office of Naval Research)	1946–73	ca. 21 ft.
National Defense Program Files (includes material on Naval ROTC, Navy Diesel School, Navy Signal School, and Navy V-12 School units)	1940–56	5 ft.
Office of Naval Research Fatigue (Engineering) Studies (in Papers of Thomas J. Dolan)	1945–58	
Louis N. Ridenour, Dean of the Graduate College and Professor of Physics (includes material relating to military research and development)	1946–50	2 ft.
Frederick Seitz, Professor of Physics and Dean of the Graduate College (restricted collection; includes material relating to naval research and development)	1935–65	ca. 18 ft.

INDIANA

Indiana Historical Society Library
315 West Ohio Street
Indianapolis, IN 46202

	Dates	*Volume*
Rear Admiral George A. Bicknell	1892–1925	121 items
Lieutenant Commander Albert Gallatin Caldwell (in the John Caldwell and Nathaniel R. Usher Collections)	1861–88	
Admiral Jonas Howard Ingram	1938–47	26 items
Chaplain George Jones	1852	1 item
Vice Admiral Albert P. Niblack	1880–1933	167 items
Rear Admiral Nathaniel R. Usher	1871–84	77 items

Indiana State Library
Indiana Division
140 North Senate Avenue
Indianapolis, IN 46204

Richard Wigginton Thompson, Secretary of the Navy, 1877–80	1818–99	400 items

Indiana University
Lilly Library
Bloomington, IN 47401

Commander George A. Bicknell (journal kept on board USS *Iroquois*)	1866–67	1 vol.
Charles Brothers (journal kept on board USS *Hartford*)	1862–65	1 vol.
Dr. George F. Holland, apothecary (journal kept on board USS *Vicksburg*)	1897–99	1 vol.
Howard Ship Yards and Dock Company, Jeffersonville, Indiana, naval contractor	1834–1942	250,000 items

Crew of an Eleven-Inch Dahlgren Gun during the Civil War

	Dates	Volume
Chaplain and Purser A. Y. Humphreys	1814–25	1 journal, 1 letterbook
Taulman A. Miller (draft of history of U.S. Naval Aviation)	1945	1 item
Commander Charles Thompson (in U.S. History Manuscripts; journal of cruise on board USS *Guerriere*)	1830–31	1 item
Richard W. Thompson, Secretary of the Navy, 1877–80	1837–99	382 items

University of Notre Dame Archives
Box 513
Notre Dame, IN 46556

John Francis O'Hara, Auxiliary Bishop of the Army and Navy during World War II	1940–45	13 ft.
Chaplain William Henry Ironsides Reaney	1894–1930	3 boxes, 3 packages

IOWA

Herbert Hoover Presidential Library
West Branch, IA 52358

	Dates	Volume
Herbert Hoover Papers (Cabinet Offices—documents relating to the Navy; Foreign Affairs—documents relating to disarmament)	1929–33	6 ft.
Vice Admiral John Franklin Shafroth	1938–67	6 ft.

Iowa State Historical Department

Division of Historical Museum and Archives
East 12th and Grand Avenue
Des Moines, IA 50319

	Dates	Volume
Rear Admiral George Collier Remey (restricted collection)	1862–1931	80 boxes

Division of the State Historical Society
402 Iowa Avenue
Iowa City, IA 52240

	Dates	Volume
Rear Admiral George Collier Remey (typescript volumes prepared by his son, Charles Mason Remey, entitled "Life and Letters")	1841–1928	6 vols.
Remey Family Correspondence (in the David Rorer Papers)	1856–67	8 items
Reserve Officers Association of the United States. Department of Iowa (includes material on Naval Reserve Officers)	1930–42, 1946–63	5 ft.

Guide: Harris, Katherine, comp. *Guide to Manuscripts.* Iowa City: State Historical Society of Iowa, 1973.

KANSAS

Dwight D. Eisenhower Library
Abilene, KS 67410

	Dates	*Volume*
Vice Admiral Evan P. Aurand	1934–71	20 ft.
Captain Edward Latimer Beach	1935–62	14 ft.
Rear Admiral John Duncan Bulkeley	1928–60	1 ft.
Captain Harry C. Butcher, USNR	1942–46	7 ft.
Captain A. Dayton Clark	1936–63	less than 1 ft.
Naval Aides to the President	1953–61	13 ft.
Rear Admiral William Woodward Outerbridge	1924–69	11 ft.
Vice Admiral Harry Sanders	1944–55	less than 1 ft.
Captain Alfred B. Stanford	1944	less than 1 ft.
Vice Admiral John Wilkes	1916–57	less than 1 ft.

Guide: *Historical Materials in the Dwight D. Eisenhower Library.* Abilene, Kansas: Dwight D. Eisenhower Library, 1977.

Kansas State Historical Society
10th and Jackson Streets
Topeka, KS 66612

Carl Cross (reflects service in the Navy and Army)	1916–19	11 items
Jesse Marvin Hawker (reflects service in the Navy, 1942–43; and the Marine Corps, 1943–59)	1942–59	1 box
Navy League of the United States, Kansas Branch, Topeka, Kansas	1917	ca. 50 items
Rear Admiral Charles Wilkes	1837–42	5 vols.

U.S. Naval History Sources

Wichita State University Library
Special Collections
Wichita, KS 67208

	Dates	*Volume*
Nicaragua and Isthmian Canal Commission Papers	1899–1904	600 items
Rear Admiral John Grimes Walker	1865–1907	5,400 items

LOUISIANA

Dillard University
Amistad Research Center
New Orleans, LA 70122

	Dates	Volume
Amistad (Schooner) Case Collection (microfilm of documents from many different repositories that include materials on the Navy's role in the capture of this slave ship)	1839–1968	6 reels of microfilm

Louisiana Historical Association Collection
Special Collections Division
Howard-Tilton Memorial Library
Tulane University
New Orleans, LA 70118

Confederate Navy and Marine Corps Records	1861–1963	2,725 items
Captain William W. Hunter, Union and Confederate naval officer	1861–65	709 items
Captain Alfred C. Van Benthuysen, Confederate States Marine Corps	1861–65	66 items

Louisiana State University Library
Department of Archives and Manuscripts
Baton Rouge, LA 70803

General Nathaniel Banks, USA (includes material on naval participation in Banks's Red River Campaign)	1863–64	1 letterbook
Nathaniel Buckley Record Book (official reports of officers of USS *Dale*)	1846–48	1 vol.
Ensign John Murphy Caffery (in Donelson Caffery Papers)	1897–1906	

85

	Dates	Volume
Midshipman George William Chapman (in the Eleanor Percy Ware and Catherine Ann Ware Papers)	1835, 1837	3 items
Lemuel Parker Connor and Family Papers (includes letters concerning the visit of USS *Mississippi* to Natchez, 1909)	1909	6 items
Rear Admiral Bartlett Jefferson Cromwell (letters concerning USS *Rio Bravo*)	1878, n.d.	4 items
Josephus Daniels, Secretary of the Navy, 1913–21	1917–36	4 items
Freeman Foster, Jr., sailor serving in the Mississippi River Campaign	1862	3 items
Ernest Lee Jahncke, Assistant Secretary of the Navy, 1929–33	1852–1960	1,528 items, 6 vols.
Lieutenant Edward J. Means, CSN	1864	1 vol.
Alexander R. Miller, sailor serving in the Navy during the Civil War	1861–64	1 diary
Gunner's Mate Oscar E. Peterson	1916–44	23 items, 4 vols.
Lauren Chester Post, radioman during World War I	1917–20	100 items
Rear Admiral Raphael Semmes, Union and Confederate naval officer (in the Walter L. Fleming Collection)	1866–1911	21 items
Acting Third Assistant Engineer William H. Smith	1862–63	5 items
Harold H. Staples (typescript of diary concerning USS *Allen*)	1916–17	1 item
Gideon Welles, Secretary of the Navy, 1861–69	ca. 1878	1 item

Guide: Hogan, William Ransom, ed. *Guide to the Manuscript Collections in Louisiana Department of Archives, Louisiana State University.* University, La.: Department of Archives, LSU, 1940.

MAINE

Maine Historical Society
485 Congress Street
Portland, ME 04111

	Dates	Volume
Captain Edward Preble	1799–1805	1 vol., 1 envelope
Thomas Gilbert Thornton, U.S. Marshal, Saco, Maine (includes letters of marque and other papers concerning privateers, prize vessels, and prisoners of war in the War of 1812)	1798–1824	7 boxes, 1 vol., 1 envelope
Midshipman Alexander Wadsworth		
Midshipman Henry Wadsworth		

University of Maine
Raymond H. Fogler Library
Orono, ME 04473

	Dates	Volume
Remick Family Collection (includes papers pertaining to the U.S. Navy and to the Naval Shipyard at Kittery)	1686–1945	15 ft.
Clark G. Reynolds, naval historian	ca. 1974	2 ft.

U.S. Naval History Sources

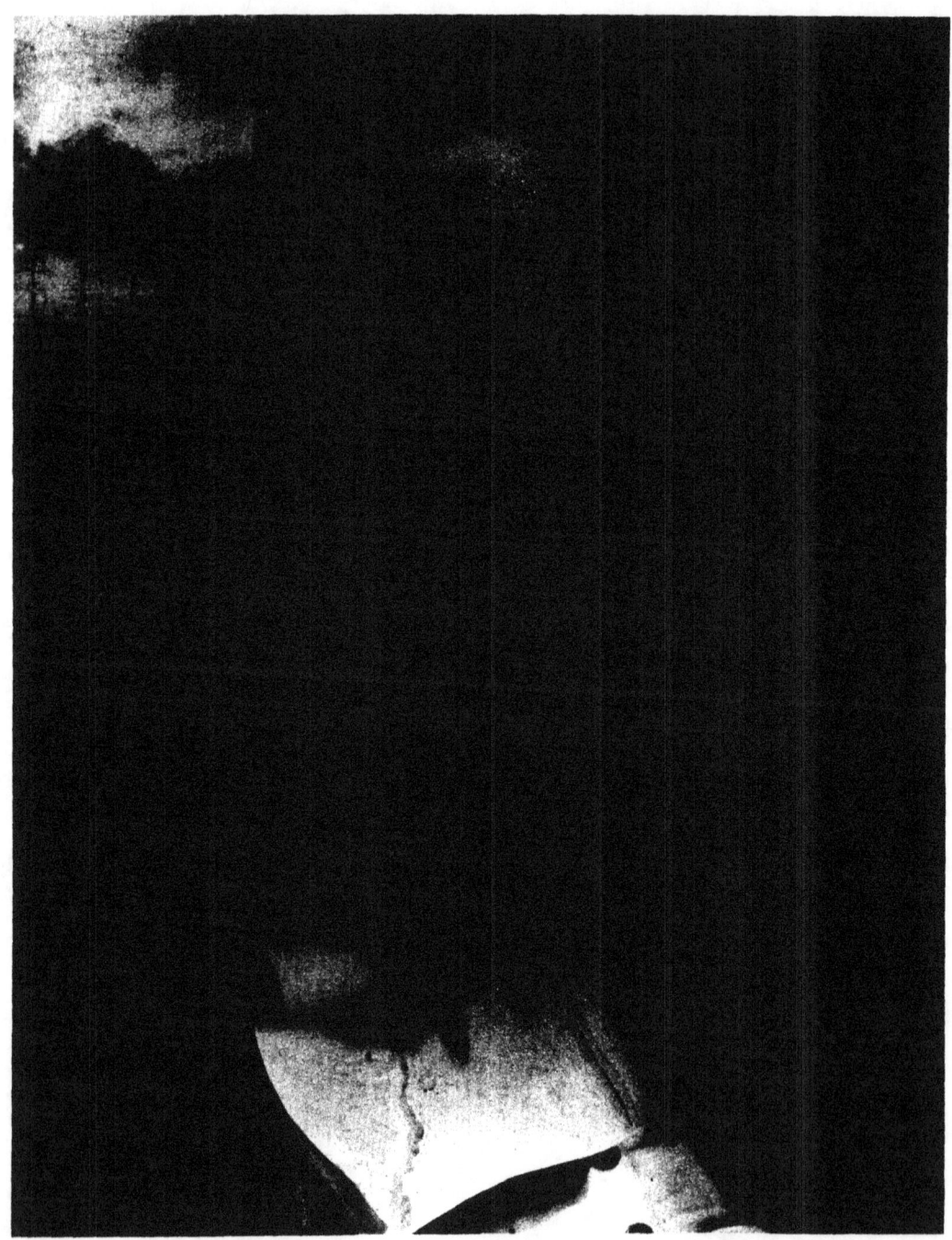

Commodore Edward Preble, a notable leader of the early American Navy

MARYLAND

Applied Physics Laboratory
Archives
Johns Hopkins Rd.
Laurel, MD 20810

	Dates	*Volume*
Records relating to the development and production of the VT fuse	1940–46	ca. 3 ft.

David W. Taylor Naval Ship Research and Development Center

Carderock Laboratory
Bethesda, MD 20084

This laboratory traces its history back to the Experimental Model Basin established in 1896 in the Washington Navy Yard. It became the David W. Taylor Model Basin in 1940 and in 1967 was enlarged and called the Naval Ship Research and Development Center. The name David W. Taylor was restored in 1975.

A collection in the Public Affairs Office includes correspondence, biographical materials, and photographs related to Rear Admiral David W. Taylor and Captain Harold E. Saunders. A pamphlet on the history of the Model Basin titled "The David Taylor Model Basin, A Brief History," has been published by the Naval Historical Foundation. Files of miscellaneous historical records include documents collected in preparation for the laboratory's 75th anniversary. Historical background on the management aspects of the organization are in the bound manuscript "A Case Study of the David W. Taylor Model Basin," by E. L. Livingstone, February 1954. Also available are the Command Histories and accompanying annexes.

Annapolis Laboratory
Annapolis, MD 21402

This laboratory began as the U.S. Naval Engineer Experiment Station and Testing Laboratory at Annapolis in 1903. It evolved into the U.S. Navy Marine Engineering

Laboratory, and in 1967 was merged into the Naval Ship Research and Development Center.

A historical collection in the Public Affairs Office includes early correspondence, annual reports starting in 1911, early photographs of personnel and plant, facility descriptions, and accident reports. Useful documents are included in the scrapbook "History of Engineer Experiment Station, 1908–1944."

Enoch Pratt Free Library
George Peabody Department
17 East Mount Vernon Place
Baltimore, MD 21202

	Dates	Volume
John Pendleton Kennedy, Secretary of the Navy, 1852–53	1812–70	130 vols.

Fort McHenry National Monument and Historic Shrine
Baltimore, MD 21230

Fort McHenry houses 1,500 drawings, paintings, and objects pertaining to the Fort and the city of Baltimore, 1776–1958; and 20,000 microfilmed documents relating to Fort McHenry, 1776–1958, including materials dealing with the British Chesapeake Bay Campaign during the War of 1812.

Hall of Records Commission of Maryland
Box 828
Annapolis, MD 21404

The Maryland Hall of Records includes among its Archives the personal papers of Captain Samuel Smith, 1776; Captain John David, 1777; Captain Thomas Conway, 1777; Captain Ignatius Taylor of the Sloop *Molly*, 1777; and Richard Smith, Sergeant in the Marines on board *Conqueror*. Other items relating to naval history include scattered financial, political, and military material dealing with the Revolutionary War, particularly in the Annapolis area; records of the Continental Admiralty Board, 1776; articles of seamen on board the *Resolution*, 1776; letters in various collections pertaining to military action during the War of 1812–15; letters of Captain Charles Gordon, Commander of USS *Constellation*, 1815–16; Enrollment and Muster Rolls, U.S. Navy, 1864–73; Muster Pay and Receipt Rolls, 1st Maryland Naval Battalion, Maryland National Guard, 1896; and records of the Maryland Naval Brigade at Camp Smith, 1901.

Guides: Papenfuse, Edward C., Gregory A. Stiverson and Mary D. Donaldson. *An Inventory of Maryland State Papers, Volume One: The Revolutionary War Era, 1775–1789.* Annapolis: Maryland Hall of Records Commission, 1977.

Maryland Hall of Records Commission. *Calendar of Maryland State Papers.* Baltimore: Genealogical Pub. Co., 1967– .
    number 3 *The Brown Books,* by Roger Thomas, 1948, reprinted 1973.
    number 4 Part One *The Red Books,* 1950, reprinted 1972.

Vanorny, Patricia M. *A Guide to the Microfilm Holdings of the Maryland Hall of Records,* 1978.

Johns Hopkins University
John Work Garrett Library
4545 North Charles Street
Baltimore, MD 21210

	Dates	*Volume*
John Hancock, member of the Continental Marine Committee (letters on naval matters)	1776–77	2 items
Richard Henry Lee, member of the Continental Marine Committee (letters on naval matters)	1776–77	2 items
Other naval related material (includes letters from George Washington, Francis Hopkinson, Edward Rutledge, and William Whipple)	1777–78	5 items

Maryland Historical Society
Museum and Library of Maryland History
201 West Monument Street
Baltimore, MD 21201

America, privateer schooner (log)	1812	1 vol.
George Jones Armiger (enlisted man lost at sea on board USS *Cyclops*)	1918–38	5 items
Commodore John Henry Aulick Expedition Papers	1851–57	5 items
Battle of Baltimore Records (restricted collection; microfilm of British Admiralty Records; originals held at the Public Record Office, London, England; Admiralty Group)	1814	1 microfilm reel
Captain William Joseph Belt (includes journals kept on board USS *Washington, Columbus, Hudson, Natchez,* and *Marion*)	1811–56	2 boxes, 7 vols.
Charles J. Bonaparte, Secretary of the Navy, 1905–06	1905–26	300 items
Bordley Family (includes material on Stephen Bordley, naval officer)	1612–1955	2 ft., 24 items
Electrician Harry S. Bowman and Ziba Bowman (diaries kept on board USS *Dixie*)	1898	2 vols.

U.S. Naval History Sources

	Dates	Volume
William Dunlop Brackenridge (includes material on the Wilkes Expedition, 1838)	1834–54, 1931–33	2 portfolios
Franklin Buchanan	1820–74	1 box
Thomas McKean Buchanan (letterbook concerning USS *Calhoun*)	1862	1 vol.
Chasseur (log of this private armed brig)	1814–15	1 vol.
Captain William Tipton Conn	1902–19	3 items
Constellation papers (material relating to the restoration of USS *Constellation*)	1959–72	2 boxes, 1 item
Defence, Maryland state naval ship commissioned in 1776 (records compiled from papers in the Land Office of Maryland)	1896	1 vol.
Apothecary Assistant C. Marion Dodson	1812–96, 1929	1 vol., 1 box
Rear Admiral Edward Donaldson	1834–77	10 items
Midshipman John Dorsey	1804	1 vol.
Acting Ensign Henry F. Dorton	1861–70	1 vol.
John L. Dubois (journal of a cruise around the world in USS *Potomac*)	1831–34	1 vol.
Lieutenant (j.g.) Hammond Dugan (naval aeronaut in lighter-than-air program)	1924–51	ca. 4 ft.
Captain Bladen Dulany	1836–55	3 vols.
Captain David Geisinger	1809–56	124 items
Hambleton Family Papers (includes letters, 1813–32, and diary, 1813–14, of Purser Samuel Hambleton; and letters 1820–32, of Purser John N. Hambleton)	1775–1914	91 items
Hammond-Harwood House Manuscript Collection (includes letters from Surgeon Nicholas Harwood on the capture and burning of USS *Philadelphia* during the Barbary Wars in 1803)	1679–1845	28 items
Harford and Cecil County Families (includes papers of a naval surgeon who accompanied Perry to Japan)		
Surgeon Henry Stump Harlan (papers are included in the Harlan Family Collection)		
Captain George N. Hollins, Union and Confederate naval officer (in Winder Family Papers)	ca. 1812–62	
John Mifflin Hood, CSN and CSA	1873–1951	ca. 100 items, 1 box

	Dates	Volume
Colonel Osmun Latrobe, G. A. R. (history of the Washington Navy Yard)	1816–53	2 boxes
Robert K. Lowry, American Consul at La Guayra (letters written to Captain Robert T. Spence)	1793–1825	9 items
Commander William May	1831–57	7 vols.
Captain Isaac Mayo	1842–53	1 vol.
Lieutenant George B. McCulloh (in McCulloh Family Papers)	1820s	2 folders
Assistant Paymaster Edward McKean	1863–64	200 items, 1 vol.
Assistant Surgeon Richard McSherry	1817–85	5 items
Military and Naval Collection	1784–1887	112 items, 8 vols.
Military Units Records	1775–1926	15 vols., 2 folders
USS *Mount Vernon* Record Books	1920	2 vols.
Murray Family Papers (includes material on Captain Alexander Murray and Rear Admiral Alexander Murray)	1812–68	54 items
Muse Family Papers (includes papers of William S. Muse, USMC)	1697–1908	4 boxes
Naval Militia Scrapbook	1901–03	1 vol.
Naval Veteran Post 76, Grand Army of the Republic, Records	1903–26	5 vols.
Lieutenant Jameson Parker USNR	1908–72	ca. 2 ft.
Ports and Customs Papers	1751–1919	550 items, 107 vols., 1 box, 25 cartons
Rear Admiral John Augustus Rodgers	1872–75	
Master's Mate James Lloyd Rogers (includes journals kept on board USS *Powhatan* and *Lexington*)	1846–56	2 vols.
Robert Lyon Rogers, Captain's Secretary on board USS *Cumberland*, 1850 (mainly correspondence with Captain William K. Latimer)	1849–65	41 items
John Ross, Colonial Naval Officer of the Patuxent (account book)	1735–71	1 vol.
Scharf Papers, Maryland Military and Naval Papers (includes the Maryland Naval District Papers)	1747–1865	5 vols.

U.S. Naval History Sources

The frigate United States *defeats HMS* Macedonian, *October 1812*

	Dates	*Volume*
Rear Admiral Edward Simpson	1840–43, 1858–62	1 vol., 2 items
Robert Smith, Secretary of the Navy, 1801–09	1779–1844	90 items
Samuel Spafford, seaman during the War of 1812 (in Spafford Family Papers)	1785–1934	2 boxes
Surgeon Guy Steele	1891–94	55 items
Surgeon Thomas B. Steele	1845–94	100 items
General John Stricker, naval agent	1789–1823	2 vols.
Fireman John Taylor, USS *Mississippi* (in Robert Taylor Papers)	1849–51, 1855	21 items
Rear Admiral Kemp Tolley	1914–27, 1941–45, 1966	21 items, 10 vols.
Ultor and *Decatur*, privateers	1814–15	8 items
War of 1812 Collection	1794–1916	7 boxes
Otho Holland Williams, naval officer and collector of the port of Baltimore	1773–1839	1,515 items, 1 vol.

Guide: Pedley, Avril J. M., comp. *The Manuscript Collections of the Maryland Historical Society.* Baltimore: Maryland Historical Society, 1968.

National Library of Medicine
8600 Rockville Pike
Bethesda, MD 20014

	Dates	*Volume*
J. H. Hobart Burge (essays concerning naval medicine)	ca. 1865	2 items
Assistant Surgeon John L. Fox (journal of a cruise on board USS *Vincennes*)	1838–40	1 vol.
Assistant Surgeon James Duncan Gatewood (includes material on naval hospitals)	1893	2 vols.
Assistant Surgeon John E. Gillespie (includes medical journal kept on board USS *Mohican*)	1865–72	2 vols., ca. 20 items
Surgeon Gustavus R. B. Horner (medical journal kept on board USS *Delaware* by Horner and Surgeons Charles A. Hassler, Howard Smith, and Stephen A. McCreery)	1841–44	1 vol.
New York Seamen's Retreat Hospital Records	1831–73	2 reels of microfilm
Thomas Otis, druggist (includes lists of medicines sold to ships)	1852–67	2 vols.
Captain Charles W. Shilling, Medical Officer, U.S. Naval Submarine Base, New London (history of submarine medicine in World War II, written by Captain Shilling and Mrs. Jessie W. Kohl)	1947	1 vol.
Ship fever (manuscript)	ca. 1850	1 vol.
Zuriel and George Waterman, surgeons on board an American privateer	1774–1817	1 box

Steamship Historical Society Library
University of Baltimore Library
1420 Maryland Avenue
Baltimore, MD 21201

Photograph Collection (includes photographs of U.S. and foreign naval ships)	ca. 1860–present	ca. 20,000 items
U.S. Coast Guard, Governor's Island, N.Y. Intelligence Photographs	ca. 1941–45	2,500 items

U.S. Naval History Sources

United States Naval Academy
Annapolis, MD 21402

Naval Academy Archives

	Dates	Volume
United States Naval Academy Records	1929–present	1,319 ft., 1,241 microfilm reels, 8,647 photographs

Naval Academy Museum

The Naval Academy Museum is an important source of reference objects, graphics, and manuscripts of the U.S. Navy and the Naval Academy. The Museum houses over 50,000 items. Significant collections include the Henry Huddleston Rogers Ship Models; over 500 marine, naval, and portrait paintings by famous artists, including Gilbert Stuart, Thomas Sully, J. W. Jarvis, Thomas Birch, Robert Hinckley, and Edward Moran; the U.S. Navy Trophy Flags; the Malcolm Storer Naval Medals; the Beverley R. Robinson Naval Battle Prints; John Paul Jones memorabilia; photographs; and manuscripts dating from the 18th to the 20th century.

Among the notable manuscript collections held by the Museum are:

	Dates	Volume
Captain Ernest L. Ackiss		10 items
Rear Admiral W. B. Bayley	1864–1906	
Boston Naval Library and Institute	1842–85	13 vols.
Boston (Charlestown) Navy Yard	1800–79	
Joseph C. Bradford, sailmaker		47 items
Brooklyn Naval Lyceum	1833–82	14 vols., 150 items
Lieutenant Commander George W. De Long (includes the "ice-journals" for *Jeanette* expedition)	1861–81	7 vols.
Captain John Downes	1814–34	2 vols.
Captain Charles Edison		
Admiral David Glasgow Farragut (includes journals, letters, and an autobiography to 1848)	1817–70	100 items, 4 vols.
Robert Fulton, naval inventor	1809–1925	16 items
Captain Charles Gauntt	1812–47	1 vol.
Admiral Albert Gleaves	1917	1 vol.

	Dates	Volume
Rear Admiral Francis Gregory (collected naval autographs)	1811–?	
Acting Master John F. Harden	1861–68	69 items
Captain John Paul Jones	1778–89	1 vol., 100 items
Journals, diaries, and logs	1779–1942	ca. 160 items
Paymaster William T. Keeler (manuscripts relating to USS *Monitor*; personal log)	1862–65	900 pages
Rear Admiral Joseph Lanman	1869–70	1 vol.
Captain John Marston	1850	1 vol.
Captain Charles S. McDonough	1835–67	26 items
Naval Consulting Board (minutes)	1915–19	
Navy Department (intelligence memorandum book)	1870s	1 vol.
Admiral Horatio Lord Nelson, RN	1798–1805	48 items
New York Navy Yard	1941	1 vol.
USS *Panay* (records of proceedings of Court of Inquiry)		
Admiral Woodward Philip	1865–68, 1898–99	3 vols.
Commodore Charles W. Pickering	1828–65	144 items
Admiral David Dixon Porter	1863–90	6 vols.
Admiral Joshua R. Sands	1830–79	
Admiral Winfield Scott Schley (includes the Winfield Scott Collection)	1884–1935	ca. 4 vols.
Admiral David Foote Sellers Autograph Collection	ca. 1784–1945	
Captain Henry S. Stellwagen	1852–57	2 vols.
Captain Thomas Truxtun		1 vol.
United States Naval Academy (includes correspondence file, log and letter books, autograph books, and other related material)	ca. 1845–98	11 vols.
Rear Admiral John G. Walker	1851–94	3 vols.
George Washington (account books of his estate)	ca. 1762–84, 1823	2 vols.
Assistant Surgeon Charles K. Yancey		10 items

The Museum also holds many individual letters, scrapbooks, account books, and related documents in its manuscript collection. Journals written by many of the officers listed here appear in the collection under the names of their ships. In addition, there are a number of miscellaneous commissions, letters, and papers signed by naval officers, U.S. Presidents, and Secretaries of the Navy. Other items are described in the following catalogs published by the Museum: *Catalogue of the Rosenbach Collection of Manuscripts* (1956); *Catalogue of the Christian A.*

U.S. Naval History Sources

Zabriskie Manuscript Collection (1956); and *Catalogue of Manuscripts* (1957). Further information can be obtained from the Director, U.S. Naval Academy Museum, Annapolis, Maryland 21402.

Nimitz Library

The Library of some 490,000 books and periodicals contains the materials necessary for a good college library with a scientifically oriented academic program. The Library's Special Collections Department contains approximately 20,000 volumes (including rare books and many unique naval items), as well as the Library's collections of manuscripts, photographs, and films. The Library's manuscript collection includes personal papers, ship logs, journals, order books, letterbooks, and watch/station/quarter bills dating from 1759 to the present. The Edward J. Steichen Collection of Photography includes World War II naval combat photographs, as well as works by such notable American photographers as Edward Weston, Dorothea Lange, Gordon Parks, and many others. The Nimitz Library's own Picture Collection contains several thousand photographs, including numerous 19th century prints, relating to the U.S. Navy and the U.S. Naval Academy.

The following manuscript collections are in the Special Collections Department:

	Dates	*Volume*
Captain Joel Abbot	1815–55	25 reels of microfilm
Carroll Storrs Alden, professor at the Naval Academy, 1904–41	1904–41	1 box
Commander George Mifflin Bache	1855–96	2 boxes
Vice Admiral Wilson Brown	1902–55	7 boxes
Campaigns of a British officer in Europe and America, with an account of operations in the United States	1814–15	1 vol.
Franklin Buchanan, first Commandant and Superintendent of the Naval Academy	1842–47	2 vols.
Captain Robert Dexter Conrad	1929–45	5 ft.
Rear Admiral John A. Dahlgren	1855	1 vol.
Captain Richard Dale	1802	1 vol.
Commander Edwin Jesse DeHaven	1835–79	2 boxes
Rear Admiral Daniel Vincent Gallery	1870–1977	90 boxes
Robert Hutchings Goddard, physicist (rocketry research notebooks)	1921–43	23 vols.
Passed Assistant Surgeon George H. Harmon	1884	1 vol.
Captain John D. Henley	1808–12	1 vol.
Chief Naval Constructor Samuel Humphreys	1824–45	1 vol.

Maryland

	Dates	*Volume*
Richard B. Jones, U.S. Consul at Tripoli	1814–19	1 vol., 4 items
Rear Admiral Husband E. Kimmel (originals at University of Wyoming)	1938–68	35 reels of microfilm
Admiral Harry S. Knapp	1877–1923	1 box
Logs, journals, letterbooks, order books, and watch/station/quarter bills	1796–1938	158 vols.
Albert Abraham Michelson, physicist and naval officer	ca. 1829–1970	16 ft.
Rear Admiral William Adger Moffett	1869–1933	6 ft.
Captain Matthew C. Perry	1820	1 vol.
Lieutenant Lloyd Phoenix	1862–63	1 vol.
Rear Admiral Winfield Scott Schley	1885–91	1 vol.

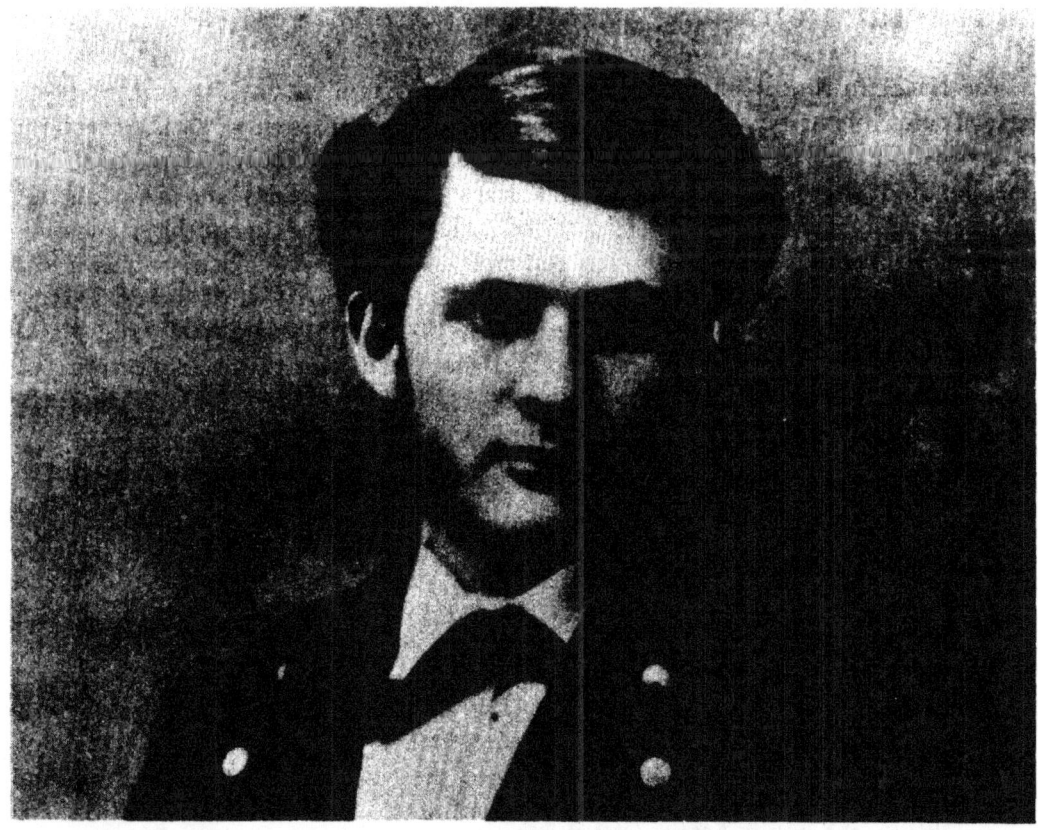

Albert A. Michelson, 1873 graduate of the U.S. Naval Academy and Nobel Prize winner, whose classic measurements of the speed of light began while serving as an instructor at the Academy

	Dates	Volume
Erastus Washington Smith, naval engineer	1850–81	2 boxes, 1 package
Rear Admiral Charles Stewart	1843–55	1 vol.
Vertical File (collection of miscellaneous items, including biographical and bibliographical materials, clippings, pamphlets, ships' histories, command histories, and other related items)		
Lieutenant James I. Waddell, CSN	1863	1 vol.
Acting Volunteer Lieutenant George E. Welch	1862–65	1 vol.
Captain Samuel Woodhouse	1823–39	1 vol.

United States Naval Institute
Naval Museum Building
United States Naval Academy
Annapolis, MD 21402

The Naval Institute sponsors an oral history program which is now in its tenth year. Transcripts of taped interviews record the personal experiences and reflections of men who have participated in naval events of historic significance. To date almost one hundred volumes are available and many additional ones are in process. A complete card index is maintained for the collection. The collection also includes clusters of single interviews with men and women on special subjects such as: Fleet Admiral Nimitz, the WAVES, Naval Aviation, the U.S. Coast Guard, and POLARIS.

A special collection of approximately 250,000 photographs is in the Naval Institute Library. The entire James C. Fahey and *Our Navy* collections of photographs covering U.S. and foreign naval vessels are included. In addition, there is an extensive collection of photographs on World War II and Vietnam.

The Naval Institute has a complete collection of the volumes of *Proceedings*, dating from the first issue in 1874. A comprehensive index is available.

White Oak Laboratory
Naval Surface Weapons Center
Silver Spring, MD 20910

This laboratory evolved from the Mine Unit and Experimental Ammunition Unit established at the Washington Navy Yard in 1919. It became the Naval Ordnance Laboratory that in 1974 was consolidated into the Naval Surface Weapons Center. Eighty cubic feet of historical records relating to NSWC from 1917–75 are controlled by the Public Affairs Office.

MASSACHUSETTS

American Antiquarian Society
Salisbury Street and Park Avenue
Worcester, MA 01609

	Dates	*Volume*
George Bancroft, Secretary of the Navy, 1845–46	1819–1901	2 boxes
Commander Amos Binney	1810–14	458 items
Commodore George Smith Blake	1857–63	19 items
Captain Isaac Hull-William Eaton letterbook	1804–05	1 vol.
William Mann (British privateer ship carpenter)	1803–05	1 journal
Rear Admiral George Henry Preble	1861–82	7 vols., 6 items
William G. Scandlin, seaman	1849–1946	1 box, 2 vols.
Ship Logbook Collection	1716–1874	26 vols.
Spalding Family (includes diary of Lieutenant Lyman Greenleaf Spalding, 1862)	1806–1904	24 items
Tripolitan War Collection	1804–05	4 items
U.S. Records Collection (includes naval documents)	1784–1827	
U.S. Revolution Collection (includes naval documents)	1754–1928	

American Jewish Historical Society Collections
2 Thornton Road
Waltham, MA 02154

American Jewish Committee, Office of War Records (contains material on Jewish naval personnel during World War I)	1918–21	10 ft.
Mark Jacob Katz (includes material relating to the sinking of the USS *Maine* and USS *Yosemite*)	1898–1919	200 items
Captain Uriah Phillips Levy	1787–1944	129 items
National Jewish Welfare Board, Bureau of War	1940–69	672 boxes

U.S. Naval History Sources

	Dates	Volume
Records (concerns Jewish servicemen, including those in the Navy, during World War II)		
Midshipman Joseph B. Nones	1812–22	200 items

Beverly Historical Society
117 Cabot Street
Beverly, MA 01915

	Dates	Volume
William Bartlett Account Books (includes material on Washington's Navy)	1775–77	
U.S. Naval Office at Beverly, Records of	1784–1800	13 vols.
Ships' Papers (various ships)	1712–1868	

Boston Athenaeum Library
10½ Beacon Street
Boston, MA 02108

	Dates	Volume
Charlestown, Massachusetts Navy Yard: Account Books	1798–99	2 vols.
J. Greenleaf (supplier of medicine to Continental Navy)	1748–77	9 vols.
Captain Isaac Hull	1810–41	18 vols.

Boston Federal Archives and Records Center
Archives Branch
380 Trapelo Road
Waltham, MA 02154

	Dates	Volume
Naval Reserve Officers Training Corps, Yale University, New Haven, Connecticut	1941–69	1 box
United States Districts and Circuit Courts for Massachusetts, Connecticut, Vermont, Maine, New Hampshire, and Rhode Island (includes records and documents of admiralty and customs violation cases and for prize cases of the Quasi-War with France, War of 1812, and Civil War)	1789–1949	10,000 ft.
United States Coast Guard Unit Logs (includes logs of cutters, light houses, light ships, and shore units; other material relating to revenue cutters appears in the records of the United States Customs Service)	1963–74	31 ft.

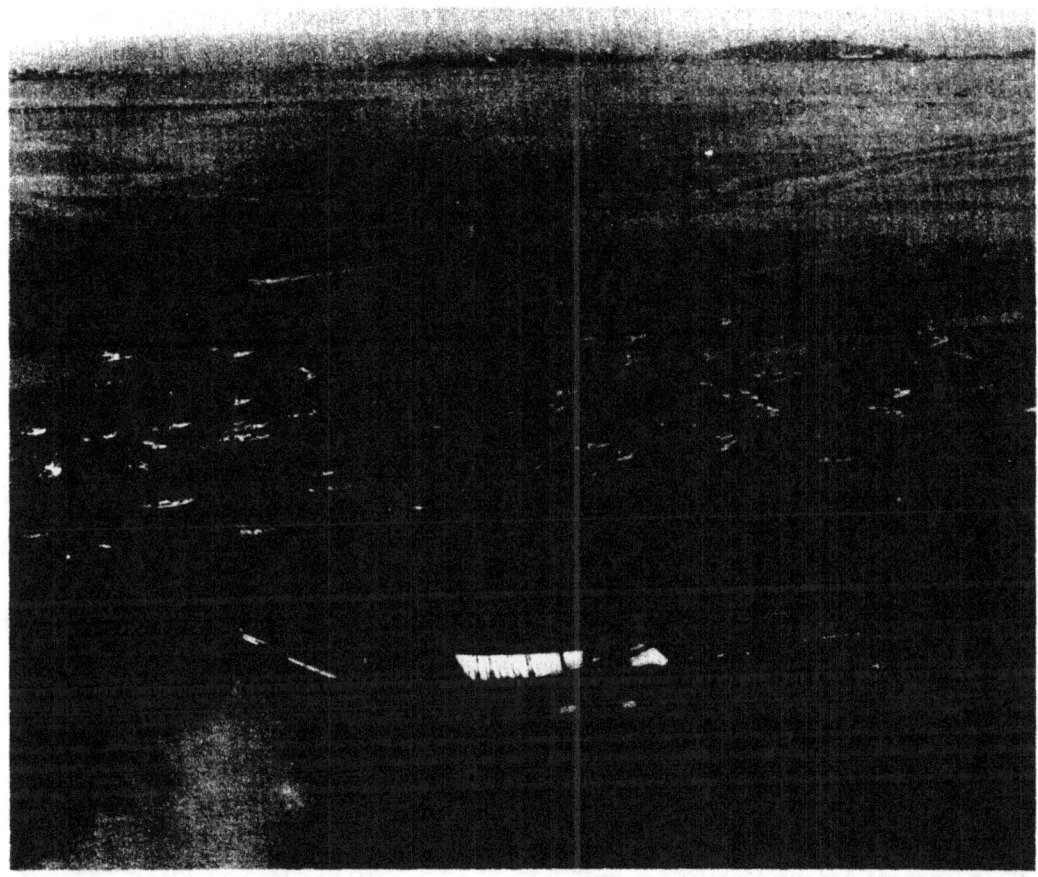

The frigate Constitution, *first commissioned in 1797, during Bicentennial ceremonies in Boston Harbor, 1976*

Boston Public Library
Department of Rare Books and Manuscripts
Boston, MA 02117

	Dates	*Volume*
Josiah Barker, naval constructor (correspondence with the Navy Department concerning *Great Western*)	1838	27 items
USS *Beagle*	1824–25	1 log
Sir Roger Curtis, RN	1809–15	114 items
Charles Kimball Cummings (voyages in USS *Mount Vernon*)	1917–19	1 vol.
Richard D. Harris (claims to land occupying Charlestown Navy Yard; includes correspondence with several naval officials)	1820–40	

U.S. Naval History Sources

	Dates	Volume
Captain Elisha Hinman	1877	1 item
Captain John Hitch	1775–76	16 items
USS *John Adams* (watch, quarter and station bills)	1855	1 vol.
E. Kent (log of service on board USS *Nonsuch*, 1821–24; *Cyane*, 1825–27; and *Erie*, 1830–31)	1821–31	1 vol.
Massachusetts Commissary General (receipts for supplies issued to state ships and units)	1778–79	
Naval Battles During Revolution (notebook with lists and short accounts of naval battles during Revolution)	1775–83	notebook
USS *Plymouth* (watch, quarter and station bills, ship's regulations)	1844?	1 vol.
Commodore William David Porter	1838–64	3 vols.
USS *Trenton* (includes watch, quarter and station bills)	1877–79	1 vol.
USS *United States* (navigational log)	1827	1 item
USS *Vincennes* (orderly book and muster roll)	1861	1 vol.

Boston University Libraries
771 Commonwealth Avenue
Boston, MA 02215

	Dates	Volume
Rear Admiral Arthur Ainsley Ageton	1920–71	10 ft.
Rear Admiral Winfield Scott Cunningham	1923–70	2 ft.
Major James Patrick S. Devereux, USMC	1940–71	20 ft.
Captain Harvey S. Haislip	1942–77	2 ft.
Richard Newcomb, naval author	ca. 1960–70	3 ft.

Commonwealth of Massachusetts
Archives Division
Office of the Secretary of State
State House
Boston, MA 02133

The Archives Division contains naval documents of the American Revolution in many of its collections, including the Council Papers, Journals of the House of Representatives, and Records of the Provincial Congress. The Revolution Rolls include information on Prize Courts. In the Council Papers are five ship logs including the log of the privateer *Winthrop*, 1782–83, and two logs of HMS *Rainbow*, 1771–74.

Massachusetts

Concord Free Library
129 Main Street
Concord, MA 01742

	Dates	*Volume*
Admiral David G. Farragut	1862–64	7 items
U.S. Marshal for Massachusetts John Shepard Keyes (contains documents concerning prize cargoes)	1861–67	1 box
Samuel Southard, Secretary of the Navy, 1823–29	1828	2 items

The Essex Institute
James Duncan Phillips Library
132 Essex Street
Salem, MA 01970

Joseph Vincent Browne, naval agent	1822–69	6 vols.
Rear Admiral Charles Edgar Clark	1898–1904	1 envelope
Benjamin Williams Crowninshield, Secretary of the Navy, 1815–18 (in Crowninshield Family Papers)	1801–31	7 folders
Acting Master Caleb A. Curtis	1861–63	1 envelope
Gregory Family (includes pension claims for soldiers and sailors in the Revolutionary War)	1840–65	13 vols.
Senator Henry Alexander Wise, Chairman of House Committee on Naval Affairs, 1842–43	1836–59	1 vol.

Manuscripts relating to privateers in the American Revolution appear in various collections, including the Ward Family Papers, the Goodhue Family Papers, and the Derby Family Papers. The Institute also holds journals and logs of privateers.

Harvard University
Cambridge, MA 02138

Baker Library

	Dates	*Volume*
Electric Boat Company (naval contractor)	1910–23	1 box
Navy Units and Offices in New York (includes account books and journal, 1849–51, kept by Midshipman R. C. Chandler on board USS *Vincennes*)	1849–64	4 vols.

U.S. Naval History Sources

Gray Herbarium Library

	Dates	Volume
Rear Admiral Charles Wilkes	1848–73	50 items

Harvard University Archives

	Dates	Volume
Frederick V. Hunt, physicist at Harvard Underwater Sound Laboratory	ca. 1927–70	10 ft.

Rear Admiral Samuel Eliot Morison, USNR, whose distinguished historical writings included many volumes dealing with the U.S. Navy

Massachusetts

	Dates	Volume
Donald H. Menzel, Harvard astronomer and naval officer		
Samuel Eliot Morison, naval historian and naval officer		
Navy Supply Corps School	1941–45	8 ft.
Underwater Sound Laboratory (Harvard)	1941–46	10 ft.
U.S. Naval Radio School (Harvard)	1919–21	½ ft.
U.S. Naval Training School (Harvard)	1942–45	12 ft.

Guide: Elliott, Clark A., comp. *A Descriptive Guide to the Harvard University Achives.* Cambridge, Mass: Harvard University Library, 1974.

Houghton Library

	Dates	Volume
Captain John Paul Jones (in the Sparks and Lee Collections)		
Senator James Lloyd, Chairman of Senate Committee on Naval Affairs, 1823–25		
Admiral Horatio Nelson, RN (includes log of HMS *Victory*)	1760–1869	250 items
President Theodore Roosevelt (includes papers as Assistant Secretary of the Navy)	1868–1919	
Captain Samuel Tucker	1774–1884	6 vols.

Haverhill Public Library
99 Main Street
Haverhill, MA 01830

	Dates	Volume
William Henry Moody, Secretary of the Navy, 1902–04	1892–1952	500 items

Holy Cross College
Worcester, MA 01610

	Dates	Volume
Senator David I. Walsh, Chairman of the Senate Naval Affairs Committee, 1936–46	1890–1946	30 ft.

U.S. Naval History Sources

International Marine Archives, Inc.
(formerly the Whaling and Marine Manuscript Archives)
93 Main Street
P.O. Box 1826
Nantucket, MA 02554

	Dates	*Volume*
Alaska Revenue Cutter Service:		
Letters Received	1869–1910	
The Bering Sea Patrol, Telecommunications of the Alaska Section	1912–14	
Point Barrow Refuge Station	1884–98	
Alaska Operations, Reports and Summaries	1884–1911	
Samuel R. Knox (Naval Signal Book)	ca. 1840	1 vol.
Ship Logbooks and Journals (materials from more than 75 naval ships and privateers, primarily for the 18th and 19th centuries, are found. These include a number of items relating to the U.S. Exploring Expedition of 1838–42.)	ca. 1777–1918	

Guide: A Compilation of the Holdings of the Whaling and Marine Manuscript Archives. Nantucket, Mass.: The Whaling and Marine Manuscript Archives, 1971. (With subsequent addenda).

John F. Kennedy Library
380 Trapelo Road
Waltham, MA 02154

Admiral Arleigh Burke (oral history)	1967	
Paul B. Fay, Jr., Under Secretary of the Navy, 1961–65 (restricted collection)		1 ft.
Rear Admiral John Harllee	1945–69	3 reels of microfilm
Admiral Alan Kirk (oral history)	1961	

Longfellow National Historic Site
Cambridge, MA 02138

Midshipman Henry Wadsworth (includes journal kept on board USS *Chesapeake*)	1796–1804	1 box, 1 journal

Marblehead Historical Society
161 Washington Street
Marblehead, MA 01945

	Dates	Volume
Jonathan Glover (includes material on Washington's Navy)	1775–96	2 vols.

Massachusetts Historical Society
1154 Boylston Street
Boston, MA 02215

	Dates	Volume
Gardner Weld Allen, naval historian	1811–1935	3 boxes
George Bancroft, Secretary of the Navy, 1845–46	1817–90	54 vols., 47 boxes
Samuel Brown, naval agent	1799–1805	3 boxes
Godfrey L. Cabot (includes service as Lieutenant, USNR, in World War I)	1872–1961	35 ft.
Seaman John Richards Child	1731–1892	50 items
Congressman Benjamin Williams Crowninshield, Chairman of House Committee on Naval Affairs, 1823–25		
Lieutenant James A. Dudley	1814	1 journal
Chaplain Charles Folsom	1732–1871	5 vols.
Vice Admiral Samuel Graves, RN		
Seaman Ezra Green	1819–40	
Samuel Higginson, naval agent		
Joshua Huntington, RN		
James Lloyd, Chairman of the Senate Committee on Naval Affairs, 1823–24	1801–26	30 items
John Davis Long, Secretary of the Navy, 1897–1902	1862–1922	115 vols., 68 boxes
George Von Lengerke Meyer, Secretary of the Navy, 1909–13	1900–18	55 vols., 21 boxes
Captain's Clerk John Eliot Parkman	1853–94	2 vols.
Captain John Percival	1826–40	1 box
Rear Admiral George Henry Preble	1732–1887	44 vols., 6 boxes
David I. Walsh, Chairman of the Senate Committee on Naval Affairs, 1936–46	1915–36	8 items
Ralph Randolph Wormeley, RN	1802–65	1 box

Guide: Massachusetts Historical Society. *Catalog of Manuscripts.* Boston: G. K. Hall, 1969. (7 vols.)

Memorial Hall Library
Andover, MA 01810

	Dates	Volume
Naval Records of Andover, Massachusetts	1861–65	

New England Historic Genealogical Society
101 Newbury Street
Boston, MA 02116

	Dates	Volume
HMS *Boxer*	1817	
USS *Constitution* (morning report)	1804	1 item
Lieutenant John B. Dale (journals kept on board USS *Vincennes, Constitution,* and *Porpoise*)	1831–46	7 vols.
Privateer *Dash*	1814	
USS *Essex*	1801	1 item
Captain Isaac Hull (letterbook)	1838–39	ca. 500 pp.
Professor of Mathematics David McClure	n.d.	1 vol.
Miscellaneous papers dealing with privateers in the American Revolution and in the War of 1812; pension applications and transcriptions of accounts of voyages and battles		
Rear Admiral Nathan Eric Niles	ca. 1847–1930	1 vol.
USS *Ohio* (account books)	1839–41	3 vols.
Rear Admiral George Henry Preble (includes journals)	ca. 1839–70	ca. 8 vols.

Old Dartmouth Historical Society and Whaling Museum
18 Johnny Cake Hill
New Bedford, MA 02740

	Dates	Volume
Logbooks (includes logbooks or journals of USS *Boston*, 1832; *Brandywine*, 1828; *Enterprise*, 1902; *Falmouth*, 1831; *Narragansett*, 1859; *Portsmouth*, 1850; and *United States*, 1815)	1745–1922	65 ft.

Guide: *Checklist of Logbooks in the Old Dartmouth Historical Society and Whaling Museum* (available from the museum)

Peabody Museum
Salem, MA 01970

	Dates	Volume
Charlestown, Massachusetts Navy Yard (diary of transactions in papers of Robert Knox, Sr.)	1838	2 vols.

Massachusetts

	Dates	Volume
Benjamin Crowninshield, Secretary of the Navy, 1815–18	1814–29	2 boxes
USS *Essex*	1798–1800	4 vols., 960 items
Naval Constructor Josiah Fox	1794	4 vols., 960 items
Lieutenant Samuel R. Knox (journal)	1839–48	2 vols.
Logbooks, journals, station books	1812–73	30 items
Miscellaneous Navy-related documents	pre-Revolution–1918	20 boxes
Corporal Austin Quinby, USMC (journal kept on board USS *Kearsarge*)	1862–64	1 vol.
Joseph Waters, merchant, sea captain, and naval agent	1790–1838	500 items

Radcliffe College
Arthur and Elizabeth Schlesinger Library on the History of Women in America
Cambridge, MA 02138

	Dates	Volume
Elizabeth Reynard (includes materials relating to her position as Assistant Director of the WAVES during World War II)	1934–62	14 file boxes
U.S. Defense Advisory Committee on Women in the Services	1951–55	2 file boxes
WAVES (Women Accepted for Volunteer Emergency Service)	1954–57	1 folder

Guide: Arthur and Elizabeth Schlesinger Library on the History of Women in America. *The Manuscript Inventories and the Catalog of the Manuscripts, Books and Pictures, Radcliffe College.* Boston: G. K. Hall, 1973. (3 vols.)

Smith College
College Archives and the Sophia Smith Collection
Northampton, MA 01063

	Dates	Volume
London Naval Conference (collection of Josephine Schain)	1930	1 folder
WAVES (Women Accepted for Volunteer Emergency Service)	1942–46	10 items

U.S. Naval History Sources

State Library of Massachusetts
State House
Boston, MA 02133

	Dates	*Volume*
USS *Constitution* (journal of Midshipman John Pope)	1825—26	1 vol.

Tufts College Library
Medford, MA 02155

William H. Ryder Collection (records of the Confederate States of America including material relating to the Office of the Secretary of the Navy, Stephen R. Mallory)	1861—65	755 items

Guide: Historical Records Survey, WPA. *A Calendar of the Ryder Collection on Confederate Archives at Tufts College.* Boston: Historical Records Survey, 1940.

MICHIGAN

Detroit Public Library
Burton Historical Collection
5201 Woodward Avenue
Detroit, MI 48202

	Dates	*Volume*
Edwin Denby, Secretary of the Navy, 1921–24	1918–24	12 boxes
Alexander Harrow, RN	1779–1930	6 boxes
Second Assistant Engineer Myron H. Knapp	1862–67	4 vols.
Truman Handy Newberry, Secretary of the Navy, 1908–09	1879–1936	17 vols., 414 boxes
Captain Melancthon Taylor Woolsey (includes material on Commodore Melancthon Brooks Woolsey)	1804–92	27 vols., 13 boxes

Greenfield Village and Henry Ford Museum
Robert Hudson Tannahill Research Library
Dearborn, MI 48121

Rear Admiral Charles Henry Davis, 1807–77, and Rear Admiral Charles Henry Davis, 1845–1921	chiefly 1850–70	3 boxes, 24 items

Other naval documents, photographs, and posters appear throughout the library's holdings.

University of Michigan
William L. Clements Library
Ann Arbor, MI 48104

Sir Robert Barrie, RN	1812–31	63 items
William Bentinck, RN	1783–84	2 items
Purser Thomas J. Chew	1809–50	2 ft.

U.S. Naval History Sources

	Dates	Volume
Lieutenant Charles W. Christopher (in Hawaiian Islands Collection)	1868–83	14 items
Rear Admiral George Clinton, RN, naval officer and Colonial Governor of New York	1697–1759	6 ft.
Edwin Denby, Secretary of the Navy, 1921–24 (in Miscellaneous Manuscripts)	1845–46, 1801–1929	2 ft.
D'Estaing Manuscript (signal book of the French Fleet during the American Revolution)	1780	1 items
Admiral Sir James Douglas, RN	1738–87	4 ft.
Purser Thomas Cochrane Dudley (purser's clerk on USS *Powhatan* during Perry's voyage to Japan)	1852–55	81 items
Surgeon Amos Evans (Prescription book from USS *Constitution*; vol. 2 in Yale Library)	1812–13	1 vol.
Germain Papers (Lord George Sackville, afterwards Germain; includes correspondence with British naval commanders during the American Revolution)	1683–1785	8 ft.
Sir Anthony Hiley Hoskins, RN (on the North American Station)	1869–72	2 items
Gene Frank Howard (letters written while serving in the U.S. Navy during World War II)	1945–51 RICHA)RD	150 items
Howe Family (includes material relating to Richard Howe, commander of British naval forces in North America, 1776–78)	1758–1812	51 items
Sumner Howard (includes letters relating to service in the U.S. Navy during World War II)	1942–53	500 items
Admiral Sir Pulteney Malcolm, RN (includes logbooks and letters regarding the War of 1812)	1814–17	46 items
Vice Admiral Christopher Mason, RN	1780–95	1 vol.
Melville Papers (includes material on Henry Dundas, first Viscount Melville and treasurer of the Navy, 1782–1800; and Robert Saunders Dundas, second Viscount Melville and First Lord of the Admiralty, 1812–30; includes material related to the War of 1812)	1600–1851	14 ft.
Michigan Naval Militia	1861–1917	
Miscellaneous Manuscripts (includes a journal, 1832–33, of an officer on board USS *St. Louis;* Japanese "instructions for receiving Perry's mission;" 37 reports of a British spy in Paris concerning French and Spanish Fleets in 1780; and other naval related documents)		

Commodore Oliver Hazard Perry proceeding to a new ship during the Battle of Lake Erie, 1813, after his flagship was heavily damaged by the enemy

	Dates	Volume
Chevalier de Monteil, French Navy (includes logbooks for several French ships and material concerning service under Admiral De Grasse during the American Revolution)	1781–82	5 items
Captain Charles Morris	1801–51	65 items
Lord Horatio Nelson, RN (in Smith Naval Collection)	1781–1805	100 items
Captain Oliver Hazard Perry	1795–1864	4 ft.
Porter Papers (papers of Captain David Porter and Admiral David Dixon Porter)	1805–1908	4 ft.
Alexander Robinson, American captain of a sea fencible corps, War of 1812	1813–43	1 ft.
President Theodore Roosevelt (includes material on his service as Assistant Secretary of the Navy)	1885–1919	1 ft.

	Dates	Volume
Schoff Civil War Collection (includes logs of USS *Marion*, *Moro Castle*, and CSS *Southern Rights*, and other naval related items)	1856–69	12 ft.
Rear Admiral Thomas O. Selfridge (in Smith Naval Collection and Aaron Cooke Collection)	1810–62	
Smith Naval Collection (the bulk of this collection relates to English and American naval history from 1800–89)	12th c.–1915	4 ft.
Midshipman George William Taylor	1828–32	19 items
War of 1812 Collection	1806–60	250 items
Sir Peter Warren, RN (officer on the North American Station; includes material on capture of French Fort Louisbourg, 1745)	1744–51	200 items
Captain Abraham Whipple (includes material on *Providence*)	1763–87	180 items
James Aldrich Whipple (submarine engineer and inventor)	1847–60	3 ft.
USS *Yosemite* (in Mortimer Elwyn Cooley Collection; includes log of the ship during the Spanish-American War)		3 vols.

Guides: Shy, Arlene Phillips, and Barbara A. Mitchell. *Guide to the Manuscript Collections of the William L. Clements Library.* 3rd. ed. Boston: G. K. Hall, 1978.

Ewing, William S. *Guide to the Manuscript Collections in the William L. Clements Library.* 2nd. ed. Ann Arbor: Clements Library, 1953.

Peckham, Howard H. *Guide to the Manuscript Collections in the William L. Clements Library.* Ann Arbor: Clements Library, 1942.

MINNESOTA

Historical Committee of the Baptist General Conference
Bethel College and Seminary
1480 North Snelling Avenue
St. Paul, MN 55108

	Dates	Volume
Acting Ensign John A. Edgren	1871–87	

Minnesota Historical Society
Division of Archives and Manuscripts
1500 Mississippi Street
St. Paul, MN 55101

	Dates	Volume
Lieutenant James Edward Calhoun	1823	1 vol.
Passed Midshipman William Harrison Cheever	1853–54	2 items
Lieutenant William Sitgreaves Cox (relates to family investigation of the court martial charges brought against this officer during the War of 1812)	1905–53	
Midshipman Robert S. Furber (diary maintained at U.S. Naval Academy)	1903	1 vol.
Chester A. Gile (letters written during World War I from Naval Training Station, Newport, R.I. and USS *Kittery*)	1917–19	11 items
Henry Harrison Hodgkin	1857–99	8 items
Lieutenant (j.g.) Lloyd Lafot (in Edward Lafot and Family Papers)	1917–23	1 box
Acting Master William H. Maies (includes logs and journals maintained in USS *Cambridge*, *Nantucket*, and *Oneida*)	1861–63, 1867	442 pp.
Commander Lewis H. Maxfield (in Alexander Henry Cathcart and Family Papers)	1907–21	1 ft.

U.S. Naval History Sources

	Dates	*Volume*
Rear Admiral George Collier Remey (in Charles Mason Remey Family history)	1939	35 vols.
USS *Winona* (materials on operations during Civil War in Thomas Hunter Dixon and Family Papers)		1 vol.

Guide: Lucas, Lydia, comp. *Manuscripts Collections of the Minnesota Historical Society*. St. Paul: Minnesota Historical Society, 1977. (guide no. 3; see also guides no. 1 and 2)

MISSISSIPPI

Mississippi Department of Archives and History
P.O. Box 571
Jackson, MS 39205

	Dates	*Volume*
Admiral Richard Henry Leigh	1887–1942	87 items
Adalia (Jacobs) Morgan (includes letters written by her brothers, Captain Charles Clark Jacobs and PFC Fred Clark Jacobs, who served during World War II in the Marine Corps)	1897–1946	65 items
Commander William F. Shields	1821–70	280 items, 8 vols.
Lieutenant Charles A. Sisson, USNR (Flag Secretary to Vice Admiral John S. McCain)	1944–45	63 items, 8 vols.

Mississippi State University Library
Starkville, MS 39762

Commander William F. Shields	1814–1912	187 items

MISSOURI

Federal Archives and Records Center
Archives Branch
2306 East Bannister Road
Kansas City, MO 64131

	Dates	Volume
U.S. Coast Guard Unit Logs	1969–76	
U.S. Coast Guard (records of the U.S. Coast Guard and its predecessor agencies within the Fourth and Fifth Inspection Districts)	1835–1958	120 ft.

Harry S. Truman Library
Independence, MO 64050

	Dates	Volume
Lieutenant Commander Mark Edwin Andrews, USNR (includes material relating to his service in the Navy's Office of Procurement and Material)	1942–46	5 ft.
Clark M. Clifford (includes material relating to his service as a naval officer)	1946–56	16 ft.
Admiral Robert Lee Dennison	1946–56	16 ft.
George M. Elsey (includes material relating to his service as a naval officer)	1941–53	42 ft.
Vice Admiral James H. Foskett	1919–54	1 ft.
W. John Kenney, Under Secretary of the Navy, 1947–49	1946–49	1 ft.
Dan A. Kimball, Secretary of the Navy, 1951–53	1949–53	3 ft.
John T. Kohler, Assistant Secretary of the Navy, 1949–51	1949–51	less than 1 ft.
Francis P. Matthews, Secretary of the Navy, 1949–51	1932–52	29 ft.
Oral History Interviews: John Abbott, Navy Department Liaison Officer	1942–53	5 items

	Dates	Volume

to the Special U.S. Senate Committee Investigating the National Defense Program (Truman Committee)
Admiral Robert L. Dennison
Captain Donald J. MacDonald
Commander William M. Rigdon
John L. Sullivan, Secretary of the Navy, 1947–49

Guide: *Historical Materials in the Harry S. Truman Library.* Independence, Mo.: The Library, 1976.

Missouri Historical Society
Jefferson Memorial Building
St. Louis, MO 63112

	Dates	Volume
Lieutenant Theodore Hunt	1779–1840	125 items
Lieutenant Commander S. Ledyard Phelps	1861–64	360 items
Gideon Welles, Secretary of the Navy, 1861–65 (in the Abraham Lincoln Papers)	1865	

University of Missouri Library
Western Historical Manuscript Collection
Columbia, MO 65201

	Dates	Volume
Yeoman Royal Daniel Michael Bauer	1916–19	200 items
Collection of World War II Letters (includes about 300 items from Radioman Roe L. Johnson; Lieutenant (j.g.) Ralph C. Patterson, USNR; and Radio Technician Joseph P. Powell)	1941–45	
Naval Diesel Training School (in University of Missouri President's Office Papers)	1942–43	9 folders
Naval Reserve Officers Training Corps (in University of Missouri President's Office Papers)	1945–52	12 folders
William M. Trenholme, naval officer and physicist (restricted collection)	1931–63	98 folders
U.S. Naval Academy, Board of Visitors (in University of Missouri President's Office Papers)	1917–21	22 folders
U.S. Navy Correspondence (in Papers of Frederick A. Middlebrush, President, University of Missouri)	1932–62	75 folders

NEBRASKA

Nebraska State Historical Society
1500 R Street
Lincoln, NE 68508

	Dates	*Volume*
Gunner John Clapham	1818–1903	600 items
Willard Bunce Cowles, Navy radio operator	1917–19	ca. 100 items
USS *Nebraska*	1909–38	ca. 100 items

Surrender of the German High-Seas Fleet, 1918. Rear Admiral Hugh Rodman and Vice Admiral William S. Sims are in the left foreground

NEW HAMPSHIRE

Dartmouth College Library
Hanover, NH 03755

	Dates	Volume
Lieutenant Commander Robert Steed Dunn, USNR	1896–1955	ca. 1600 items
Lieutenant William Kimball Flaccus (restricted collection)	1942–49	
Senator John Parker Hale, Chairman of the Senate Committee on Naval Affairs, 1861–65	1777–1904	ca. 600 items
Levi Woodbury, Secretary of the Navy, 1831–34	1811–51	100 items

New Hampshire Historical Society
30 Park Street
Concord, NH 03301

Richard Hazen Ayer (naval storekeeper, Portsmouth Navy Yard)	1803–61	350 items
William Eaton Chandler, Secretary of the Navy, 1882–85	1829–1917	5 vols., 40 diaries, 109 boxes
John Emery, Naval Agent, Bilboa, Spain	1777–79	1 ledger
Senator John Parker Hale, Chairman of Senate Committee on Naval Affairs, 1861–65	1822–74	2 vols., 23 boxes
Captain Hamilton Hutchins	1873–79	4 vols.
John Langdon, Continental Agent for New Hampshire (includes material on the Continental Navy)	1770–1819	2 boxes, 1 envelope
John Fabyan Parrott, sea captain, ordnance inventor, and U.S. Senator	1792–1878	2,500 items
Commodore George Hamilton Perkins	1858–85	10 vols., 2 boxes
Rear Admiral George Henry Preble (manuscript	1868	1 vol.

	Dates	Volume
of History of Portsmouth Navy Yard, 1603–1868)		
Edmund Roberts, U.S. envoy to Siam, Muscat, and Cochin China	1805–39	1 box
John Salter, sea captain (includes documents on Navy Yard at Kittery, Maine)	1813–57	97 items
Levi Woodbury, Secretary of the Navy, 1831–34	1813–51	110 items

Phillips Exeter Academy Library
Exeter, NH 03833

	Dates	Volume
George Bancroft, Secretary of the Navy, 1845–46	1824–87	44 items

Strawberry Banke, Inc.
P.O. Box 300
Portsmouth, NH 03801

	Dates	Volume
Historic Photograph Collection (includes prints of naval ships)	19th and 20th centuries	
Isaac S. Mullen (ledger kept on board USS *Portsmouth*)	1859–61	1 vol.
Portsmouth Naval Shipyard Collection		

NEW JERSEY

Gloucester County Historical Society Library
Woodbury, NJ 08096

	Dates	Volume
Lieutenant Richard Somers	1749–1804	ca. 170 items

Morristown National Historical Park
P.O. Box 1136R
Morristown, NJ 07960

The Lloyd W. Smith Collection of about 30,000 manuscripts and the Park Collection, containing 2,000 manuscripts, are filmed together on 69 reels of microfilm. They contain the correspondence of many naval officers active during the American Revolution and 19th century, and other documents dealing with American and British naval activities.

Guide: Stewart, Bruce W. and Hans Mayer. *A Guide to the Manuscript Collection, Morristown National Historical Park.* Morristown, N.J.: Morristown National Historical Park, 1967.

New Jersey Historical Society
230 Broadway
Newark, NJ 07104

	Dates	Volume
Sailmaker Thomas J. Boyce (journal kept on board USS *Peacock, St. Louis,* and *North Carolina*)	1829–31; 1833–39	1 vol.
Admiral Arthur S. Carpender	1913–58	54 items
USS *Constellation* (record book of Commander Charles Stewart)	1812–13	1 item
Mahlon Dickerson, Secretary of the Navy, 1834–38	1782–1852	1,000 items
Captain Lawrence Kearny (includes logbook of USS *Warren*)	1814–44	5 vols.

U.S. Naval History Sources

	Dates	Volume
USS *Lancaster* (journal kept by Chaplain Donald MacLaren)	1865–67	1 item
Assistant Surgeon Edward A. Pierson	1796–1872	116 items
Surgeon William Turk (includes journal maintained in USS *Constitution*, *Concord*, and *Washington*)	1824–33	

James V. Forrestal, Secretary of the Navy, 1944–1947

New Jersey

Princeton University Library
Princeton, NJ 08540

Vice Admiral Harold Gardiner Bowen	1940–50	12 cartons
Joachim du Perron, Comte de Revel, French naval officer		
James Vincent Forrestal, Secretary of the Navy, 1944–47, and first Secretary of Defense	1944–49	20 file drawers
Blair-Lee Papers (includes materials of Rear Admiral Samuel Phillips Lee)	1733–1916	50 boxes
Philadelphia Naval Shipyard, League Island	1831–65	1 box
Samuel Lewis Southard, Secretary of the Navy, 1823–29, and Chairman of the Senate Committee on Naval Affairs, 1833–36		20,000 items
Stockton Family Collection (includes papers of Captain Robert Field Stockton)	1702–1866	12 boxes

Guide: Clark, Alexander P. *The Manuscript Collections of the Princeton University Library: An Introductory Survey.* Princeton University Library, 1958.

Rutgers University
Archibald Stevens Alexander Library
New Brunswick, NJ 08901

American Revolution—American, British, French Ship Drawings (in Johannes Reuber military journal)	1776–82	295 pp.
Lieutenant Silas Bent (includes a journal kept on board USS *Mississippi* during the U.S. naval expedition to Japan)	1853, 1858, 1868–85	3 vols.
Lieutenant Charles Stuart Boggs (other material is located in the David Bishop Papers)	ca. 1845	1 vol.
Midshipman Henry Booraem, Jr. (journal kept on board USS *Warren* and USS *Porposie*)	1829, 1830–31	1 vol.
Commodore Oscar Bullus		12 items
Admiral George Dewey (in Dr. George V.W. Voorhees Papers)		1 item
Mahlon Dickerson, Secretary of the Navy, 1834–38	1783–1857	66 items
James C. Dobbin, Secretary of the Navy, 1853–57 (in Moore Furman Papers)	1855	1 item
Acting Master Walter E. H. Fentress	1846–85	1 vol.
Robert Fulton, naval inventor	1814	1 item

U.S. Naval History Sources

	Dates	Volume
Mate Benjamin Heath, Jr. (journal kept on board USS *Delaware*)	1864–65	1 item
Captain Adam Huyler (in Charles H. Voorhees manuscript)	1888	1 vol.
William H. Jaques, Commander of Naval Reserve of New Jersey (material relates to USS *Ajax*)	1896–97	40 items
USS *Merrimack* (CSS *Virginia*)	1862	1 item
USS *Nantucket*	1865	1 item
Frederick Bernard Newman, sailor (journal kept on board USS *Kentucky*)	1900–04	1 vol.
Captain Matthew C. Perry (Expedition to Japan)	1848–52	10 items, flag journal
Lieutenant Oliver Hazard Perry, 1825–70 (journal kept on board USS *Mississippi* on the U.S. naval expedition to Japan)	1853–54	1 item
Woodburne Potter, naval inventor		42 items

Commodore Matthew C. Perry's Expedition making its initial landing in Japan, 1853

New Jersey

	Dates	*Volume*
James Parker (journals kept on board USS *Warren* and USS *Wizard*)	1827, 1828	1 vol.
Midshipman Burritt Shepard (journal kept on board USS *Lexington*)	1827–30	1 vol.
Purser Francis Barton Stockton (includes letters from Captain Hiram Paulding)	1810–84	93 items
William W. Van Cleaf (served on board USS *Benton*, 1862–63)	1861–97	114 items
Wholesaler of Naval Stores	1829–34	1 vol.
Ensign Robert Wilkinson		

Guide: Smith, Herbert, comp. *Guide to the Manuscript Collection of the Rutgers University Library.* New Brunswick, N.J.: Rutgers University Press, 1964.

Stevens Institute of Technology
S.C. Williams Library
Castle Point Station
Hoboken, NJ 07030

Stevens Family, naval contractors	1664–1870	6,500 items
USS *Monitor* (original design drawings)	1861–62	

NEW YORK

American Geographical Society Library
Broadway at 156th Street
New York, NY 10032

	Dates	*Volume*
Passed Midshipman Samuel Palmer Griffin (includes rough log maintained on board USS *Rescue*)	1850–51	2 vols.
Henry Grinnell (includes material on USS *Rescue*)	1849–67	8 vols.

Guide: American Geographical Society. *Research Catalog.* Boston: G.K. Hall, 1962 (15 vols.) and 1st Supplement, 1972, 1974 (4 vols.)

American Museum of Natural History
Central Park West at 79th Street
New York, NY 10024

Lieutenant William Leverreth Hudson	ca. 1838–42	journal

Buffalo and Erie County Historical Society
25 Nottingham Court
Buffalo, NY 14216

Master Daniel Dobbins	1800–49	3 ft.
Henry Randolph Storrs, Chairman of the House Committee on Naval Affairs, 1825–26	1825–30	6 vols.

Chemung County Historical Society Inc.
425 East Market Street
Elmira, NY 14901

Arctic Expedition of Robert E. Peary, naval	1906	ca. 5 vols.

	Dates	Volume
officer and explorer (material relating to Ross Marvin, a member of the expedition)		
USS *Chemung* (logbooks and other items)	1941–65	11 items

Columbia University Libraries
Butler Library
New York, NY 10027

	Dates	Volume
Acting Master Henry M. Bonney	1863	1 vol.
John Emery (journal kept on board USS *Constitution*)	1798	1 vol.
Thomas J. Ferrell (journal kept on board USS *Germantown*)	1850–53	1 vol.
Robert Fulton, naval inventor	1796–97, 1809–15	21 items
Lester B. Granger, Special Representative of Secretary of the Navy James Forrestal		oral history
George Braxton Pegram, physicist (includes information on nuclear engineering and the Navy)	1903–54	35,000 items
Frank Smith, confidential clerk to Secretary of the Navy Josephus Daniels		

Additional manuscripts relating to naval matters during the American Revolution are located in several other collections, including the Gouverneur Morris Collection, the John Jay Collection, and the Otis Collection.

Columbia University's well-known Oral History Collection, located in Room 221-M of the Butler Library, has many oral reminiscences relating to the Navy. *The Oral History Collection of Columbia University*, edited by Elizabeth B. Mason and Louis M. Starr (New York: Oral History Research Office, 1979) is a comprehensive guide to this material.

Cornell University Libraries
Department of Manuscripts and University Archives
John M. Olin Library
Ithaca, NY 14853

	Dates	Volume
George Bancroft, Secretary of the Navy, 1845–46	1811–1901, 1826–1941	2 ft.
Passed Assistant Engineer Asa M. Mattice	1862–99	5 boxes
Jean-Frederic Phelypeaux, Comte de Maurepas, French Minister of Marine and Secretary of State	1731–51	3 ft.

	Dates	Volume
Ernest George Merritt, physicist and university professor (includes material relating to the New London Naval Research Station)	1890–1940	4 ft.
Midshipman Robert Burns Reynolds (includes correspondence written while at the U.S. Naval Academy)	1863–65	
President Theodore Roosevelt (Assistant Secretary of Navy, 1897–98)	1883–1916	115 items
Judge Ferris Shoemaker, USMC	1861–66	80 items, 4 vols.
Rear Admiral Montgomery Sicard (in Floyd Family Collection)	1855–73	
Edward Guild Wyckoff (includes correspondence with Robert E. Peary regarding Peary's Arctic explorations)	1899–1910	515 items

Explorers Club
46 E. 70 Street
New York, NY 10021

Rear Admiral George W. Melville (materials relating to Arctic Expeditions)

Franklin D. Roosevelt Library
National Archives and Records Service
Hyde Park, NY 12538

	Dates	Volume
Vice Admiral Wilson Brown	1935–55	750 pp.
Louis McHenry Howe (assistant and personal secretary to Franklin D. Roosevelt; some of the papers are closely related to Roosevelt's papers as Assistant Secretary of the Navy)	1913–36	42 ft.
Vice Admiral John L. McCrea	1942–43	700 pp.
Vice Admiral Ross T. McIntire	1939–60	11 ft.
Commander William McKinley Rigdon	1943–45	500 pp.
Franklin D. Roosevelt—Collection of Naval and Marine Manuscripts (includes logs of USS *Adams, Constitution, Essex, Philadelphia,* and *St. Louis;* and papers of such naval officers as John Almy, David Conner, David Dixon Porter, Robley D. Evans, Matthew C. Perry, and Winfield S. Schley)	1731–1942	36 ft.

	Dates	Volume
Franklin D. Roosevelt's Naval Pictorial Collection	ca. 1776–ca. 1945	6,000 items
Franklin D. Roosevelt—Papers as Assistant Secretary of the Navy	1913–20	51 ft.
Franklin D. Roosevelt—Papers as President:		
Official File	1933–45	1,174 ft.
Personal File	1933–45	608 ft.
President's Secretary's File	1933–45	130 ft.
Map Room File	1941–45	81 ft.
Major James Roosevelt, USMC (restricted collection)	1937–67	212 ft.

Guide: *Historical Materials in the Franklin D. Roosevelt Library.* Hyde Park: Franklin D. Roosevelt Library, 1977.

Grumman Aerospace Archives
Plant 5
Bethpage, Long Island, NY 11714

Grumman Company Records (naval contractor)

Museum of Modern Art
11 West 53 Street
New York, NY 10019

Captain Edward Steichen, USNR, photographer and naval officer	1879–1973	4 file cabinets

New York Historical Society
170 Central Park West
New York, NY 10024

Rear Admiral John Jay Almy	1873–76	3 vols.
USS *Argus*	1803	1 item
Army and Navy Club of New York (formerly Military-Naval Club)	1933–73	
Commodore William Bainbridge		
Thomas Barclay, British agent for American prisoners of war	1812–15	
Samuel L. M. Barlow ("Narrative of Expedition Against Charleston, S.C.")		
Lieutenant Commander John Sanford Barnes		
Captain John Barry	1781–1801	

	Dates	Volume
USS *Boston* (Purser's book)	1828–29	1 vol.
Lieutenant Peter Brooke	1804–16	14 items, 7 boxes, 1 package
John Bullus, naval agent	1806–15, 1818–39	
Commodore Oscar Bullus	1806–77	
USS *Cambridge* (letters from Master's Mate W. B. Smith)		2 items
USS *Cayuga* (log and journal of Assistant Engineer Richard Hodgson)	1862–63	1 vol.
Captain French Ensor Chadwick	1886–88	12 vols.
Rear Admiral Ralph Chandler (in Porter R. Chandler Papers)	1847–87	1 box
Commodore Isaac Chauncey	1805–21	7 vols.
USS *Chocura*	1864	
Civil War	1861–65	47 vols., 28 boxes
John Clarkson, RN	1791–92	2 vols.
Acting Assistant Surgeon Titus Munson Coan		
James B. and Joseph T. Collins, Union Navy sailors	1862–63	66 items
USS *Constitution* (includes log books)	1798, 1844	5 vols., 11 items
Captain Gustavus Conyngham	1777–79	3 vols., 1 portfolio
James Fenimore Cooper (includes naval manuscripts)		11 vols., 1 box
Sir William Cornwallis, RN	1776–82	12 vols.
Rear Admiral William S. Cowles		
Rear Admiral John Adolphus Bernard Dahlgren	1848–49	
Lieutenant Francis Gregory Dallas	1837–59	
George H. Daniels, USMC	1860–64	
Rear Admiral John DeCamp	1805–77	100 items
Mrs. Stephen Decatur	1824–25	2 items
Captain Stephen Decatur, Jr.	1806–07	2 items
HMS *Defiance*	1807–09	4 vols.
Admiral of the Navy George Dewey		
W. Duane (letters relating to use of Robert Fulton's torpedoes against the enemy on the Delaware)	1813	3 items
Commander George R. Durand	1861–65	6 vols.

New York

	Dates	Volume
Captain James D'Wolf	1812–16	
Lieutenant Charles Phillips Eaton	1883–1921	65 items, 3 vols.
Rear Admiral Henry Erben	1848–1903	2 ft.
John Ericsson, naval inventor	1831–88	1 vol., 49 boxes
Assistant Paymaster Charles Fairchild		
Admiral David G. Farragut	1862–64	8 items
Rear Admiral John C. Febiger (journal kept on board USS *Chipola, Concord,* and *Macedonian*)	1838–43	1 vol.
Gustavus Vasa Fox, Assistant Secretary of the Navy, 1861–66	1841–83	11 vols., 19 boxes
Mrs. Virginia L. Fox (wife of the Assistant Secretary of the Navy Gustavus Vasa Fox)	1860–80	1 box
Admiral S. R. Franklin (journal kept on board USS *Pensacola*)	1885–87	1 vol.
Robert Fulton, naval inventor		4 vols., 2 boxes
Alexander Gallop (journal kept on board *Brandywine* and *Dolphin*)	1827–29	1 vol.
David Gelston (includes material on return of British seaman taken prisoner)	1813–15	
Georgia (mail steamer) (logbooks while under the command of David Dixon Porter)	1850–51	3 vols.
Phipps D. Goffe (typed manuscript, "How Battles were Fought in the Navy in the Days Before Steam")	1840	1 vol.
Captain Caspar Frederick Goodrich	1863–1909	2 boxes
Commander Samuel Dana Greene	1869–83	10 vols.
Captain Theodore P. Greene	1863–64	1 vol.
Acting Master Alexander Hamilton, Jr.		
Captain John Dandridge Henley		
Commander William L. Herndon	1828–50	
Captain Isaac Hull	1808–40	15 vols.
HMS *Hunter*	1807–08	
Lieutenant William M. Hunter	1814	1 vol.
Acting Volunteer Lieutenant Commander Samuel Huse	1863–64	1 vol.
Rear Admiral John Irwin	1863–98	
Captain John Paul Jones		
Captain Beverly Kennon	1822–43	8 items
Admiral R. H. King, RN	1830	

U.S. Naval History Sources

	Dates	*Volume*
Randall J. LeBoeuf, Jr. (includes material on Robert Fulton, naval inventor)	1764–1857	ca. 215 items
First Assistant Engineer Oscar C. Lewis (diary while on board USS *Port Royal*)	1862–63	1 vol.
Logbooks of U.S. Naval Ships:		
Hornet	1826–27	1 vol.
Camilla	1834–35	
Ontario		
Constellation	1838	
Grampus	1839–40	
Vincennes	1843–44	
Portsmouth	1848–49	
Brandywine	1848–50	
Republic	1850–52	
Decatur	1854–55	
Saratoga	1855–56	
Arctic	1856	
Florida	1863	1 vol.
America		
General Grant	1864	1 vol.
Pensacola	1885–87	1 vol.
Porter	1900	
Rear Admiral Stephen Luce		
Assistant Surgeon William Cullen Lyman	1859–1917	2 ft.
Captain Alexander Slidell MacKenzie	1842–43	100 pp.
Rear Admiral Edward Yorke McCauley	1845–76	224 items, 3 vols.
Allen McLane, Revolutionary War and War of 1812 military officer (includes materials on naval matters)		3,253 items
Rear Admiral Richard Worsam Meade, III	1839–95	18 vols., 3 boxes
Master Samuel Jordan Morrill	1812–15	89 items
Captain Charles Morris	1806–46	39 items
Ensign Dennis W. Mullan (diary kept in USS *Monongahela*)	1864	1 vol.
Naval and Military Order of the Spanish American War	1902–54	19 vols., 21 boxes, 6 letterpress books
Naval Historical Society Records:		
Letters from U.S. Naval Officers	1870–90	225 items

	Dates	Volume
Papers relating to Bristol, R.I.	1801–55	3 vols.
Papers relating to Bristol and Warren, R.I.	1818–55	3 vols.
Miscellaneous manuscripts		8 boxes
Naval Order of the United States	1890–ca. 1960	7 vols., 6 boxes
Naval Papers	1796–1851	153 items, 16 vols.
Naval Ship Construction and Outfitting		
U.S. Naval Ships Register	1863	1 vol.
Midshipman James Nicholson	1803–29	1 box
Lieutenant James Lawrence Parker	1831–33	1 vol.
USS *Peacock*	1839	58 items
Commodore Oliver H. Perry	1813	1 item
Admiral David Dixon Porter	1841–70	55 items
Evelina Anderson Porter (Wife of Admiral David Porter)	1813–91	81 items
Captain Edward Preble	1802	1 vol.
Lieutenant Commander John N. Quackenbush	1864	
Assistant Naval Constructor Richard Hallett Meredith Robinson	1898–1912	9 vols.
Rear Admiral Christopher Raymond Perry Rodgers	1861–66, 1840–42	
Captain John Rodgers	1796–1835	900 items (microfilm)
Admiral George Brydges Rodney, RN	1779–81	1 vol.
Roll of Navy Enlisters at New York (includes name, age, occupation and ship assignment of 26,418 men)	1861–64	
USS *St. Paul*	1898	
Edward Hallam Saltonstall (includes copy of his naval diary and copies of letters of Lieutenant Thomas Holdup Stevens, commanding officer of USS *Ottawa*)	1861–62	
Rear Admiral Benjamin F. Sands		
USS *San Jacinto*	ca. 1865	
Secretaries of the Navy (correspondence relating to Secretaries)	1795–1851	
Rear Admiral William Branford Shubrick	1823–56	15 items
Signal Books (includes signal books of Vice Admiral Marriot Arbuthnot, RN, and Commodore John Barry)	1779–1862	3 vols.

U.S. Naval History Sources

	Dates	Volume
Robert M. Smith, Secretary of the Navy, 1801–09	1801–11	53 items
Commander Richard Somers	1799–1803	24 items
Lieutenant Thomas H. Stevens	1861–62	
William H. Stiner, correspondent for the *New York Herald* (includes eyewitness description of battle of *Monitor* and *Merrimack*)	1861–65	
Richard Thompson, Secretary of the Navy, 1877–80	1877	
Smith Thompson, Secretary of the Navy, 1819–23	1796–1843	106 items
Rear Admiral Thomas Turner	1869–70	
George Van Duzer, Union sailor	1861–64	
Master's Mate John B. Van Duzer	1860–63	26 items
USS *Viking*	1898	1 vol.
USS *Wabash*	1862	
War of 1812	1812	14 items, 8 vols., 7 boxes, 1 package
Andrew Warner, military inspector (includes letters from Dr. Henry O. Mayo on board USS *Savannah* and *Powhattan*)		
Sir Peter Warren, RN		
Midshipman William H. Weaver	1848–49	1 vol.
G. Creighton Webb, Army officer (includes correspondence relating to naval aspects of Cuban campaign of Spanish-American War)	1898–1937	1,700 items
Lieutenant Commander William K. Wheeler	1871	1 vol.
Rear Admiral Cameron McRae Winslow		
Rear Admiral John Ancrum Winslow		
Captain Henry Augustus Wise	1855–68	17 vols.
World Cruise of American Fleet in 1908 (memorabilia collected by Lieutenant William R. Henderson)	1908	

Guide: Breton, Arthur J. *A Guide to the Manuscript Collections of the New York Historical Society.* Westport, Conn.: Greenwood Press, 1972. (2 vols.)

The Great White Fleet off San Francisco, 1908, during its cruise around the world

New York Public Library
Manuscript and Archives Division
Fifth Avenue and 42nd Street
New York, NY 10018

	Dates	Volume
Rear Admiral John Jay Almy	1857–66	2 vols.
George Bancroft, Secretary of the Navy, 1845–46	1748–ca. 1880	ca. 288 vols.
Commodore Homer Crane Blake	1840–69	2 vols.
Naval Constructor Francis Tiffany Bowles	1885–96	5 vols.
Master William N. Brady	1848–60	125 items
British Navy (a number of items, in addition to those listed here, concerning the Royal Navy, some of which relate to the American Revolution and the War of 1812)		
William B. Burtis (journal kept on board USS *Delaware*)	1867–70	1 vol.

	Dates	Volume
James Leander Cathcart (U.S. Consul at North Africa during the Barbary Wars)	1785–1806, 1824–44, 1862–66	457 items
Commander William Chandler	1832–64	15 vols.
William Conant Church, founder and editor of *The Army and Navy Journal*	1860s	2 boxes
Rear Admiral Charles Edgar Clark (in S. Weir Mitchell Papers)	1898–1900	24 items
Captain Richard S. Collum, USMC	1885	1 item
Captain David Conner	1816–56	2,600 items
Rear Admiral Thomas Tingey Craven (in John Bigelow Papers and in Thomas Turner Letterbooks)	1865, 1868–69	ca. 19 items
Captain James Creighton, RN	1813–19	1 vol.
Captain John Orde Creighton (includes logs of USS *Hudson*, USS *Boston*)	1828–29	1 vol.
Rear Admiral John Adolphus Bernard Dahlgren	1829–85	2 vols.
Comte Francois Joseph Paul DeGrasse, French Navy		
Admiral George Dewey	1864–65, 1898	2 items
Sir Kenelm Digby, RN	1633–35	1 vol.
Bartholomew Diggins, seaman in USS *Hartford*	1862–64	1 vol.
Captain Percival Drayton	1860–65	115 items
Surgeon Amos A. Evans	1815–16	1 vol.
Captain Samuel Evans	1815–25	1 vol.
Admiral David Glasgow Farragut	1863–70	5 items
Yeoman 2nd Class Harold Footman (letters while serving in USS *Yankee* during the Spanish-American War)	1898	9 items
Lieutenant George Clayton Foulk	1884–87	1,000 items
Rear Admiral Samuel R. Franklin		1 vol.
Robert Fulton (includes material in Gilbert Holland Montague Collection)	1790–1815	86 items
Rear Admiral Louis M. Goldsborough	1821–73	2 vols., 3 boxes
Rear Admiral Franklin Hanford	1881–1927	1 box, 1 vol.
Second Assistant Engineer John T. Hawkins (includes an account of the voyages of USS *Pensacola*, 1861–63)	1861–64	1 vol.
Levi Hayden, Marine engineer (includes material relating to his service in the Civil War)	1864–84	4 vols.

	Dates	Volume
Sir William Hoste, RN	1855–56	1 vol.
Rear Admiral Aaron Konkle Hughes	1839–94	6 vols.
Surgeon James Inderwick (journal kept on board the USS *Argus*)	1813	1 vol.
USS *Kearsarge*	1874–75	68 sheets
Master's Mate John R. C. Lewis (diary kept on Perry's Expedition to Japan)	1853–55	1 vol.
Logbooks (an extensive collection of logbooks for naval and merchant ships, in addition to those mentioned here under the names of individuals)		
Lieutenant Gordon G. MacDonald, RN	1745–1831	1 vol.
McBlair Family (includes material relating to Captain Charles H. McBlair, U.S. and Confederate naval officer and his brother Thomas P. McBlair, purser, U.S. Navy)	1793–1874	12 folders
Midshipman J. T. McLaughlin	1831–32	1 vol.
Ensign Haile C. T. Nye (logs kept on board USS *Kansas* and USS *Richmond*)	1872–73	1 vol.
Midshipman Joseph Parrish (journal kept on board USS *Congress*)	1846–47	1 vol.
Assistant Surgeon Dinwiddie B. Phillips (includes log of USS *Mississippi*)	1857–58	1 vol.
Frank H. Pierce (scrapbook of clippings and manuscripts relating to action of *Monitor* and *Merrimack*)	1860s	1 vol.
Captain David Porter	1803–39	30 items
Rear Admiral George Campbell Read	1846–49	1 vol.
F. Ross (journal of the voyage of HMS *Tagus*, describing capture of USS *Essex*)	1813–14	1 vol.
Vice Admiral Sir Herbert Sawyer, RN	1810–15	5 vols.
Secretaries of the Navy and Other Naval Officials (including Secretaries Woodbury, Paulding, Upshur, and Bancroft)	1832–63	25 items
Captain Robert W. Shufeldt	1871–73	160 items
Samuel L. Southard, Secretary of the Navy, 1823–29	1823–28	1 vol.
Spanish American War (transcripts of logbooks of 11 U.S. ships when the fleet was before Santiago, Cuba)	1898	2 vols.
Francis Stanfell, RN	1812–31	1 vol.
Simeon A. Stearns (journal while on board USS	1838–41	1 vol.

	Dates	Volume
Vincennes during the Wilkes Exploring Expedition)		
Stevens' Battery (ironclad steamer)	1862–71	11 items
George Stone (account of the *Merrimack* and *Monitor* encounter)	1861–64	23 vols.
Rear Admiral Thomas Turner	1858–60, 1862–63, 1868–70	10 vols.
U.S. Navy (workbooks and other items of gunners John Lord and John R. Covington; includes material on USS *Constitution* and *Franklin*)	1820–40	4 vols., 5 items
Washington Navy Yard (day book of articles ordered)	1861–68	1 vol.
Rear Admiral Aaron Ward Weaver	1851–87	77 items
Gideon Welles, Secretary of the Navy, 1861–69	1825–85	1,400 items
Rear Admiral Charles Wilkes	1838–52	33 items

Guide: New York Public Library, Research Libraries. *Dictionary Catalog of the Manuscript Division*. Boston: G. K. Hall, 1967 (2 vols.).

New York State Historical Association
Cooperstown, NY 13326

	Dates	Volume
Midshipman James H. Gillis (journal while on board USS *Dale* and *Germantown*)	1850	1 vol.
Midshipman Alexander A. Semmes (journals of cruises on board USS *Vandalia, Macedonian, Saratoga,* and *Vincennes*)	1842–47	1 vol.
Chaplain Charles Samuel Stewart	1822–41	3 boxes

Pickering-Beach Historical Museum
Sackets Harbor, NY 13685

Captain Horace Sawyer	1807–58	

Pierpont Morgan Library
33 East 36th St.
New York, NY 10016

Autographs of Generals of the American Revolution (includes naval related material)
Autographs of Presidents of the United States

New York

Rear Admiral Charles Wilkes, leader of the U.S. Exploring Expedition and Civil War naval officer

U.S. Naval History Sources

	Dates	Volume
(includes letters from Secretaries of the Navy)		
Autographs of Signers of the Declaration of Independence (includes naval documents)		
John Paul Jones Autograph Letters		
Lafayette Correspondence		1 item
John Davis Long, Secretary of the Navy, 1897–1902 (copy of his book, *The New American Navy*, which contains 50 letters of naval officers concerning the Spanish-American War)		50 items
New York City (New Netherlands) (includes naval related material)		1 item
Siege of Yorktown and Surrender of Cornwallis		
Joseph Yorke, British Ambassador to the Hague (includes naval documents)	1775–79	

Letters from prominent naval officers of the 19th century can be found throughout the library's collections.

Rensselaer Polytechnic Institute
Archives
Troy, NY 12181

	Dates	Volume
Eben Norton Horsford, chemist (includes plans for the Horsford submarine, 1862, and material relating to the North Pacific Exploring Expedition, 1852–56)		14 ft.
Pamphlet collection of Charles H. Haswell, Chief Engineer of the Navy (includes *Report of the Board . . . Armament of Our Vessels of War*, 1845)	1842–74	25 items

The State Education Department
The New York State Library
The University of the State of New York
Albany, NY 12234

	Dates	Volume
Rear Admiral Charles Dwight Sigsbee	1845–1923	17 boxes
Sergeant-Major William Mitchell Stetson, Naval Brigade, New York Volunteers (includes an account of the *Merrimack-Monitor* action)	1861–64	489 pp.

New York

	Dates	*Volume*
State Office of Audit and Control Accounts (in New York State Archives Collection; includes material on military and naval operations in the War of 1812)	1783–1858	24 vols.

Syracuse University
The George Arents Research Library
Syracuse, NY 13210

	Dates	Volume
Vice Admiral Bernard Lige Austin	1937–66	½ box
Rear Admiral Theodorus Bailey	1828–85	220 items
Rear Admiral Thomas Tingey Craven	1841–69	170 items
Rear Admiral John Adolphus Bernard Dahlgren	1823–1945	2 ft.
Admiral of the Navy George Dewey	1844–1912	¼ ft.
Admiral David Glasgow Farragut	1864–70	10 items
Senator Frederick Hale, Chairman, Senate Naval Affairs Committee, 1923–31	1917–40	2 boxes
Captain Purnell F. Harrington	1884–1919	½ box
Admiral James L. Holloway, Jr.	1930–64	3 ft.
Paymaster Samuel B. Massa	1861–68	1 box
Admiral David Lamar McDonald	1930–65	1½ ft.
Lynn J. Montross, military author	1923–61	6 ft.
Admiral David Dixon Porter	1806–90	1/5 ft.
Vice Admiral William Francis Raborn, Jr.	1951–63	1 ft.
Charles M. Remey (restricted collection; includes materials on his father, Rear Admiral George C. Remey)	1874–	9 ft.
Mate Horatio G. Robinson		19 items
Rear Admiral Henry Knox Thatcher	1867–68	1 letterbook

U.S. Military Academy Library
West Point, NY 10996

	Dates	Volume
Captain William Bainbridge (in Swift Papers)	1817, 1826	3 items
Captain James Biddle (in Thayer Papers)	1815	1 item
USS *Brandywine* (logbook, and abstract of cruise of USS *Boston*)	1832	1 vol.
Rear Admiral Thomas Crabbe	1815	1 journal
Surgeon Edmund Louis DuBarry	1845–54	295 items
Admiral Albert Gleaves (in Porter Collection)	1917	1 item
Charles Haynes Haswell (in Porter Collection)	1900	1 item
Rear Admiral Alfred Thayer Mahan	1859	1 item

	Dates	Volume
Admiral David Dixon Porter (in Beebe Papers, Delafield Papers, Porter Collection, and Grant Papers)	1866, 1856, n.d., 1863	4 items
Captain Francis Asbury Roe (in Porter Collection)	n.d.	1 item
Rear Admiral Henry Knox Thatcher (in Delafield Papers)	1851	1 item

University of Rochester Library
Department of Rare Books, Manuscripts and Archives
River Campus
Rochester, NY 14627

Rear Admiral William Harkness, naval officer and astronomer	1849–1900	1½ ft.
Elwell Stephen Otis Papers (include letters to Admiral George Dewey)	1856–1928	2 ft.

Washington's Headquarters State Historic Site
84 Liberty Street
Newburgh, NY 12550

Confederate States Naval Laboratory Records (ammunition issues)	1861–65	1 ledger
Navy Related Documents	1776–1862	15 items

Other materials in this repository concern privateering, armed sloops and the "secret committee" which obstructed Hudson River navigation during the American Revolution.

NORTH CAROLINA

Duke University
Manuscript Department
William Perkins Library
Durham, NC 27706

	Dates	Volume
Rear Admiral Edwin Alexander Anderson, Jr.	1915–18	13 items, 1 vol.
Samuel A'Court Ashe (includes letters from Alfred Thayer Mahan, 1840–1914)	1856–1950	100 items
Sir Robert Barrie, RN	1765–1953	733 items, 2 vols.
Mate James L. B. Blauvelt	1862–67	5 items
Rear Admiral Samuel Livingston Breese	1823–78	5 items, 4 vols.
Great Britain: Papers (Military and Naval) (includes documents relating to the British Navy in the American Revolution and naval activities during the Napoleonic Wars)	1730–1914	1,079 items, 1 vol.
Sir Benjamin Hallowell Carew RN	1794–1831	55 items
Clark Family Papers (includes material on CSS *Virginia*, formerly USS *Merrimack*)	1764–1890	3 vols., 174 items
John Wilson Croker, British Admiralty official (includes correspondence relating to naval operations during the French Revolution and Napoleonic Wars)	1793–1861	2,874 items
James Cochran Dobbin, Secretary of the Navy, 1853-57	1821–56	16 items
Sir William Henry Dillon, RN	1819–55	141 items
Henry Archibald Duc, Sr. and Jr. (includes material relating to student life at the U.S. Naval Academy and activities of USS *Charleston*)	1840–1909	248 items

U.S. Naval History Sources

	Dates	Volume
William P. S. Duncan	1847–68	7 items
Edwin Fairfield Forbes, American seaman with the British Navy	1861–65	1 vol.
Rear Admiral Louis Malesherbes Goldsborough	1827–77	523 items, 1 vol.
William Alexander Graham, Secretary of the Navy, 1850–52	1841–96	58 items
John Berkley Grimball, jurist and officer in Union and Confederate Navies	1727–1930	1,605 items, 5 vols., 2 reels of microfilm
Sir Andrew Snape Hamond, RN	1783–1862	230 items, 1 vol.
Surgeon Isaac Henry	1794–1841	59 items
Lieutenant Robert E. Johnson	1804–66	57 items
Commander John McIntosh Kell, Union and Confederate naval officer	1785–1921	4,288 items, 8 vols.
Surgeon Edward Kershner	1861–1902	375 items, 2 vols.
Rear Admiral Elie A. F. Lavallette	1826–1928	558 items, 10 vols.
Charles MacGill (includes letters while in USS *Potomac* during Vera Cruz campaign, 1847)	1786–1906	1,038 items
Hugh MacRae (includes papers of Lieutenant Archibald MacRae)	1817–1943	4,222 items, 37 vols.
Senator Willie Person Mangum, Chairman of Senate Committee on Naval Affairs, 1841–43	1763–1861	1 vol., 142 items
Commander Matthew Fontaine Maury, Union and Confederate naval officer	1829–71	167 items
Rear Admiral Samuel McGowan	1910–35	228 items
Lieutenant Alfred Augustus McKethan	1860–1927	513 items
Second Viscount Robert Saunders Dundas Melville, British statesman and First Lord of the Admiralty	1811–49	213 items
Fleet Pay Master Sir John Samuel Moore, RN	1843–92	139 items
Purser Thomas B. Nalle	1805–1905	641 items, 1 vol.
U.S. Navy (includes logbooks and papers relating to naval officers, seamen, and naval administration)	1804–1944	445 items, 10 vols.
Thomas A. Nicholson, naval dentist (journal kept on board USS *Powhatan*)	1857–60	1 vol.

North Carolina

	Dates	Volume
Acting Third Engineer John O'Neil	1862	2 items
Commander Thomas Jefferson Page, Union and Confederate naval officer (includes unpublished autobiography)	ca. 1875	17 items
Rear Admiral Enoch Greenleafe Parrott	1831–1929	433 items, 2 vols.
John E. Patterson, physician (served in various hospital ships and hospitals during the Civil War)	1825–69	118 items, 2 vols.
Admiral David Dixon Porter	1847–77	14 items
Rear Admiral Stephen Platt Quackenbush	1867–68	2 items
Clifton Quinn, naval volunteer during World War I	1917–19	1 vol.
Rear Admiral George Collier Remey	1939	1 vol.
Lieutenant Hilary H. Rhodes	1819–44	16 items
Lieutenant James Henry Rochelle	1811–1907	965 items
Commander Raymond Perry Rodgers	1876–79	2 items
Robert Smith Rodgers	1827–97	1,382 items, 7 vols.
Second Lieutenant Dabney M. Scales, CSN	1861–63	1 vol.
Surgeon Albert S. Schriver	1867	1 diary
Franklin E. Smith, sea captain and naval officer	1818–90	939 items
Lieutenant Lyman Greenleaf Spalding	1835–89	237 items
Rear Admiral Charles Steedman	1835–1905	170 items, 2 vols.
Rear Admiral Thomas Holdup Stevens, II	1823–1902	144 items
Claude Augustus Swanson, Secretary of the Navy, 1933–39, and Chairman of the Senate Naval Affairs Committee, 1918–19	1867–1935	62 items

Guide: Tilley, Nannie M. and Norma Lee Goodwin. *Guide to the Manuscript Collections in the Duke University Library, 1947.* Reprint. New York: AMS Press, 1970.

East Carolina University
Naval Collections
East Carolina Manuscript Collection
Greenville, NC 27834

	Dates	Volume
Vice Admiral Walden Lee Ainsworth	1942–48	100 items
Rear Admiral John Conner Atkeson, Sr.		oral history
Captain Alexander B. Coxe, Jr.	1928–33, 1941–45	1 vol.

U.S. Naval History Sources

	Dates	Volume
Vice Admiral Glenn B. Davis	1913–53	136 items, oral history
Captain Louis Poisson Davis	1917–18	221 pp.
Commodore George Leland Dyer	1863–1924	ca. 2,400 items
Captain Alvin A. Fahrner, USNR	1941–47	250 items
Colonel Karl E. Faser, USMC		oral history
Major General Paul J. Fontana, USMC	1940–73	43 items, oral history
Vice Admiral George H. Fort	1917–53	319 items
William J. French (diary of naval enlisted man)	1942	1 vol.
Vice Admiral Jules James	1904–56	1,800 items
Captain C. Brooke Jennings		oral history
Lieutenant General William K. Jones, USMC	1946–72	6½ reels of microfilm, oral history
Rear Admiral William A. Kirkland	1894–1901, 1958–60	46 items
Rear Admiral John E. Kirkpatrick (USS *North Carolina* Battleship Collection)	1941–44	2 microfilm reels
Commander Warren S. Lane, USNR	1944–45	35 items, oral history
Captain Henry C. Lauerman	1938–45	oral history
Edward P. Leahy, USMC	1942–45	116 pp.
North Carolina Shipbuilding Collection (material gathered for the writing of a pamphlet on the Liberty Ship SS *Zebulon B. Vance*)	1941–56	291 items
Major General Bennet Puryear, Jr., USMC	1884–1943	oral history
Brigadier General Paul A. Putnam, USMC	1926–49	ca. 250 items, oral history
Rear Admiral Robert S. Quackenbush, Jr.	1927–57	oral history
Rear Admiral Alston Ramsay	1942–62	25 items
Major General Carson Abel Roberts, USMC		ca. 250 items
Lieutenant General Ralph K. Rottet, USMC	1929–69	ca. 600 items
Captain William James Ruhe	1939–41	oral history
Rear Admiral Archibald H. Scales (located in Alfred Moore Scales Papers)	1888–97	20 items
William N. Still, Jr., naval historian (includes correspondence (1954–56) while serving in the Navy in the Mediterranean)	1862–1972	ca. 800 items
Rear Admiral Joe W. Stryker (see also USS *North Carolina* Battleship Collection)	1926–29, 1941–42	2 vols.

	Dates	Volume
Commander H. A. I. Sugg		oral history
Captain John H. Turner	1936–66	oral history
Rear Admiral T. J. Van Metre	1942–44	141 items, oral history
Lieutenant Beverly W. White	1942	1 item
USS *North Carolina* Battleship Collection	1941–45	ca. 1,000 items, 12 vols.

Includes papers of:
    Captain Francis Lee Albert
    Captain Ben W. Blee
    Rear Admiral Robert J. Celustka
    Rear Admiral John E. Kirkpatrick
    Rear Admiral Timothy J. O'Brien
    Lt. J. T. Stevenson, USNR
    Lt. G. G. Strott
    Rear Admiral Joe W. Stryker
    Rear Admiral Kemp Tolley
    Commander Richard C. Walker, USNR
    Admiral A. G. Ward
and following enlisted personnel:
    Gregory L. Baker
    H. E. Cleaver
    Edward F. Cope
    Charles Gilbert
    J. A. Halas
    Richard S. Piper
    Milbern Frank Stelljes
    John W. Tuber
    William A. Watkins
    Paul A. Wieser

The collection also contains oral history memoirs for 36 officers and enlisted personnel of USS *North Carolina*.

Guide: East Carolina Manuscript Collection Bulletins.

North Carolina Department of Cultural Resources
Division of Archives and History
Raleigh, NC 27611

Samuel A'Court Ashe Papers (includes material relating to World War I naval service of James L. Sprunt and Lyman A. Cotten)	mainly 1849–1940	ca. 700 items

U.S. Naval History Sources

	Dates	Volume
George Edmund Badger, Secretary of the Navy, 1841	1822–61	48 items
Commander Johnston Blakeley	1814–18, 1841–42	38 items
Commander Victor Blue (memoir of the Spanish-American War)		1 item
John Branch, Secretary of the Navy, 1829–31	1819, 1830–33	7 items
Congressman John Herritage Bryan (includes naval materials relating to the Barbary Wars and War of 1812)	1716–1907	2,300 items
Otway Burns, privateer commander during the War of 1812 (in Romulus A. Nunn Papers)		
James Cochran Dobbin, Secretary of the Navy, 1853–57	1846–57	14 items
William Alexander Graham, Secretary of the Navy, 1850–52	1779–1918	2,050 items
Lieutenant John Julius Guthrie, Union and Confederate naval officer	1859–1918	65 items
Iconographic Collection (includes photographs relating to the Coast Guard and maritime matters)	1899–1972	50 items
Commander S. Phillips Lee	1861	1 item
Senator Willie Person Mangum, Chairman of Senate Committee on Naval Affairs, 1841–43	1809–94	2,000 items
Commander Charles H. McBlair, Union and Confederate naval officer	1875	1 item
North Carolina Naval Militia (in Romulus A. Nunn Papers)		1 item
Ocracoke Lifesaving Station	1883–94	
Commodore Harry Phelps	1830–1946	2,000 items
Captain James Iredell Waddell, Union and Confederate naval officer	1755–1919	103 items
Charles W. Welsh, Acting Secretary of the Navy, 1855	1855	1 item

Guide: Crabtree, Beth. *Guide to Private Manuscript Collection in the North Carolina State Archives.* Raleigh: State Department of Archives and History, 1964.

North Carolina

University of North Carolina Library
Southern Historical Collection
Chapel Hill, NC 27514

	Dates	*Volume*
Lieutenant Edward Clifford Anderson	1813–82	63 items
Rear Admiral Edwin Alexander Anderson	1878–1939	800 items
George Edmund Badger, Secretary of the Navy, 1841	1829–58	11 items, 2 reels of microfilm
Bagley Family Papers (includes material relating to Ensign Worth Bagley)	1848–1939	1,300 items
Rear Admiral George Beall Balch	1830–1924	420 items
Lieutenant Joseph Nicholson Barney	1839–52	1 vol.
Surgeon Steven Chaulker Bartlett	1865, 1908	28 items
John Young Bassett (includes correspondence concerning Surgeon H. W. Bassett)	1822–71	153 items
Rear Admiral Charles H. Bell (restricted collection)	1813–22	1 vol.
Robert Watson Winston Papers (includes material on Joseph R. Bird, U.S. naval officer)	1793–1944	3,000 items
Surgeon George Blacknall	1831–45	2 logs
Rear Admiral Victor Blue	1884–1919	340 items
Richmond Pugh Bond, World War II naval officer	1943–45, 1949	65 items
Branch Family Papers (includes material on John Branch, Secretary of the Navy, 1829–31)	1784–1919	2 ft.
Commander John Mercer Brooke, Union and Confederate naval officer	1859–98	12 items
Admiral Franklin Buchanan, Union and Confederate naval officer	1829–34, 1862–63	2 vols.
James W. Patton Papers (includes material on Midshipman George Calder)	1798–1903	240 items
William Gerard Chapman (correspondence with Secretary of the Navy Josephus Daniels)	1913–14	14 items
Lieutenant Francis Thornton Chew, CSN	1841–81	5 items
Civil War Papers, Federal (miscellaneous) (includes naval correspondence)	1860–67	50 items
Captain Harrison Henry Cocke, Union and Virginia Navy	1762–1876	200 items
Captain Lyman Atkinson Cotten	1886–1947	7,500 items
Passed Assistant Surgeon Richard P. Daniel	1855–58	1 vol. (microfilm)

U.S. Naval History Sources

	Dates	Volume
Francis Asbury Dickins Family (includes naval enlisted members)	1713–1934	4½ ft.
Ferebee, Gregory, and McPherson Family (includes material on Surgeon Nelson McPherson Ferebee)	1822–1913	184 items
CSS *Florida* (log)	1862–63	1 vol.
Rear Admiral Percy Wright Foote	1905–36	60 items
Forrest Family Papers (includes papers of Captain French Forrest, Union and Confederate naval officer, and his son, Lieutenant Douglas F. Forrest, CSN)	1847–97	30 items
Master Thomas Nicholas Gautier	1789–1926	100 items
Lieutenant George Washington Gift, Union and Confederate naval officer	1862–70	188 items
William Alexander Graham, Secretary of the Navy, 1850–52	1750–1927	7 ft.
Lieutenant Charles Iverson Graves, Union and Confederate naval officer	1831–1962	1,500 items
Vice Admiral Osborne Bennett Hardison	1912–53	2,000 items
Brigadier General William Curry Harllee, USMC	1685–1944	2 ft.
George W. Harris, sailor in USS *Richmond*	1861–63	3 items
Midshipman Thomas Locke Harrison (photographs)	1860	41 items in 1 photograph album
Hilary A. Herbert, Secretary of the Navy, 1893–97	1864–1931	1½ ft.
Surgeon James Fountain Heustis	1851–53	2 logs
Joseph Hewes, member of Naval Committee of the Continental Congress	1765–76	6 items
William Alexander Hoke (includes material dealing with the U.S. and Confederate navies)	1750–1925	6 ft.
Captain William Leverreth Hudson	1840–42	1 log (microfilm)
Rear Admiral Rufus Z. Johnston	1895–1950	493 items
Lieutenant Catesby ap Roger Jones	1836–45	1 diary (microfilm)
Thomas Butler King, Chairman of House Committee on Naval Affairs, 1847–48	1763–1925	5½ ft.
Langdon, Young, Meares Family Papers (includes letters from members of the Langdon family who were naval officers)	1771–1877	74 items
Rear Admiral Andrew Theodore Long	1876–1943	400 items

Union naval units bombard Fort Fisher, North Carolina, 1865, preceding the fort's capture by a combined Navy and Army force

	Dates	Volume
Macay and McNeely Family Papers (includes naval enlisted members)	1746–1918	320 items
Commander John Newland Maffitt, Union and Confederate naval officer	1833–1911	600 items
Stephen Russell Mallory, Confederate Secretary of the Navy, 1861–65	1835–73	2 vols., microfilm of 95 items
Senator Willie Mangum, Chairman of the Senate Naval Affairs Committee, 1841–43 (in Mangum Family Papers)	1777–1956	2 ft.
William Francis Martin (includes material dealing with the construction of Confederate gunboats)	1787–1884	1,900 items

U.S. Naval History Sources

	Dates	Volume
John Young Mason, Secretary of the Navy, 1844–45, 1846–49	1843–98	300 items
Maurice Family Papers (includes papers of family members who served in the U.S. Navy during the 19th century)	1796–1959	10 ft.
Commander Matthew Fontaine Maury, Union and Confederate naval officer	1788–1888	77 items
Vice Admiral Newton Alexander McCully	1923–24	1 diary
Vice Admiral Aaron Stanton Merrill	1912–48	4 ft.
Rear Admiral Edward Middleton	1810–93	200 items
Norfleet Family Papers (includes diary, 1891–92, of Surgeon Ernest Norfleet)	1784–1895	42 items
USS *North Carolina*	1825–27	1 log
Lieutenant James Heyward North, Union and Confederate naval officer (in Chisolm Family Papers)	1849, 1856, 1861–66	33 items
USS *Oneida*	1862–63	1 ship diary
Commander Richard Lucian Page, Union and Confederate naval officer	1825–64	5 logs (microfilm)
Acting Master Henry A. Phelon	1861–1906	140 items
Philadelphia Navy Yard, League Island, Pa. (office files of successive commandants, including James Barron)	1832–77	1,500 items
Salley (Rowan) Saufley Papers (includes material on Lieutenant (j.g.) R. Caswell Saufley	1864–1916	115 items
Rear Admiral Archibald H. Scales (scrapbooks)	1883–1929	1,100 items
Rear Admiral Winfield Scott Schley (in papers of Isidore Rayner)	1866–1921	1 ft.
Thomas Settle (includes information on naval enlisted service)	1812–79	92 items
Frederic Sherman (Union sailor)	1862–63	14 items
Rear Admiral William O. Spears	1914–34	481 items
Rear Admiral Adolphus Staton	1907–36	4,400 items
Chief Engineer James H. Tomb, CSN, and Captain William V. Tomb	1855–1936	350 items
Trenholm Family Papers (includes information on naval enlisted service)	1865–1933	18 items
Major General William Peterkin Upshur, USMC	1898–1928	1,000 items
Lieutenant Leonard Charles VanNoppen, USNR	1888–1947	8 ft.
Lewis Neale Whittle Papers (includes material on Commander William Conway Whittle, Union and Confederate naval officer)	1826–1919	800 items

	Dates	Volume
George Tayloe Winston (includes manuscript book, 1900-06, of Lieutenant Commander Hollis T. Winston)	1868–1906	16 items
Wirt Family Papers (includes material relating to Rear Admiral Louis M. Goldsborough and Lieutenant James McCutcheon Baker, CSN)	1802–1925	464 items
Senator Henry Alexander Wise, Chairman of House Committee on Naval Affairs, 1842–43	1833–96	32 items
Captain John Taylor Wood, Union and Confederate naval officer	1858–1915	201 items
Benjamin Cudworth Yancy (includes information on naval enlisted service)	1800–1931	4 ft.

Guides: Blosser, Susan Sokol, and Clyde Norman Wilson. *The Southern Historical Collection: A Guide to Manuscripts.* Chapel Hill, N.C.: University of North Carolina, 1970.

Smith, Everard H., III. *The Southern Historical Collection: Supplementary Guide to Manuscripts, 1970–1975.* Chapel Hill, N.C.: University of North Carolina, 1976.

OHIO

American Jewish Archives
3101 Clifton Avenue
Cincinnati, OH 45220

	Dates	*Volume*
Captain Uriah Phillips Levy	1816–61	13 items, 8 reels of microfilm

Bowling Green State University
Northwest Ohio-Great Lakes Research Center
5th Floor, University Library
Bowling Green, OH 43403

Defoe Shipbuilding Company (naval contractor)	1907–76	175 ft., 50 films, several thousand photographs
Erik Heyl, maritime historian	1945–73	6½ ft.
Captain Oliver Hazard Perry	1777–1819	microfilm of correspondence

Case Western Reserve University
Special Collections
11161 East Blvd.
Cleveland, OH 44106

Warner and Swasey Company Records (includes material on U.S. Naval Observatory contracts)	1880–1967	29 ft.

Cincinnati Historical Society
Eden Park
Cincinnati, OH 45202

Joseph B. Boyd (includes correspondence with Union gunboat crewmen)	1780–1884	85 items

Ohio

	Dates	Volume
Midshipman Charles Daniel Drake (autobiography to 1830)	1879	1 vol.
Rear Admiral Sylvanus W. Godon	1831–49	91 items
Miles Greenwood, iron founder (includes material on Civil War ordnance)	1861–65	30 items
Lieutenant Augustus R. Strong	1823–34	5 folders
Midshipman Thomas Henry Yeatman (includes material on service in USS *Macedonian*)	1822–25	4 items

Inland Rivers Library
Department of Rare Books and Special Collections
Public Library of Cincinnati and Hamilton County
800 Vine Street
Cincinnati, OH 45202

	Dates	Volume
Acting Master Charles Ackley (personal log kept on board USS *Tyler*)	1865	1 item
Acting Volunteer Lieutenant Commander William R. Hoel	1862–66	3 vols.
Acting Volunteer Lieutenant Jacob S. Hurd	1863–64	100 items, 1 vol.
USS *Ozark* (Yeoman James Noble, Jr.'s quarterly and monthly returns)	1864–65	1 vol.

Ohio Historical Society

Ohio Historical Center
1982 Velma Avenue
Columbus, OH 43211

	Dates	Volume
John W. Bricker, U.S. Senator, 1947–58, Governor of Ohio, 1939–45 (includes information about the Armed Services Committee and Navy related subjects)	1939–59	205 ft.
Clarence J. Brown, U.S. Congressman, 1939–65 (includes information on the Armed Services Committee)	1891–1965	74 ft.
Acting Ensign Symmes Evans Browne, Union gunboat officer, 1862–64	1803–1927	5 ft.
Commodore John C. Carter, Commander of USS *Michigan*	1864–66	4 items

U.S. Naval History Sources

	Dates	Volume
Isaac Craig, Marine Captain and Major, 1776–83	1766–1907	3 microfilm reels
Acting Volunteer Lieutenant Benjamin C. Dean (served in gunboat USS *Midnight* and schooner USS *Dan Smith*)	1816–65	¼ ft.
Ex-Soldiers' and Sailors' League of Franklin County Records	1899–1902	¼ ft.
John J. Gilligan, naval officer, 1943–45, and Governor of Ohio	1938–75	738 ft.
Warren G. Harding, President of the United States, 1921–23 (includes material on numerous Navy related topics)	1888–1923	250 ft., 263 microfilm reels
Lieutenant Commander Newton D. Mansfield	1933–52	1 ft.
Ohio Naval Brigade Rosters	1896–1904	2 vols.
USS *Shenandoah*, naval airship (in James G. May Collection)	1925	1 box
United States Department of the Navy Records	1877–81	27 microfilm reels
Frank B. Willis, U.S. Congressman, Senator, Governor of Ohio (includes material on Vice Admiral Louis R. De Steiguer; Theodore Roosevelt, Jr., Assistant Secretary of the Navy; and other Navy related topics)	1892–1928	41 ft.

Rutherford B. Hayes Library
1337 Hayes Avenue
Fremont, OH 43420

Rear Admiral Purnell Frederick Harrington	1879–1920	½ ft.
President Rutherford B. Hayes (contains correspondence of Richard W. Thompson, Secretary of the Navy, 1877–80, Rear Admiral Daniel Ammen, and other naval officers)	1829–97	170 ft.
Lieutenant (j.g.) Walter Sherman Hayes, USNR (diaries)	1914–23	2 vols.
Commodore Webb Cook Hayes, II	1914–57	11 ft.
William G. Moorhead, U.S. Consul and naval agent at Valparaiso, Chile (in Eleutheros Cooke Family Papers)	1848–49	
Rear Admiral Charles O'Neil	1871–99	½ ft.
Reynolds' (John P.) Escutcheons (records of a	1865–92	1½ ft.

	Dates	Volume
company specializing in painting escutcheons of military and naval officers)		
Richard W. Thompson, Secretary of the Navy, 1877–80	1877–89	5 ft.

Guide: Lentz, Andrea D., ed. *A Guide to Manuscripts at the Ohio Historical Society*. Columbus: The Ohio Historical Society, 1972.

Western Reserve Historical Society
10825 East Boulevard
Cleveland, OH 44106

	Dates	Volume
B. G. Benyon, RN (journal kept on board HMS *Menelaus* during War of 1812)	1813–14	1 vol.
Civil War Miscellany (includes material relating to Union Navy)	1860–75	5 boxes
Coffinberry Family (includes material relating to Acting Master Henry D. Coffinberry, Civil War naval officer)	1767–1830	3 boxes
Diaries and journals (includes naval items)	1813–1909	2 items, 28 vols., 1 reel of microfilm
Captain Stephen Decatur, 1779–1820 (includes report on defense and fortification of Chesapeake Bay and related British material)	1817	2 items
Freeman H. Morse, U.S. Consul in London, 1861–70 (includes affidavits of seamen of CSS *Alabama* and USS *Kearsarge*)	1861–88	½ box
William Pendleton Palmer Papers (includes journals and accounts of the following naval personnel: Stephen F. Blanding, USS *Louisiana*, 1862–64; Acting Master John M. Butler White, USS *New Ironsides*, 1863; Alexander Robert Chisolm, bombardment of Fort Sumter 1861; Assistant Surgeon Henry A. Richardson, USS *Cambridge*, 1861–62; John Simpson, USS *Brooklyn, Richmond, Metacomet*, 1861–65)	1861–1927	46 boxes
Brigadier General Samuel Holden Parsons (letter to Captain Esek Hopkins, commander of the Continental Navy, concerning British naval movements)	1777	1 item
President Theodore Roosevelt	1904	2 items

U.S. Naval History Sources

	Dates	*Volume*
Royal Marines	1813—14	1 vol.
Commodore Peter Turner	1823—73	3 vols., 1 folder

Guide: Pike, Kermit J. *A Guide to the Manuscripts and Archives of the Western Reserve Historical Society.* Cleveland: The Society, 1972.

OKLAHOMA

University of Oklahoma
Western History Collections
Room 452, Monnet Hall
630 Parrington Oval
Norman, OK 73019

Assistant Surgeon Alfred Griffith	1861–80	243 items
Grace E. Ray Photographic Collection (includes photographs of the Naval Air Station, Norman, Oklahoma)	1942–45	75 items

Fleet Admiral William F. Halsey, Jr. on board his flagship New Jersey *in Philippine waters, 1944*

OREGON

Oregon Historical Society
235 S.W. Park Avenue
Portland, OR 97205

	Dates	*Volume*
Puget Sound Navy Yard	1933	1 item
USS *Oregon* (includes material on proposed use of *Oregon* as a museum)	1898–1957	5 vols., 2 boxes

Guide: Oregon Historical Records Survey, W.P.A. *Guide to the Manuscript Collections of the Oregon Historical Society.* Portland, Ore.: Oregon Historical Records Survey, W.P.A., 1940.

University of Oregon Library
Eugene, OR 97403

Lieutenant Spencer F.B. Biddle	1877–1925	
Lieutenant (j.g.) Lyle Fear, USNR (letters while serving in USS *Olympia*)	1917–18	
Arthur Perry (includes diary kept on board USS *West Elasco*)	1918–48	
Frederick W. Wichman (includes material relating to his experiences as seaman on board USS *Harvard*)	1898–1901	9 vols., 4 items

Guide: Schmitt, Martin. *Catalogue of Manuscripts in the University of Oregon Library.* Eugene, Ore.: University of Oregon Books, 1971.

PENNSYLVANIA

Academy of Natural Sciences Library
19th Street and the Parkway
Philadelphia, PA 19103

	Dates	*Volume*
Mahlon Dickerson, Secretary of the Navy, 1834–38	1836–46	2 items
Robert E. Peary Greenland Expedition Papers	1890–94	172 items
Lieutenant Charles Pickering	1838–41	1 journal
William Samuel Waithman Ruschenberger, Navy Medical Director	1851–94	464 items
Rear Admiral Robert Wilson Shufeldt	1885–1924	195 items
United States Exploring Expedition Papers	1846	1 item

American Philosophical Society Library
105 South Fifth Street
Philadelphia, PA 19106

Bache Family Papers (includes diaries, 1862, 1867, 1869, of Paymaster Albert Dabadie Bache)	1770–1912	64 items
Passed Assistant Surgeon Charles Luke Cassin	1745–1883	66 items
Captain John Paul Jones	1770–80	150 items
Assistant Surgeon Elisha Kent Kane	1825–57	10 ft.
William Henry Smyth, RN	1827–64	86 items
Rear Admiral Charles Wilkes	ca. 1838–50	15 items

American Swedish Historical Foundation
1900 Pattison Avenue
Philadelphia, PA 19145

Rear Admiral John Adolphus Bernard Dahlgren	1850–70	8 items
John Ericsson, naval inventor	1839–81	1,000 items

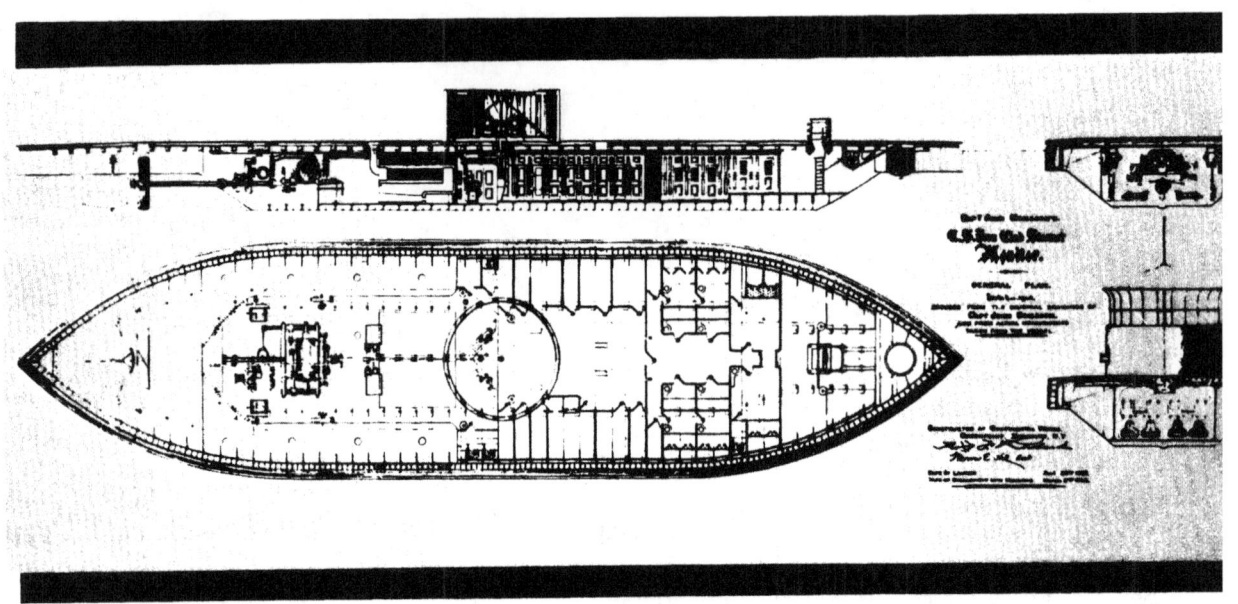

John Ericsson's plan for USS Monitor, *1861*

Carnegie Library of Pittsburgh
Pennsylvania Division
4400 Forbes Avenue
Pittsburgh, PA 15213

	Dates	Volume
Isaac Craig, Marine Captain and Major, 1776–83	1759–1834	40 vols., 4,000 items (available on 14 microfilm reels)

Dickinson College Library
Carlisle, PA 17013

Moyerman Collection (includes correspondence and other papers relating to military and naval history)	1718–1919	4 boxes

Erie County Historical Society
417 State Street
Erie, PA 16501

Lieutenant Joseph S. Day	1839–87	46 items
Boatswain John Sutton	1882–1905	75 items

Pennsylvania

Federal Archives and Records Center
Archives Branch
5000 Wissachickon Avenue
Philadelphia, PA 19144

	Dates	*Volume*
Commandant, Fourth Naval District	1943–57	77 ft.
Industrial Manager, Fourth Naval District	1955–57	17 ft.
Fifth Naval District, Norfolk, Va.	1926–43	
Norfolk Naval Air Station	1922–36	
Norfolk Navy Yard	1863–1943	
Philadelphia Naval Shipyard, Shipyard Commander	1955–57	43 ft.
Philadelphia Navy Yard	1791–1939	

Many other holdings of naval districts and shore activities in the area of Pennsylvania, Delaware, Virginia, West Virginia, and Maryland are held in this repository.

Franklin and Marshall College
Fackenthal Library
Lancaster, PA 17604

Medical Director Jonathan Messersmith Foltz	1831–77	40 vols.
Rear Admiral William Reynolds (includes diaries while serving with the U.S. Exploring Expedition)	1830–65	3 ft.

The Franklin Institute
Department of Historical Programs
Philadelphia, PA 19103

Cramp Shipyard (naval contractor)	1830–1946	15 ft.
John Lenthall, naval constructor and Chief of the Bureau of Construction and Repair	1807–82	3 ft.
Midvale Steel Collection (includes materials on the construction and testing of armor plate and guns for the Navy)	1904–15	1 ft.

Haverford College Library
Haverford, PA 19041

Charles Roberts Autograph Collection (includes extensive naval officer correspondence dating	ca. 1775–1896	ca. 300 items

primarily from the era of the American Revolution through the Civil War)

Historical Society of Pennsylvania
Manuscript Department
1300 Locust Street
Philadelphia, PA 19107

	Dates	Volume
Captain William Bainbridge		
Captain Joshua Barney	1782–1818	150 items
Lieutenant Charles Crillon Barton	1827–31	2 vols.
Charles Biddle, merchant, privateer, and public official	1763–1829	250 items
Captain James S. Biddle	1833–59	150 items
Paymaster Edmund W. Bonnaffon	1896–1903	2 vols.
Thomas Bradford, Philadelphia printer and publisher (records include paroles and bonds for delivery of American naval prisoners)	1760–1862	3,500 items
Lieutenant James Burns	1793–1860	1 box
Commodore Isaac Chauncey (in Colonel Cromwell Pearce Collection)	1855	1 vol.
Chesapeake Flotilla, War of 1812 (muster roll and enlistment records of personnel)	1813–15	2 vols.
William Bell Clark, naval historian and collector (includes material on naval casualties in World War I)	1919–20	
Second Assistant Engineer William J. Clark	1861–89	2 vols.
Commissioners of Naval Stores (accounts of the Commissioners of Naval Stores for outfitting ships of the Continental Navy, in Dr. Samuel W. Woodhouse Collection)	1776	
Senator George Mifflin Dallas, Chairman of the Senate Naval Affairs Committee, 1833	1791–1880	1 vol., 1,400 items
Alfred Day, naval agent, Philadelphia	1855	1 vol.
Captain Stephen Decatur (additional Decatur material in the Daniel Parker Papers)	1801–05, 1820	1 vol., 75 items
Drayton Family (includes correspondence of Captain Percival Drayton, 1812–65)	1796–1896	2,500 items
Julius Ferdinand Dreer (contains numerous letters of officers in the U.S. and British navies from about 1570 to 1865)	1492–1917	40,000 items
Charles Henri, comte D'Estaing	1778–79	1 vol.

	Dates	Volume
Colonel Frank M. Ettings, USA (includes letters of officers in the American and British navies, 1740–1865)	1558–1917	20,000 items
Edward Everett (manuscript of speech given at a dinner of the Naval Committee of the House of Representatives, Boston, 12 March 1864)	1864	1 vol.
Midshipman W. W. Feltus (journal kept on board USS *Essex*)	1812–14	1 vol.
Robert Fulton, naval engineer and inventor	1813–46	1 vol.
Gardiner Collection (includes material on Rear Admiral Louis Malesherbes Goldsborough)	1632–1939	
Gratz Collection (contains information on the American Navy in the Revolution, 1742–1843, 2 boxes; Board of War and Navy Board, 1776–99, 1 box; British officers in War of 1812, 1803–66, 1 box; U.S. naval officers, 1795–1906, 7 boxes; Confederate Navy, 1836–83, 1 box; and other material relating to the Navy and various wars)	1383–1921	175,000 items
George Harrison, naval agent, Philadelphia	1812–32	150 items
Alexander Henry (includes letters from Army and Navy officers, 1858–65, pertaining to defense of Ft. Delaware and other matters)	1840–76	350 items
Joshua Humphreys, naval constructor (includes plans and records of the building of such naval vessels as USS *United States, Constitution,* and *Franklin,* with detailed drawings)	1638–1835	20 vols.
Chief Naval Constructor Samuel Humphreys	1818–45	2 vols.
Joshua Huntington, Revolutionary war officer, shipbuilder (papers relating to the frigate *Confederacy*)	1776–86	525 items
Third Assistant Engineer John C. Huntly	1863	1 vol.
Surgeon Samuel Jackson	1862–63	25 items
William Jennison, Marine and Army officer	1776–80	1 vol.
William Jones, Secretary of the Navy, 1813–14 (other papers appear in the collection of Uselma C. Smith)	1792–1839	1,000 items
Assistant Surgeon Elisha Kent Kane	1853–56	2 vols.
Logbooks of naval and merchant vessels	1711–1939	25 vols.
E. Miles (extracts from Miles's historical and statistical description of the Royal Naval Service of England, and data on the building and	1841	1 vol.

	Dates	Volume
extension of the United States Navy)		
John Mitchell (agent for American prisoners of war at Halifax, Nova Scotia)	1812–14	100 items
Lieutenant John S. Muckle	1898–1915	4,000 items
Congressman Leonard Myers (includes letters from naval officers)	1854–1905	150 items
Navy League of the United States, Philadelphia Sector Records	1917–22	1,000 items
Samuel D. Patterson, naval agent, Philadelphia	1845–49	2 vols.
Daniel Parker (includes Stephen Decatur's reports on the condition of the *Chesapeake* after the battle with the *Leopard*, and information relating to the War of 1812)	1800–46	12,000 items
Pennsylvania, Court of Admiralty (includes the log of the ship *Imperial*, 1803–04, and miscellaneous papers relating to other ships)	1770–1804	1,100 items
Samuel Clarke Perkins, Philadelphia lawyer (includes correspondence relating to Naval General Court Martial, Navy Yard, Philadelphia)	1669–1899	300 items
Captain David Porter (in Gilpin Papers)	1825–27	40 items
Price Family (material relating to Samuel Price, his services in the Navy during the Civil War, and his later life as a marine engineer)		300 items
Rear Admiral George C. Read	1836–47	7 vols.
Midshipman John Reed, Jr. (in collection of Reed and Forde)	1759–1823	8,000 items
Rear Admiral George C. Remey	1841–1928	2 vols.
Rear Admiral John Rodgers	1791–1885	763 items, 168 vols.
Sir John Ross, RN	1834	1 vol.
Shaler Family (mainly papers of William Shaler, U.S. agent in Mexico and consul general to the Barbary States and Cuba, and of Nathaniel Shaler, captain of privateer during the War of 1812)	1797–1903	1,000 items
Medical Director Edward Shippen	1849–75	300 items
Floyd T. Starr, collector (includes papers, 1841–70, of Commodore James Madison Frailey, and material on Rear Admiral James R. Madison Mullaney and Rear Admiral Charles Stewart)	1750–1876	157 items

	Dates	Volume
Captain Thomas Truxtun (other materials are in the Wharton-Willing Collection)	1798–1801	3 vols.
U.S. Marine Corps Records (pay rolls and size rolls)	1811–48	51 items
U.S. Naval Home, Philadelphia (papers of John Steele, agent for the Philadelphia Marine Hospital, now called the U.S. Naval Home)	1808–12	100 items
U.S. Philadelphia Naval Shipyard, League Island	1831–77	150 items
John Wanamaker, collector (autograph album, mainly 19th century, which includes naval figures)	1779–1892	1 vol.
Wister Family Collection (contains papers of Assistant Surgeon Owen J. Wister)	1730–1940	8,000 items
Woodhouse Family (includes material on Captain Samuel Woodhouse and the ship *William Penn*)	1818–1930	5 vols.

Guide: The Historical Society of Pennsylvania. *Guide to Manuscript Collections of the Historical Society of Pennsylvania.* 2nd ed. Philadelphia: The Society, 1949.

Library Company of Philadelphia
1300 Locust Street
Philadelphia, PA 19107

(Collections maintained by the Historical Society of Pennsylvania)

	Dates	Volume
Pierre Eugene DuSimitiere (list of the Navy on Lake Champlain with names of vessels, number of men, guns, and swivels on each)	1776	1 item
Captain Thomas Truxtun (mostly letters to Charles Biddle)	1787–1820	110 items

Naval Air Development Center
Warminster, PA 18974

NADC began as the Naval Air Modification Unit of the Air Material Center in 1944 and evolved into the Naval Air Development Station (now Center) in 1947. Historical materials, available through the Public Affairs Office, include command histories, status reports on technical projects, files of Center newspapers, summaries of the Center's history, and papers on the individual organizational units making up the command.

Pennsylvania Historical and Museum Commission
Bureau of Archives and History
William Penn Memorial Museum and Archives Building
Box 1026
Harrisburg, PA 17120

	Dates	*Volume*
Senator James Donald Cameron, Chairman of the Senate Naval Affairs Committee, 1881–92		
Senator George M. Dallas, Chairman of the Senate Committee on Naval Affairs, 1833	1817–63	63 items
Midshipman Simon Cameron Mish (journal)	1840–52	1 vol.
John Mitchell Papers (sequestered papers of a contractor with the Pennsylvania Navy)	ca. 1775–85	
Pennsylvania, Records of the Comptroller General (Military Accounts, Navy)	1775–94	5 boxes
Pennsylvania's Revolutionary Governments (includes records of the Navy Board)	1775–90	microfilm edition

Guide: Evans, Frank B. and Martha L. Simonetti, comp., and Donald H. Kent, ed. *Summary Guide to the Pennsylvania State Archives.* Harrisburg: Pennsylvania Historical and Museum Commission, 1963.

Pennsylvania State University Libraries
Historical Collections
University Park, PA 16802

Lieutenant James Lawrence Parker (includes journal kept on board USS *Brandywine*, 1834–37)	1827–48	1 vol., 54 items
Mate Richard Leroy Parker (includes journal kept on board USS *Brandywine*, 1843–45)	1842–61	1 vol.

The Philadelphia Maritime Museum
321 Chestnut Street
Philadelphia, PA 19106

Commodore Henry A. Adams	1841–77	29 items
American International Shipbuilding Corporation (Hog Island) launchings	1919–20	1 vol.
Benjamin Austin (autographs of naval personages)	1800–95	24 items
Captain William Bainbridge	ca. 1829	1 vol.
Captain James Barron	1831–36	10 items
Captain James Biddle	n.d.	1 item
Thomas L. Bleyler, engineer at Cramp Shipyard	1901–27	14 items

	Dates	Volume
William Cramp and Son, shipbuilders	ca. 1850–1940s	5 boxes, 28 vols.
Captain Stephen Decatur	1804	1 item
Hepburn Collection (includes papers of Captain John Barry and other naval officers)	ca. 1780–1840	6 boxes
Captain Isaac Hull (includes journal of a cruise on board USS *United States*)	1812, 1825	2 items
Joshua Humphreys Shipyard	1782–99	1 record book
New York Shipbuilding Corporation launchings	1958–65	24 vols.
Chief Engineer Robert Potts	1859–1901	1 vol.
Captain Henry S. Stellwagen	1842–65	11 items
Benjamin Stoddert, Secretary of the Navy, 1798–1801	1798–1800	4 items
U.S. Shipping Board Emergency Fleet Corporation	1919	8 vols., 3 folders
Third Assistant Engineer James L. Vauclain	1860	1 item
Acting First Assistant Engineer James Whittaker (includes patent papers for invention of underwater gun part)	1862–75	11 items

Presbyterian Historical Society
425 Lombard Street
Philadelphia, PA 19147

	Dates	Volume

Navy Chaplains Collection:
  Clifford Merrill Drury
  Stanton Willard Salisbury
  Robert Dubois Workman
	1940–62	1,500 items, 8 vols.

U.S. Army Military History Institute
Carlisle Barracks, PA 17013

Civil War Times Illustrated Collection:

	Dates	Volume
Blockade Running	1861–65	1 item
Private Peter Doyle, USMC	1861, 1879	2 items
Lieutenant John E. Hart	1861–63	
Rowland S. True, landsman on board USS *Silver Lake*	1847–1920	
Gideon Welles, Secretary of the Navy, 1861–69	1861	1 item

U.S. Naval History Sources

	Dates	Volume
Spanish American War Naval Veterans (chiefly material from enlisted men; includes some material on their naval service after the war):		
Herman Ludvig Akerlund (handwritten account of Akerlund's service while serving in *Oregon*)	1898	1 item
Louis E. Arvin	1898	
Christopher Atkinson	1898–1906	
Deane C. Bartley (includes diary while on board USS *Minneapolis*)	1903–05	5 vols., 1 item
Frank Bennett (diary of service on board USS *Indiana*)	1901–04	1 vol.
Harry R. Bennett (diary kept on board USS *Columbia*)	1894–1905	1 vol.
Charles W. Bragg	1897–1900	2 items
Adrian Bried (diary kept on board USS *Yorktown* and *Brooklyn*)	1899–1902	1 vol.
George E. Brown (diary kept on board USS *Bancroft*)	1898	
Timothy A. Buckley	1898–1903	7 items
John Charbeneau (diary kept on board *Mississippi*)	1897–98	1 item
Augustus Danziesen	1898	1 item
Archibald M. Forbis	1898–1904	2 vols.
Daniel E. Gamero	1898	1 item
John Gray	1898	26 items
Benjamin C. Greene (diary kept on board USS *Hancock*)	1898–1905	2 items
A. G. Grunwell	1898–1910	
Leslie Guile (includes copies of his diary kept on board USS *New York*)	1901–03	
P. M. Gwin	1898–1901	1 item
Raymond J. Hanlon (includes material relating to USS *Ernest Hinds*)	1918–45, 1954, 1968	
Thomas E. Harrigan (handwritten story about USS *Birmingham*)	1908–10	1 item
Frederick Henry Holzhauser	1897–1903	
Charles J. Hauber	1898–1914	
Julius Frederick Hellweg (journal kept on board USS *Cincinnati*)	1898	1 item
E. A. Hitte	1899–1901	1 item

Pennsylvania

	Dates	Volume
Frank Rufus Hole (includes printed log of the *Newark*'s cruise)	1902–06	2 items
Curtis H. Jennings (includes diary kept on board USS *Prairie*)	1898	6 items
Frank N. Kramer	1898	1 item
Hugo Kramer	1893–1932	
Walter H. Kupfer	1898–1903	
Ernest DeKoven Leffingwell	1898	4 items
Charles Mannhardt	1898–1904	3 items
John McGrory (diary kept on board USS *Buffalo*)	1898–1901	1 vol.
George Herman Moeller	1899–1907	1 item
Harry A. Neithercott	1898	
George M. Palmer, USMC (diary kept on board USS *Brooklyn*)	1898–1904	1 item
William Siegmazer	1898	1 item

Admiral of the Navy George Dewey, victor at the Battle of Manila Bay, 1898

U.S. Naval History Sources

	Dates	*Volume*
George N. Sipps	1895	1 item
William H. Smith	1898–1909	1 item
James O. Spires	1901–18	
Lee Strobel	1898–1903	
"Wayne" (letters from unidentified seaman on board USS *Olympia*)	1896–99	4 items
Henry Williams	1898–1905	
Golson C. Young (diary kept on board USS *Bennington*)	1898–1905	1 vol.
George Zederman	1897–98	

(Included also are questionnaires filled out by veterans of approximately 80 vessels, stations, and units.)

World War I Naval Veterans:

Malcolm Aitken, USMC	1918–19	
August Arndt	1916–19	
George W. Bailey	1918	1 item
Ross A. Etter		
William A. Francis, USMC (diary of Battle of Chateau-Thierry)	1918–22	1 item
Addison H. Lowell	1917–19	2 items
Austin W. Lowell (diary concerning service in U.S. Mine Force)	1917–19	1 item
C. J. Maretti	1917–19	
Joubert S. McCrea (diary kept on board USS *Florida*)	1917–19	
Joseph F. Miller (diary kept on board USS *Lake Forest*)	1918–19	
J. C. Overbaugh	1917–19	1 item
Frank E. Schueler	1917–19	

(Included also are questionnaires filled out by veterans of 21 vessels, stations, and units.)

Other Collections:

Solomon B. Berkowich, naval communicator	1898–1945	1 transcript
Colonel Esher C. Burkart (includes documents concerning naval related service during World War II)	1942–44	
Civil War Miscellaneous Collection (includes material relating to CSS *Alabama* and USS	1864	

	Dates	Volume
Kearsarge)		
USS *Congress* (includes logbook, 1813)	1799–1836	1 box
Rear Admiral Francis H. Delano (includes papers on Panama interventions)	1901–27	
Captain Frederick H. Delano, USMC	1898–1920	
Chief Electrician Eric William Horndahl, USNR	1917–22, 1950–51	
Laning Family (includes genealogical material relating to Admiral Harris Laning and Rear Admiral Caleb Barrett Laning II)	1620–1967	
Midshipman Hubbard Taylor Minor, CSN (includes material relating to Robert Minor of the Confederate Navy)	1862–66	
Charles Nast (papers concerning the controversy between Generals Ralph Smith and Holland Smith over the Saipan Campaign)	1944–48	
William Seach	1898–1963	1 typescript
Master George Sonntag (in Sonntag Family; Halstead-Maus Family Papers)	1807–10	3 items
Rear Admiral Alexander S. Wotherspoon (in Wotherspoon Family Papers; includes transcripts of his diary kept on board USS *New York*)	ca. 1840–1960	

Guide: Sommers, Richard J. *Manuscript Holdings of the Military History Research Collection.* Carlisle Barracks, Pa.: U.S. Army Military History Research Collection, 1975.

University of Pittsburgh Libraries
Archives of Industrial Society
Pittsburg, PA 15261

	Dates	Volume
Herman Stearns Davis, Director of U.S. Naval Observatory	1896–1904	2 ft.

RHODE ISLAND

Brown University
Providence, RI 02912

	Dates	Volume

John Carter Brown Library

	Dates	Volume
John and Nicholas Brown Collection (includes materials on naval affairs)	ca. 1775–83	
D'Estaing-O'Connor Journal (siege of Savannah)	1779	
Jonathan Lawrence Journal	1778	
Manuscripts Relating to John Paul Jones		

The John Hay Library

	Dates	Volume
Samuel Sullivan Cox, Chairman of House Committee on Naval Affairs, 1883–85	1852–1909	1,000 items
Walter Nickerson Hill, chemist at the Naval Torpedo Station, Newport, Rhode Island, 1869–81	1870–84	1,200 items
Surgeon Usher Parsons	1806–66	ca. 600 items
Augustus William Smith, Professor, USN	1820–60	ca. 300 items

Other naval documents appear throughout the library's collections.

Naval Underwater Systems Center
Newport Laboratory
Newport, RI 02844

The Newport Laboratory began in 1869 as the Naval Torpedo Station, which later became the Naval Underwater Weapons Research and Engineering Station. In 1970 the Station was merged into NUSC. Several historical collections relating to torpedoes are cataloged at the Technical Library and are available at the Public

Information Office. These include photographs dating from 1880, pre-World War II handwritten logs on experiments and activities, and other test report material.

At the library, a manuscript report in seven volumes entitled "History of the Naval Torpedo Station, Newport Rhode Island," and a narrative of major activities are on file, as well as a collection of photographic torpedo prints (1810–82), and a collection of rare books.

Newport Historical Society
82 Touro Street
Newport, RI 02840

	Dates	*Volume*
Samuel Brown, naval agent for Boston accounts	1801–07	200 items
Captain Theodore F. Kane	1855–98	ca. 200 pages
Captain John Manley (account book for the Continental Navy's ships *Providence, Alfred, Hamden, Warren, Columbus*)	1776	1 vol.
Rear Admiral Charles Sigsbee	1898–1906	12 letters
Sailing Master William V. Taylor (log of USS *Lawrence*)	1813	1 vol.
William Vernon, President of Navy Board	1777–94	

Rhode Island Historical Society
52 Power Street
Providence, RI 02906

Brown Family (includes material relating to Jeremiah Brown and William S. Brown, officers in the Texas Navy)	1816–92	300 items
DeWolf Family (includes documents referring to the privateers *Yankee, Macdonough,* and *Yankee Lass*)	1751–1864	950 items, 5 vols.
Henry Sanborne Flint (typescript of reminiscences of a seaman on board USS *Brandywine*)	1841	1 vol.
Commodore Esek Hopkins	1677–1799	4 vols.
Maritime Court Minute Book No. 3	1776	1 vol.
Surgeon Usher Parsons	1812–68	15 items, 3 vols.
Providence and *Warren* (journal of the shipbuilding committee for these ships of the Continental Navy)	1776	1 vol.
Quonset Point-Davisville (material documenting the growth of the Quonset Point Naval Air	1939–46	6 ft.

U.S. Naval History Sources

	Dates	Volume
Station and Davisville Construction Battalion Center during World War II)		
Captain Silas Talbot	1775–1800	60 items
Zuriel Waterman (includes journals kept by a surgeon on board the privateers *Providence, Fortune, Rambler,* and *Chace*)	1779–81	3 vols.
Captain Abraham Whipple	1766–86	40 items, 1 vol.

State Archives
Office of the Secretary of State
Room 43
State House
Providence, RI 02903

The State Archives contains documents relating to naval affairs during the Revolutionary War and the Federal period. Included are British Admiralty papers, Admiralty Court Minute Books, Council of War papers, letters to and from the Governor, maritime papers, and Petitions to the General Assembly concerning naval matters.

U.S. Naval War College
Naval Historical Collection
Newport, RI 02840

	Dates	Volume
Documents (miscellaneous manuscripts relating to naval affairs, especially in the 19th and 20th centuries)	1784–1961	61 items
Naval War College Records	1884–present	34 record groups
Oral History Collection (includes naval officer reminiscences by Columbia University, the U.S. Naval Institute, and the Naval War College)	ca. 1960–77	23 items
Manuscript Collections:		
Rear Admiral Richard W. Bates	1932–73	19 boxes
Lieutenant Cyrus W. Breed	1865–75	½ box
Admiral William B. Caperton	1875–1951	½ box
Rear Admiral French E. Chadwick	1898–1911	6 items
Admiral Richard G. Colbert	1932–73	21 boxes
Henry Trevor Cook (letters written from the Naval Academy, Newport, RI)	1862–63	10 items
Rear Admiral Edward Durgin	1937–43	1 box

	Dates	Volume
Rear Admiral Henry E. Eccles		ca. 15 ft.
Admiral Henry Kent Hewitt	1903–57	2 boxes, 16 vols.
Professor Manley O. Hudson (frequent lecturer on international law at Naval War College)	1923–54	13 boxes
Mark Kerr (signed manuscripts of lectures on Sir Horatio Nelson prepared in connection with the commissioning of the HMS *Nelson*)	1931	8 items
Captain William McCarty Little	1880–1921	3 boxes, 3 vols.
Rear Admiral Stephen B. Luce	1876–1919	½ box
Rear Admiral Alfred Thayer Mahan	1868–1908	14 vols., 15 folders
Commodore John B. Marchand	1834–74	20 vols.
Mrs. Wilma S. Miles (includes correspondence and reports of her husband, Vice Admiral Milton E. Miles)	1922–71	4 boxes
Chester T. Minkler (ordnance engineer at the Naval Torpedo Station, Newport, RI)	1919–52	30 items
Rear Admiral Charles J. Moore	1944–63	18 items, 5 vols.
Naval Torpedo Station, Newport, RI	1915, 1937–39	4 vols.
Admiral William Veazie Pratt	1903–63	18 boxes, 22 vols.
Quonset Point-Davisville Naval Officers' Wives Club	1962–72	4 vols.
Quonset Point Naval Air Station Public Affairs Office Historical Files	1941–73	14 cartons
Daniel Sayer (Civil War family correspondence)	1862–65, 1874, 1951	12 items
Lieutenant Roy C. Smith	1876–1929	½ box
Spanish-American War (scrapbook of clippings from U.S. newspapers)	1898–99	1 vol.
Admiral Raymond Ames Spruance	1906–68	7 boxes, 5 vols.
Horatio R. Storer, naval collector	1883–1929	1 vol.
Paymaster Charles P. Thompson	1869–87, 1883–93	2 vols.
Commander Thomas K. Trotter (papers relating to Fleet Admiral Nimitz)	1964–66	½ box

	Dates	Volume
U.S. Naval Base, Newport, RI	1913–69	7 boxes, 5 folders
U.S. Naval Station, Newport, RI	1885–1974	23 boxes, 13 vols.
U.S. Navy, Bureau of Construction and Repair	1898–99	4 items
Commander Robert H. Warren (interviews with survivors of Philippines Campaign, 1941–42)	1971	4 tapes
Commander Eugene E. Wilson	1966–70	8 items
Professor George G. Wilson (lecturer at Naval War College)	1895–1927	6 items
Captain Cameron McRae Winslow	1882–1911	20 items
Vice Admiral Chester C. Wood	1928–52	4 folders
Women Officers School, Newport, RI	1913–74	1 box
Yankee (privateer)	1812–13	2 vols.

SOUTH CAROLINA

The Citadel
Memorial Archives-Museum
Charleston, SC 29409

	Dates	Volume
Admiral Arleigh A. Burke	1974–78	2 ft.
L. Mendel Rivers, Chairman of the House Armed Services Committee, 1965–1970	1945–69	80 ft.
Vice Admiral Friedrich Ruge, German Navy	1941–76	20 ft.

Clemson University Library
Clemson, SC 29631

Senator Benjamin Ryan Tillman, Chairman of Senate Committee on Naval Affairs, 1913–18 (additional letters are in the Samuel Dribble Papers)	1877–1918	215 boxes

South Carolina Department of Archives and History
1430 Senate Street
Columbia, SC 29211

Records of the Commissioners of the Navy of South Carolina	1776–80	4 vols.

South Carolina Historical Society
100 Meeting St.
Charleston, SC 29401

The Society holds Revolutionary War naval documents in the Henry Laurens Papers, in the Letters and Papers Relating to the Revolution, and in the "Return of the Rebel Army." Additional naval documents appear in other collections of the Society.

U.S. Naval History Sources

University of South Carolina
South Caroliniana Library
Columbia, SC 29208

	Dates	Volume
Second Lieutenant Richard H. Bacot, CSN (in Peter Samuel Bacot Papers)	1863–66	8 items
Blue Family (includes material on Lieutenant Commander John S. Blue and Rear Admiral Victor Blue)	1873–1955	50 items, 1 vol.
Lieutenant James Edward Calhoun	1806–89	598 items
Confederate States Navy	1861–1916	5 items
Acting Master Richard M. Cornell (additional material in Confederate States Navy Collection)	1862–1922	12 items
Rear Admiral John Adolphus Bernard Dahlgren	1864–65	2 items
Rear Admiral Samuel Francis DuPont	1862–63	3 items
Acting Midshipman E. Harleston Edwards, CSN	1859–63	67 items
Midshipman Samuel Gaillard	1820–24, n.d.	17 items
First Lieutenant John B. Grimball, Union and Confederate naval officer	1859–88	12 items
Paul Hamilton, Secretary of the Navy, 1809–12	1802–12	27 items
Midshipman Joseph L. C. Hardy (in William Moultrie Reid Collection)	1815–23	6 items
Senator Robert Hayne, Chairman of the Senate Naval Affairs Committee, 1826–31		
Lieutenant Ralph Izard, Jr. (in William W. Burrows Papers; additional material in Ralph Izard Papers)	1765–1955	ca. 333 items
Passed Midshipman Allen C. Izard	1850–1943	93 items
Paymaster Samuel McGowan, Jr.	1893–1903	1 vol.
Captain Robert Whitehead McNeely	1886–1966	8,156 items
Rear Admiral Edward Middleton	1861	1 item
Passed Midshipman James Morris Morgan, CSN	1769–1927	67 items
Acting Third Assistant Engineer James Morrow	1838–1938	355 items
Lieutenant Philip Porcher	1845–1925	401 items
Commander Thomas R. Rootes, Union and Confederate naval officer	1864	1 item
Pilot William H. Smith, CSN	1883	1 vol.
Lieutenant Henry K. Stevens, Union and Confederate naval officer	1858–62, 1960	8 items
Commander Thomas H. Stevens	1861–64	4 items
Senator Benjamin Ryan Tillman, Chairman of the Senate Committee on Naval Affairs, 1913–18	1888–1917	15 items

TENNESSEE

Lincoln Memorial University
Abraham Lincoln Museum
Harrogate, TN 37752

	Dates	*Volume*
Rear Admiral John L. Worden	1835–91	75 items

Memphis/Shelby County Public Library and Information Center
Memphis Room
1850 Peabody Avenue
Memphis, TN 38104

Admiral Harold Martin (oral history)	1915–56	1 item

Tennessee State Library and Archives
403 Seventh Avenue North
Nashville, TN 37219

Rear Admiral Albert Gleaves Berry	1865–1910	1 item
Civil War, Confederate and Federal, Collection	1858–1965	4,500 items, 150 vols.
Rear Admiral Andrew Hull Foote (in Civil War Federal Collection)	1862	7 items
USS *Kearsarge* (account of battle with CSS *Alabama*, written by a crewmember; in Civil War Federal Collection)	1864	1 item
Captain Philip Van Horn Weems (includes material on Weems System of Navigation)	1833–1965	15,000 items

U.S. Naval History Sources

University of the South Library
Archives Department
Sewanee, TN 37375

	Dates	Volume
Lieutenant William Storrow Lovell	1844–1953	1,000 items
Secretaries of the Navy Letter Collection	1813–69	69 items

TEXAS

DeGolyer Foundation Library
P.O. Box 396
S.M.U. Station
Dallas, TX 75275

	Dates	*Volume*
Rear Admiral George Albert Converse	1861—97	400 items, 52 vols.

Denison Public Library
300 West Gandy
Denison, TX 75020

Vice Admiral Adolphus Andrews	1923—44	13 items

Lyndon B. Johnson Space Center
History Office Archives
National Aeronautics and Space Administration
Houston, TX 77058

Records, interviews, press clippings, publications, sound tapes, and other documents relating to the manned spaceflight operations of NASA, including the role of naval personnel and space recovery forces.	ca. 1954—79	ca. 1,000 ft.

Rice Institute
Fondren Library
Houston, TX 77001

USS *Adams* (logbook)	1879—81	1 item
Autograph Collection (includes naval officers)	1828—1909	21 items
Admiral George Cranfield Berkeley, RN	1808—13	1,000 items

	Dates	Volume
Rear Admiral Thomas H. Stevens (letters from Edgar S. Maclay, naval author)	1894–95	3 items
USS *Jamestown* (logbook kept by Midshipman J. H. Gibbons)	1822	1 item
USS *Tuscarora* (diary kept by Midshipman William H. Southerland)	1874–75	1 diary

The Rosenberg Library
2310 Sealy Avenue
Galveston, TX 77550

	Dates	Volume
Samuel Rhoads Fisher, Texas Navy	1836	1 item
Edwin Ward Moore, Texas Navy	1842	1 item
Naval Appropriation Certificates, Texas Navy	1837–41	4 items
USS *Ontario* (plan)	n.d.	1 item
Rules and Regulations of the Texas Navy, Articles 61-78	n.d.	1 item
Signals and Pennants of the Texas Navy	n.d.	1 item
Texas Navy Papers	1836–57	265 items
Commodore John Grant Tod, Texas Navy	1808–77	4 ft.
Samuel May Williams Papers (material relating to the Texas Navy)	1819–65	42 items

Texas State Library
Box 12927, Capitol Station
Austin, TX 78711

	Dates	Volume
Alfred Gilliat Gray, Texas Navy	1839–60	2 folders
Lieutenant Edwin Fairfax Gray	1850–53	1 folder

University of Texas at Austin
Eugene C. Barker Texas History Center
Austin, TX 78712

	Dates	Volume
John Sowers Brooks, USMC	1834–56	39 items
Andrew Jackson Bryant, Texas Navy (in Charles G. Bryant Papers)	ca. 1840s	
D. H. Crisp (sketch of Texas Navy activities; in William Bollaert Papers)	1837–43	1 item
Tim Finn (includes his service in the U.S. Navy in the Civil War)	1854–96	1 vol.

	Dates	Volume
Samuel Rhoads Fisher, Secretary of the Texas Navy	1836	1 vol.
Addison C. Hinton, Commander of the Texas Navy ship *Zavala*, 1837–40	1835–53	117 items
Benjamin Franklin Hughes, Texas Navy, 1842–44, and U.S. Navy, 1853–61	1835–75, 1891	2 vols.
Surgeon Charles E. Lining, Union and Confederate naval officer	1855–1900	8 ft.
William Leake Mann, naval officer and historian	1834–1949	9 in.
Thomas Freeman McKinney, Texas naval officer and financier (additional McKinney documents appear in other collections)	1828–73	62 items
John William Thomason, Jr., author and U.S. Marine Corps officer	1926–50	216 items
John Grant Tod, Texas Navy	1833–72	187 items

Other documents relating to the Texas and U.S. navies appear throughout other collections at the Center.

Additional material at the Harry Ransom Humanities Research Center:

William Eaton, Army officer, diplomat, and naval agent		33 items

Guide: Texas University Library, Archives Collection. *The University of Texas Archives: Historical Manuscript Collections in the University of Texas Library,* comp. and ed. by Chester V. Kielman. Austin: University of Texas Press, 1967.

University of Texas at Dallas Library
Manuscript Division
Dallas, TX 75080

Vice Admiral Charles E. Rosendahl	ca. 1914–77

UTAH

Brigham Young University
Harold B. Lee Library
Provo, UT 84602

	Dates	Volume
J. Reuben Clark, Jr., Special Counsel and Expert Assistant to the Commissioners, Washington Conference on Arms Limitation (restricted collection)	ca. 1921–22	3 ft.
History of the Mine Force, U.S. Atlantic Fleet (typed manuscript)	1917–18	1 item

VERMONT

University of Vermont
Guy W. Bailey Library
Burlington, VT 05401

	Dates	Volume
William Jarvis, U.S. Consul to Portugal (includes letters from Captain Edward Preble and Commodore Samuel Barron)	1801–10	25 items
Captain Thomas MacDonough	1813–24	1 vol.

VIRGINIA

College of William and Mary
Earl Gregg Swem Library
Williamsburg, VA 23185

	Dates	Volume
Captain James Barron	1776–1899	2,742 items
Captain Samuel Barron, II (also includes some material related to Captain Samuel Barron, III and Captain Samuel Barron, IV)	1793–1942	527 items
Surgeon Thomas Ewell (in papers of Benjamin S. Ewell)	1802, 1821	3 items
Thomas Walker Gilmer, Secretary of the Navy, 1844 (correspondence in the Tyler Papers)	1827–44	34 items
Admiral John L. Hall	ca. 1913–73	ca. 8 ft.
Commander William Lewis (in Conway-Whittle Family Papers)	1801–15	105 items
Abel P. Upshur, Secretary of the Navy, 1841–43 (letters in the Tucker-Coleman Papers and in the Tyler Papers)	1836–44	89 items

Confederate Museum Library
1201 East Clay Street
Richmond, VA 23219

Confederate States of America Military Collections (includes private journals kept on board CSS *Shenandoah*, *Tennessee*, and *Florida*; logs of *Shenandoah* and *Georgia*; crew list of the *Tennessee*; and commissions and papers of naval personnel)	1861–65	50-75 items
Commander Matthew Fontaine Maury (Union and Confederate naval officer)	1864–65	50 items

191

U.S. Naval History Sources

	Dates	Volume
CSS *Shenandoah* (includes journals of Assistant Surgeon Lining and Midshipman Mason)	1864–65	3 items
CSS *Stonewall* (log of chief engineer)	1864–65	1 item

Dahlgren Laboratory
Naval Surface Weapons Center
Dahlgren, VA 22448

The U.S. Naval Proving Ground, which moved to Dahlgren from Indian Head, Maryland, in 1918, became the Naval Weapons Laboratory that was consolidated into NSWC in 1974. In preparing a history of the laboratory, the Publication Division developed a collection of documents which includes biographical files of key people, extracts from publications, photographs, press clippings, selections from congressional hearings, correspondence, and historical summaries. Of special significance is the manuscript "History, U.S. Naval Proving Ground, Dahlgren, Va., April 1918–December 1945," by Captain David I. Hedrick. There is also an oral history collection.

James Carson Breckinridge Library
U.S. Marine Corps Education Center
Building 2048
Marine Corps Development and Education Command
Quantico, VA 22134

This library has approximately 80,000 items, including books, periodicals, non-security–classified reports, maps, microfilm, microfiche, and vertical file material. There is a comprehensive collection of manuscripts, documents, and publications related to the history of amphibious warfare and the development of amphibious doctrine.

MacArthur Memorial Archives
198 Bank Street
Norfolk, VA 23510

	Dates	Volume
General of the Army Douglas MacArthur (includes naval material)	1929–73	ca. 750 ft.

Virginia

Marine Corps Aviation Museum
Brown Field
Marine Corps Development and Education Command
Quantico, VA 22134

The exhibits at the Marine Corps Aviation Museum include more than 20 aircraft plus ordnance and other aviation material spanning the period from 1941 through 1945. Earlier years will be covered in an exhibit scheduled to open in 1979.

Major portions of the Marine Corps Museum's collections of artillery and vehicles also are located at Quantico. For additional information concerning any of these collections, researchers should contact the Marine Corps History and Museums Division, Headquarters Marine Corps, Washington, D.C. 20380.

A landing force of naval bluejackets at Hankow, China, 1927

U.S. Naval History Sources

The Mariners Museum
Newport News, VA 23606

The Mariners Museum contains over 1,600 maps, 2,000 ship papers, and about 280 logs, journals, and letter books, many of which concern ships of the U.S. Navy.

Guide: The Mariners Museum, Newport News, Virginia. *Catalog of Maps, Ships' Papers and Logbooks.* Boston: G. K. Hall, 1964.

McCain Amphibious Warfare Library
Naval Amphibious School
Naval Amphibious Base
Norfolk, VA 23521

	Dates	*Volume*
Action Reports, Exercise Reports, and Operational Orders	1944–70	ca. 5,000 items

Norfolk Public Library
Sargeant Memorial Room
Norfolk, VA 23510

Captain William Conway Whittle, Union and Confederate naval officer	1863–1910	150 items

Old Dominion University Archives
Norfolk, VA 23508

Chief Engineer Thom Williamson	1853–1912	1 ft.

University of Virginia Library
Manuscripts Department
Charlottesville, VA 22901

Captain Samuel Barron, Union and Confederate naval officer	1820–99	ca. 700 items
Commander Theodore G. Ellyson	1901–28	30 items
Rear Admiral Frank Friday Fletcher	1873–1928	ca. 7,500 items
Captain Andrew Snape Hamond, RN	1766–1825	2 ft.
Medical Director Gustavus R. B. Horner	1826–92	ca. 100 vols., 13,500 items
Lieutenant Commander Marc Winthrop Larimer (journal kept on board USS *Cummings*)	1917–18	1 vol.

Virginia

	Dates	Volume
Captain Matthew Fontaine Maury, Union and Confederate naval officer (in Maury Family Papers)	1773–1917	3000 items
Passed Assistant Surgeon James Monroe Minor	1806–1901	285 items
Surgeon Lewis Willis Minor, Union and Confederate naval officer	1772–1932	150 items
Noland Family (includes material relating to Lieutenant Callender St. George Noland)	1813–1901	4,000 items
Commander Gale Aylett Poindexter	1890–1946	200 ft.
Senator William Cabell Rives, Chairman of the Senate Committee on Naval Affairs, 1836–39	1827–66	425 items
Lieutenant Commander B.F.D. Runk, USNR	1943–45	900 items
Senator Claude A. Swanson, Chairman of the Senate Committee on Naval Affairs, 1918–19, and Secretary of the Navy, 1933–39	1887–1945	ca. 20,000 items
Assistant Surgeon John S. Whittle (journal)	1838–41	2 vols.
Captain William Conway Whittle, Union and Confederate naval officer (in Whittle Family Papers)	1805–78	12 items

Virginia Historical Society
Post Office Box 7311
Richmond, VA 23221

	Dates	Volume
Allmand Family (includes material relating to contracts with the Navy)	1796–1891	573 items
Robert Coleman Bagby (attended U.S. Naval Academy)	1893–99	10 items
George Bancroft, Secretary of the Navy, 1845–46	1845	1 item
Barron Family	1858–73	6 items
USS *Brandywine* (logbook includes log of USS *Constitution*)	1825–28	1 vol.
Yeoman John Taylor Chappell, CSN	1865	1 item
Francis Asbury Dickins, lawyer (relating to bounty and military pension claims)	1848–53	1 vol.
USS *Germantown*	1857–60	2 vols.
Surgeon Gustavus Richard Brown Horner, Navy Medical Director, 1871	1837–88	509 items
Commander Catesby ap Roger Jones, Union and Confederate naval officer	1856	9 items

U.S. Naval History Sources

Commander Matthew Fontaine Maury, known as the "pathfinder of the seas" for his pioneering hydrographic studies

	Dates	*Volume*
John Pendleton Kennedy, Secretary of the Navy, 1852–53	1813–64	50 items
USS *Lexington*	1849–50	2 vols.
John Young Mason, Secretary of the Navy, 1844–45, 1846–49	1818–59	2,140 items
Commander Matthew Fontaine Maury, Union and Confederate naval officer	1846–73	140 items
Minor Family (includes material relating to Lieutenant Robert Dabney Minor)	1657–1942	4,800 items
Commander John Kirkwood Mitchell	1819–88	600 items
Surgeon Francis Smith Nash	1878–89	108 items
Ensign John Combe Pegram	1861–66	29 items
Commander Robert Baker Pegram, Union and Confederate naval officer (logbook of CSS	1861–62	1 item

	Dates	Volume
Nashville in papers of the Pegram, Johnson, and McIntosh families)		
Captain Matthew Calbraith Perry	1848	1 item
USS *Perry*	1852	1 vol.
William Ballard Preston, Secretary of the Navy, 1849–50	1840–62	418 items
Rear Admiral Raphael Semmes, Union and Confederate naval officer	1862–69	150 items
Andrew Talcott, Army Engineer (served on a board of naval officers and engineers which examined navy yards)	1834–48	23 items
USS *Vincennes*	1843–44	1 vol.
Gideon Welles, Secretary of the Navy, 1861–69	1862	1 item
Senator Henry Alexander Wise, Chairman of the House Committee on Naval Affairs, 1842–43	1819–74	255 items
Surgeon John Cropper Wise	1865–1922	7 items
USS *Wyoming*	1859–61	3 vols.

Guide: Virginia Historical Society. *Catalogue of the Manuscripts in the Collection of the Virginia Historical Society, and Also Some Printed Papers.* William Ellis Jones, Book and Job Printer, 1901.

Virginia State Library
Archives Division
Richmond, VA 23219

	Dates	Volume
Captain French Forrest, Union and Confederate naval officer	1861–64	4 vols.
Virginia Navy Records	1775–83	1,250 items, 12 vols.

WASHINGTON

Coast Guard Museum/Northwest
1519 Alaskan Way South
Seattle, WA 98134

	Dates	*Volume*
U.S. Coast Guard (includes predecessor services)	1857–present	10 ft.

Coast Guard patrol boats operating off the landing beaches at Normandy as rescue craft, 1944

Federal Archives and Records Center
Archives Branch
6125 Sand Point Way, NE
Seattle, WA 98115

	Dates	*Volume*
Records of Naval Districts and Shore Establishments (R. G. 181):		1,037 ft.
13th Naval District	1901–56	
17th Naval District	1941–56	

The Archives Branch holds extensive microfilm collections of documents located in the National Archives. These include U.S. naval records as well as naval related items in the records of other federal agencies.

Guide: Hobbs, Richard, comp. *Guide to the Seattle Archives Branch.* Federal Archives and Records Center, 1977.

University of Washington Libraries
Archives and Manuscripts Division
Suzzallo Library
Seattle, WA 98195

Thomas T. Aldwell, naval contractor (includes correspondence concerning the Puget Sound Navy Yard, Bremerton)	1912–48	22 items
Stephen F. Chadwick, attorney (includes correspondence with naval officers)	1933–45	20 items
Captain Miller Freeman, USNR	1918–44	74 items
Henry Suzzallo, President of the University of Washington (includes correspondence concerning the University's Naval Training Unit in World War I)	1917–24	55 items
Lieutenant (j.g.) Edward L. Ullman, USNR	1940–56	150 items
U.S. Navy, Mare Island Depot	1855	1 item
Mate Philip C. Van Buskirk	1851–1902	1 2/3 ft.
Lieutenant Ambrose B. Wyckoff	1880–1914	15 items

Washington State University Library
Manuscripts, Archives, and Special Collections Division
Pullman, WA 99163

George Frederick Jewett Naval History Collection	1900–55	7 ft.
Surgeon George W. Woods, Medical Director of	1883–86	31 items

U.S. Naval History Sources

	Dates	Volume
the Navy, 1895–1900 (includes journals kept on board USS *Juniata*)		
Commander John Henry Walsh	1897–1960	4 ft.

Other naval materials appear in the Homer J. Dana and Walter F. Horan Collections.

Guide: Washington State University, Pullman, Library. *Selected Manuscript Resources in the Washington State University Library.* The Library, 1974.

WEST VIRGINIA

West Virginia University Library
Morgantown, WV 26506

	Dates	Volume
Captain French Ensor Chadwick	1903–14	2 items, 1 box
Nathan Goff, Secretary of the Navy, 1881	1866–99	37 boxes, 4 cartons, 1 folder
Henderson-Tomlinson Families (includes letters and other material on Brigadier General Archibald Henderson, USMC)	1798–1859	1 microfilm reel
Nicholas Marmion Papers (includes correspondence of Surgeon Robert A. Marmion, first president of the Naval Medical School, and Assistant Surgeon William V. Marmion)	1798–1951	5 ft.

Guide: Hess, James W. *Guide to Manuscripts and Archives in the West Virginia Collection.* Morgantown, W. Va.: West Virginia University Library, 1974.

WISCONSIN

Marathon County Historical Society
Wausau, WI 54401

	Dates	Volume
USS *Brandywine* (logbook)	1834–37	1 vol.

Milwaukee County Historical Society Collections
910 N. 3rd Street
Milwaukee, WI 53203

German Naval Association (documents relating to a Marine Historical Society founded to study German naval history)	1912–62	5 folders, 157 items

State Historical Society of Wisconsin
Archives Division
816 State Street
Madison, WI 53706

Captain William Compton Bolton	1801–80	1 box
Timothy Brown (includes information on naval enlisted service)	1917–18	3 vols.
Busch-Sulzer Brothers Diesel Engine Company (naval contractor)	1895–1946	40 boxes
Isaac Cooper (sailor serving off the coast of Central America and in the Far East)	1880–95	6 items
Commander William B. Cushing	1859–63	23 items
Lieutenant James C. Gipson	1863–97	10 items
Lieutenant Commander Albert Weston Grant	1872–1930	3 boxes
Malcolm Parker Hanson (chief radio engineer on Richard E. Byrd's expedition to Little America in 1928–30)	1906–47	3 boxes
Midshipman Sidney Harrington	1837–39	1 vol.

Fleet Admiral William D. Leahy, Chief of Naval Operations (1937–1939), U.S. Ambassador to France (1940–1942), and Chief of Staff to the President (1942–1949)

	Dates	Volume
Harrison Family (includes letter written by Sylvanus T. Harrison stationed in USS *Victory*)	1862–65, 1955–58	64 pp.
Assistant Engineer John S. Hill	1865	1 item
Fleet Admiral William D. Leahy	1897–1931, 1941–45	7 vols., 11 reels of microfilm
Manitowoc Shipbuilding Corporation Records (naval contractor)	1920–51	1 reel of microfilm
Frank Earl Mason (Special Assistant to Secretary of the Navy during World War II)	1931–46	3 ft.
Admiral Marc Andrew Mitscher	1943–46	1 box

U.S. Naval History Sources

	Dates	Volume
Lieutenant (j.g.) Wells B. Nottingham (includes information on USS *Tonawanda*)	1944–45	1 folder
U.S. Navy (letters and reports relating to naval actions in which Wisconsin men participated)	1864, 1909, 1946–57	23 items
Commander Reed A. Rose, USNR (includes material on USS *Kilauea* and Naval Training School, Richmond, Virginia)	1942–46	1 vol.
Henry Salomon, Jr., naval historian (includes material from his work on naval history under Rear Admiral Samuel Eliot Morison and his production of the television series *Victory at Sea*)	1934–62	3 boxes
Horace J. Smith (World War II correspondence, including letters from Captain P. B. Smith and a daughter in the WAVES)	1857–1948	6 boxes
William O. Titus (includes letters written during World War II by Titus's son, Ensign Robert Titus)	1835–1951	11 boxes, 6 vols.
Lieutenant Nathan Crook Twining	1888–1917	86 items
Kenneth White (includes letters from his son, John White, describing his service in the U.S. Navy)	1917–49	20 boxes
Rear Admiral Charles Wilkes (with William Compton Bolton Papers)	1801–80	1 box

Guide: Smith, Alice E., ed. *Guide to the Manuscripts of the Wisconsin Historical Society.* Madison, Wisc.: State Historical Society, 1944.
    Supplement Number 1. Madison, 1957.
    Supplement Number 2. Madison, 1966.

WYOMING

University of Wyoming Library
Laramie, WY 82070

	Dates	*Volume*
Lieutenant Commander Charles C. Hiles	ca. 1935–60	
Rear Admiral Husband Edward Kimmel	1907–68	20 ft.
Navy Airship Pilots School, Pensacola, Florida (in Papers of Colonel Frank M. Kennedy, USA)		
Captain Laurence F. Safford	1941–67	4 ft.
Theodore P. Wright (Chief Inspector, U.S. Navy NC-4 flying boats, 1918; and corporate and government official in field of aviation)	1917–45	

index

A

Abbot, Joel, 98
Abbott, John, 120
Abbott, Samuel W., 24
Abraham Lincoln Museum, 185
Academy of Natural Sciences Library, 165
Ackiss, Ernest L., 96
Ackley, Charles, 159
Action and Operational Reports (1941–53), 39
Adams, Henry A., 172
Adams, James M., 60
Adams, Sherman W., 13
Adams, USS (frigate), 132
Adams, USS (gunboat), 187
Adee, Augustus Alvey, 24
Adee Family Papers, 24
Admiralty, see Great Britain
Aerial Coast Patrol Unit No. 1, 16
Ageton, Arthur Ainsley, 104
Ainsworth, Walden Lee, 149
Aitken, Malcolm, 176
Ajax, USS, 128
Akerlund, Herman Ludvig, 174
Alabama, CSS, 161, 176, 185
Alabama Department of Archives and History, 1
Alaska Revenue Cutter Service, 108
Albert, Francis Lee, 151
Alden, Carroll Storrs, 98
Aldwell, Thomas T., 199
Alexander, Archibald Stevens, Library, Rutgers University, 127–29
Alfred, Continental Ship, 15, 179
Alison, Samuel King, 78
Allen, USS, 86
Allen, Gardner Weld, 109
Allen, William A. H., 24
Allen, William Henry, 2, 24
Allied Operational and Occupational Authorities, World War II, 66
Allmand Family, 195
Almy, John Jay, 132–33, 139
America, Privateer, 91
America, USS, 136
American Antiquarian Society, 101
American Battle Monuments Commission, 66
American Geographical Society Library, 130
American International Shipbuilding Corporation, 172
American Jewish Archives, 158
American Jewish Committee, 101
American Jewish Historical Society Collections, 101
American Museum of Natural History, 130
American National Red Cross Archives, 22
American Philosophical Society Library, 165
American Swedish Historical Foundation, 165
Amistad Research Center, 85
Ammen, Daniel, 10, 160
Amphibious Force, Atlantic, 41
Anderson, Edward Clifford, 153
Anderson, Edwin Alexander, Jr., 147, 153
Anderson House Library and Museum, 63
Andover, Mass., 110
Andrew Doria, Continental Ship, 24
Andrews, Adolphus, 187
Andrews, Mark Edwin, 120
Annapolis, see also Naval Academy
Annapolis, Naval Engineer Experiment Station and Testing Laboratory, 89
Annapolis, Navy Marine Engineering Laboratory, 89
Annapolis Laboratory, Naval Ship Research and Development Center, 90
Apollon, 25
Applied Physics Laboratory, Johns Hopkins University, 43, 89
Arbuthnot, Marriot, 137
Archibald Stevens Alexander Library, Rutgers University, 127–29
Archives of American Art, Washington Center, Smithsonian Institution, 59
Arctic, USS, 136
Arctic Expedition of Robert E. Peary, 130, 132, 165
Arents, George, Research Library, Syracuse University, 145
Argus, USS, 133, 141
Armiger, George Jones, 91
Armour, Lester, 4
Arms, Frank H., 14
Army and Navy Club of New York, 133

Army and Navy Journal, 25, 140
Army Military History Institute, 173-77
Arndt, August, 176
Arthur and Elizabeth Schlesinger Library on the History of Women in America, 111
Arvin, Louis E., 174
Ashe, Samuel A'Court, 147, 151
Asiatic Fleet and Asiatic Defense Campaign, 39
Associated Negro Press, 76
Atkeson, John Conner, Sr., 149
Atkinson, Christopher, 174
Atlanta Federal Archives and Records Center, 72
Atlantic Fleet, 41, 44, 190
Auburn University Archives, 1
Audiovisual Division, National Archives, 64
Augur, Christopher C., 77
Aulick, John Henry, 91
Aurand, Evan P., 83
Austin, Benjamin, 172
Austin, Bernard Lige, 145
Aviation Flight Logs, 69
Aviation History Unit, Office of the Deputy Chief of Naval Operations (Air), 22, 40
Awards Branch, Office of the Chief of Naval Operations, 40
Axtell, Richard, 47
Ayer, Richard Hazen, 123

B

Babbitt, Edward B., 47
Baber, George Francis Burleigh, 74
Bache, Albert Dabadie, 165
Bache, George Mifflin, 98
Bache Family Papers, 165
Bacot, Richard H., 184
Bacot, Peter Samuel, 184
Badger, George Edmund, 152–53
Badger, Oscar C., 43
Bagby, Robert Coleman, 195
Bagley, Worth, 153
Bagley Family Papers, 153
Bailey, George W., 176
Bailey, Guy W., Library, 190
Bailey, Theodorus, 9, 145
Bailey, Thomas A., 4
Bailey, Vernon Howe, 59
Bailey-Ryan Collection, 4
Bainbridge, Joseph, 76
Bainbridge, William, 47, 133, 145, 168, 172
Baker, Gregory L., 151
Baker, James McCutcheon, 157
Baker, Wilder D., 4
Baker Library, Harvard University, 105
Balch, George Beall, 153

Baldridge, Harry A., 47
Baldwin, Hanson W., 16, 54
Baltimore, USS, 57
Baltimore, Md., 90–91, 94
Bancroft, USS, 174
Bancroft, George, 24, 101, 109, 124, 131, 139, 141, 195
Bancroft-Bliss Papers, 24
Bancroft Library, University of California, Berkeley, 10
Banks, Nathaniel P., 77, 85
Baptist General Conference, 117
Barbey, Daniel E., 43
Barclay, Thomas, 133
Barker, Albert S., 54
Barker, Eugene C., Texas History Center, 188–89
Barker, Josiah, 103
Barleon, John S., 55
Barlow, Samuel L. M., 133
Barnes, Guy, 55
Barnes, John Sanford, 133
Barnett, Claude A., 76
Barney, Joseph Nicholson, 153
Barney, Joshua, 24, 168
Barrie, Robert, 113, 147
Barron, James, 14, 47, 156, 172, 191
Barron, Samuel (1765–1810), 190–91
Barron, Samuel (1808–88), 191, 194
Barron, Samuel (CSN), 191
Barron Family, 191, 195
Barry, John, 20, 24, 133, 137, 173
Bartlett, Steven Chaulker, 153
Bartlett, William, 24, 102
Bartley, Deane C., 174
Barton, Charles Crillon, 168
Base Maintenance Division, Office of the Chief of Naval Operations, 40
Bassett, H. W., 153
Bassett, John Young, 153
Batchelder-Nelson Family Papers, 10
Bates, John A., 47
Bates, Richard W., 47, 180
Batione, Benecia, 12
Batione, Dominick B., 12
Bauer, Daniel Michael, 121
Bayard, Richard Henry, 24
Bayard Family Papers, 24
Bayley, W. B., 96
Beach, Albert Douglas, 2
Beach, Edward Latimer, 83
Beagle, USS, 103
Beale, Edward F., 9
Beale Family Papers, 25
Bear, USCG, 9
Beardslee, Lester A., 47
Beaufort, Francis, 2

Beebe Papers, 146
Belknap, George E., 47
Belknap, Reginald R., 47, 55
Bell, Charles H., 153
Bell, Henry H., 47
Bellamy, John H., 47
Belt, William Joseph, 91
Bemis, Harold M., 55
Benedict, Edwin R., 72
Bennett, Frank, 174
Bennett, Frank M., 47
Bennett, Harry R., 174
Bennington, USS, 176
Benson, William S., 25
Bent, Silas, 127
Bentinck, William, 113
Bentley, John W., 14
Benton, USS, 129
Benyon, B. G., 161
Bering Sea Patrol, 108
Berkeley, George Cranfield, 187
Berkowich, Solomon B., 176
Bermuda, Naval Air Station, 41
Bernice Pauahi Bishop Museum, 75
Berry, Albert Gleaves, 185
Berry, Joseph, 47
Berry, Robert W., 5
Bethel College and Seminary, 117
Beverly Historical Society, 102
Beverly, Naval Office, 102
Bicknell, George A., 80
Biddle, Charles, 168, 171
Biddle, James, 25, 145, 168, 172
Biddle, Nicholas, 24
Biddle, Spencer F. B., 164
Bigelow, John, 140
Bilboa, Naval Agent, 123
Billings, Luther G., 47
Binford, Thomas H., 5
Bingham, Donald C., 47
Binney, Amos, 101
Biological Computer Laboratory, University of Illinois, 79
Birch, Thomas, 96
Bird, Joseph R., 153
Birmingham, USS, 174
Bishop, Bernice Pauahi, Museum, 75
Bishop, David, 127
Bixby, W. H., 25
Blacknall, George, 153
Blackwell, Edward M., 68
Blair, James L., 3, 16
Blair-Lee Papers, 127
Blake, Charles F., 47
Blake, George Smith, 101
Blake, Homer Crane, 139
Blakeley, Johnston, 152

Blakeslee, Victor F., 55
Blanding, Stephen F., 161
Blandy, William H. P., 55
Blauvelt, James L. B., 147
Blee, Ben W., 151
Bleyler, Thomas L., 172
Bloch, Claude C., 47
Blount, Fernando Moreno, 71
Blow, George P., 55
Blue, John S., 184
Blue, Victor, 152–53, 184
Blue Family, 184
Boarman, Charles, 47
Boggs, Charles Stuart, 127
Bolander, Louis H., 5
Bollaert, William, 188
Bolton, William Compton, 202, 204
Bonaparte, Charles J., 25, 91
Bond, Richmond Pugh, 153
Bonnaffon, Edmund W., 168
Bonney, Henry M., 131
Boone, Joel T., 25
Booraem, Henry, Jr., 127
Bordley, Stephen, 91
Bordley Family, 91
Boston, USS, 110, 134, 140, 145
Boston Athenaeum Library, 102
Boston, Federal Archives and Records Center, 102
Boston Naval Library and Institute, 96
Boston Navy Yard, *see* Charlestown, Mass., Navy Yard
Boston Public Library, 103–04
Boston University Libraries, 104
Bouche, Louis, 59
Bowen, Harold Gardiner, 47, 55, 127
Bower, Lawrence F., 3
Bowles, Francis Tiffany, 139
Bowling Green State University, 158
Bowman, Harry S., 91
Bowman, Ziba, 91
Boxer, HMS, 110
Boyce, Thomas J., 125
Boyd, Joseph B., 158
Brackenridge, William Dunlop, 92
Braden, Charles J., 77
Bradford, John, 25
Bradford, Joseph C., 96
Bradford, Thomas, 168
Brady, William N., 139
Bragg, Charles W., 174
Braisted, Frank, 47
Branch, John, 152–53
Branch Family Papers, 153
Brandywine, USS, 110, 135–36, 145, 172, 179, 195, 202
Breck, Edward, 47
Breck, John, 47

Breck Family, 47
Breckenridge, James Carson, Library, 33, 192
Breed, Cyrus W., 180
Breese, Samuel Livingston, 147
Bremerton, see Puget Sound Navy Yard
Brent, Joseph L., 47
Bricker, John W., 159
Bried, Adrian, 174
Brigham Young University, 190
Bristol, Mark L., 25, 47
Bristol, R. I., 137
British Navy, see Great Britain
Brodhead, Daniel Dodge, 25
Bronson, Walter A., 31
Brooke, John Mercer, 153
Brooke, Peter, 134
Brooklyn, USS (Sloop), 161
Brooklyn, USS (CA-3), 174–75
Brooklyn Naval Lyceum, 96
Brooklyn Navy Yard, see New York Navy Yard
Brooks, John Sowers, 188
Brooks, William Param, 72, 74
Broome, John L., 31
Brothers, Charles, 80
Brown, Clarence J., 159
Brown, George E., 174
Brown, Harry Fletcher, 19
Brown, Jeremiah, 179
Brown, John Carter, Library, Brown University, 178
Brown, John and Nicholas, Collection, 178
Brown, Timothy, 202
Brown, Samuel, 109, 179
Brown, Wilburt S., 32
Brown, William S., 179
Brown, Wilson, 98, 132
Brown Books (Maryland State Papers), 90–91
Brown Family, 179
Brown University, 178
Browne, John M., 47
Browne, Joseph Vincent, 105
Browne, Symmes Evans, 159
Browning Family, 47
Browning, Robert L., 48
Brownson, Willard H., 48
Bryan, John Herritage, 152
Bryant, Andrew Jackson, 188
Bryant, Charles G., 188
Buchanan, Franklin, 92, 98, 153
Buchanan, Thomas McKean, 92
Bucher, Lloyd M., 5
Buckley, Christopher A., Collection, 8
Buckley, Nathaniel, Record Book, 85
Buckley, Timothy A., 174
Buckmaster, Elliott, 5
Buenos Aires, 20

Buffalo, USS, 175
Buffalo and Erie County Historical Society, 130
Bulkeley, Charles, 15
Bulkeley, John Duncan, 83
Bullus, John, 134
Bullus, Oscar, 127, 134
Bureau of Aeronautics, 65
Bureau of Construction and Repair, 167, 182
Bureau of Medicine and Surgery, 65, 67–68
Bureau of Naval Personnel, 42, 65
Bureau of Ordnance, 61, 65
Bureau of Ships, 65
Bureau of Supplies and Accounts, 65
Bureau of War Records, National Jewish Welfare Board, 101–02
Bureau of Yards and Docks, 7, 65
Burge, J. H. Hobart, 95
Burkart, Esher C., 176
Burke, Arleigh A., 27, 55, 108, 183
Burns, James, 168
Burns, Otway, 48, 152
Burrows, William W., 184
Burtis, William B., 139
Burton Historical Collection, 113
Busch-Sulzer Brothers Diesel Engine Company, 202
Bushnell, David, 15
Butcher, Harry C., 83
Butler, Albert L., 13
Butler, Smedley D., 32
Butler Library, Columbia University, 131
Byrd, Richard E., 43, 202
Byrne, Edmund, 48

C

Cabot, Godfrey L., 109
Cadwaleder, John, 55
Cady, Horatio Nelson, 25
Caffery, Donelson, 85
Caffery, John Murphy, 85
Calder, George, 153
Caldwell, Albert Gallatin, 80
Caldwell, John, Collection, 80
Calhoun, USS, 92
California Historical Society, 2
Calhoun, James Edward, 23, 117, 184
Callan, John L., 48
Cambridge, USS, 117, 134, 161
Cameron, James Donald, 172
Camilla, USS, 136
Canaga, Alfred B., 48
Caperton, William B., 48, 180
Carderock Laboratory, Naval Ship Research and Development Center, 90
Carew, Benjamin Hallowell, 147
Carlin, James W., 48
Carnegie Library of Pittsburgh, 166

210

Carpender, Arthur S., 125
Carpenter, Dudley N., 48
Carter, John C., 159
Carter, Samuel P., 48
Cartographic Division, National Archives, 64
Cary, Clarence, 48
Case Western Reserve University, 158
Casey, Silas, 48
Cassin, Charles Luke, 165
Castine, USS, 68
Cates, Clifton B., 32
Cathcart, Alexander Henry, and Family Papers, 117
Cathcart, James Leander, 140
Catholic Conference (U.S.), 23
Catholic University of America, 23
Causten, Joseph H., 23
Cayuga, USS, 134
Cecil, John L., 55
Cecil Field, Naval Air Station, 72
Celustka, Robert J., 151
Central Division, Office of the Chief of Naval Operations, 41
Chace, Privateer, 180
Chadwick, French Ensor, 134, 180, 201
Chadwick, Stephen F., 199
Chaisson, John R., 5
Chambers, Washington I., 48
Chandler, Porter R., 134
Chandler, Ralph C., 105, 134
Chandler, William, 140
Chandler, William E., 25, 123
Chapelle, Howard I., 60, 62
Chapelle Collection, 62
Chapman, George William, 86
Chapman, Leonard F., Jr., 32
Chapman, William Gerald, 153
Chappel, Church A., 5
Chappell, John Taylor, 195
Charbeneau, John, 174
Charleston, USS, 147
Charleston Navy Yard, 72
Charleston Harbor Defense Papers, 72
Charlestown, Mass., Navy Yard, 54, 96, 102–03, 110
Chart Room, Commander in Chief, U.S. Fleet, 44
Chase, Philander, 48
Chasseur, Privateer, 92
Chateau-Thierry, Battle, 176
Chatham, HMS, 75
Chauncey, Isaac, 55, 134, 168
Cheever, William Harrison, 117
Chemung, USS, 131
Chemung County Historical Society, 130
Chesapeake, USS, 20, 61, 108, 170
Chesapeake Bay Campaign (1814), 90
Chesapeake Bay Fortifications, 161
Chesapeake Flotilla, War of 1812, 168

Chester, Colby M., 48
Chew, Francis Thornton, 153
Chew, Thomas J., 113
Chicago, Federal Archives and Records Center, 76
Chicago Historical Society, 76
Chief of Naval Operations, *see* Office of the Chief of Naval Operations
Child, John Richards, 109
China, Naval Group, 41
China Lake, Naval Ordnance Test Station, 8
China Lake, Naval Weapons Center, 8
China Repository, Naval Historical Center, 40
Chipola, USS, 135
Chisolm, Alexander Robert, 161
Chisolm Family Papers, 156
Chocura, USS, 134
Christopher, Charles W., 114
Church, William Conant, 25, 140
Cilley, Greenleaf, 48
Cincinnati, USS, 174
Cincinnati and Hamilton County, Public Library, 159
Cincinnati Historical Society, 158
Circuit Courts, 102
Citadel, The, 183
Civil Affairs/Military Government Branch, Office of the Chief of Naval Operations, 40–41
Civil War Papers, Federal, 153, 185
Clapham, John, 122
Clark, A. Dayton, 83
Clark, Charles Edgar, 105, 140
Clark, George Warren, 56
Clark, J. Reuben, Jr., 190
Clark, Joseph G., 25
Clark, William Bell, 48, 168
Clark, William J., 168
Clark Family Papers, 147
Clarkson, John, 134
Claxton, Alexander, 48
Cleaver, H. E., 151
Clements, William L., Library, University of Michigan, 16, 113–16
Clemson University Library, 183
Clifford, Clark M., 120
Clinton, George, 114
Clover, Richardson, 56
Coale, Griffith Baily, 60
Coan, Titus Munson, 134
Coast and Geodetic Survey, U.S., 65
Coast Guard, 2, 16, 62, 65, 75–76, 95, 100, 102, 120, 152, 198; *see also* Revenue Cutter Service
Coast Guard Academy Library, 16
Coast Guard Museum/Northwest, 198
Cochrane, Alexander F. I., 48
Cochrane, Henry C., 32
Cockburn, George, 25

Cocke, Harrison Henry, 153
Coffinberry, Henry D., 161
Coffinberry Family, 161
Cohen, Albert M., 48
Colbert, Richard G., 180
Colburn, Oliver, 14
Colhoun, Edmund R., 48
Collins, James B. and Joseph T., 134
Collum, Richard S., 140
Colorado State Historical Society, 12
Colt, Samuel, 13
Columbia, USS, 174
Columbia University Libraries, 44, 131, 180
Columbus, Continental Ship, 179
Columbus, USS, 91
Colvocoresses, George M., 16
Commissioners of Naval Stores, Continental Navy, 168
Concord, USS, 126, 135
Concord Free Library, 105
Cone, Hutch I., 56
Confederacy, Continental Ship, 169
Confederate Museum Library, 191
Confederate States Army and Navy Surgeons Association, 74
Confederate States Naval Laboratory, 146
Confederate States of America, 25, 72, 112
Confederate States of America, Navy and Marine Corps, 72, 74, 85, 169, 184, 191
Confederate States of America, Navy Secret Service, 72
Congress, USS (frigate, 1799–1834), 20, 177
Congress, USS (frigate, 1842–62), 48, 141
Congress, U.S., House and Senate, *see* Senate and House entries
Congress, U.S., Joint Committees, 66
Conn, William Tipton, 92
Connecticut, Naval Veterans Association, 13
Connecticut, Shipbuilding and Naval Records, 13
Connecticut Historical Society, 13
Connecticut State Library, 13
Conner, David, 16, 25, 132, 140
Connor, Lemuel Parker, and Family Papers, 86
Conqueror, Maryland Navy, 90
Conrad, Daniel B., 48
Conrad, Robert Dexter, 98
Constellation, USS, 20, 90, 92, 125, 136
Constitution, USS, 14, 16, 37, 48, 56, 58, 110, 112, 114, 126, 131–32, 134, 142, 169, 195
Constitutional Convention, 67
Construction Forces (Seabees), 7
Continental Admiralty Board, 90
Continental and Confederation Congresses, 67
Continental Congress, Marine Committee, 91
Continental Navy, 90–91, 123, 168, 179
Continental Congress, Naval Committee, 154
Converse, George Albert, 48, 187

Convoy and Routing Section, Commander in Chief, U.S. Fleet, 44
Conway, Thomas, 90
Conway-Whittle Family Papers, 191
Conyngham, Gustavus, 134
Cook, Henry Trevor, 180
Cook, John A., 48
Cooke, Aaron, Collection, 116
Cooke, Charles M., Jr., 5
Cooke, Eleutheros, Family Papers, 160
Cooke, Harold D., 48, 51
Cooley, Mortimer Elwyn, Collection, 116
Cooper, Isaac, 202
Cooper, James Fenimore, 16, 134
Cope, Edward F., 151
Cornell, Richard M., 184
Cornell University Libraries, 131–32
Cornwallis, William, 134, 144
Corona, Naval Ordnance Laboratory, 8
Cotten, Lyman Atkinson, 151, 153
Cotton, Charles S., 48, 56
Couthouy, Joseph P., 48
Covington, John R., 142
Cowles, Willard Bunce, 122
Cowles, William S., 134
Cox, Samuel Sullivan, 178
Cox, William Sitgreaves, 117
Cox and Stevens Company, 14
Coxe, Alexander B., Jr., 149
Crabbe, Thomas, 145
Craig, Isaac, 160, 166
Cramer, Ambrose C., 45
Cramer, John, 10
Cramp, William and Son, Shipyard, 167, 172
Craven, Thomas Tingey, 140, 145
Creighton, James, 140
Creighton, John Orde, 140
Crisp, D. H., 188
Croker, John Wilson, 147
Cromwell, Bartlett Jefferson, 86
Crosby, Allyn J., 48
Crosley, Paul C., 56
Cross, Carl, 83
Cross Cultural Survey Staff, Yale University, 7
Crowninshield, Benjamin Williams, 105, 109, 111
Crowninshield Family Papers, 105
Cruiser Division Seven, 44
Cumberland, USS, 93
Cummings, USS, 194
Cummings, Charles Kimball, 103
Cummings, Damon E., 56
Cunningham, Winfield Scott, 104
Curator Branch, Naval Historical Center, 35
Cushing, Leonard F., 48
Cushing, William B., 202
Cushman, William H., 25

Curtis, Caleb A., 105
Curtis, Roger, 103
Customs Service, U.S., 102
Cyane, USS (frigate), 104
Cyane, USS (sloop), 10
Cyclops, USS, 91

D

Dabney, John B., 48
Dahlgren, John Adolphus Bernard, 19, 25, 48, 77, 98, 134, 140, 145, 165, 184
Dahlgren, Naval Proving Ground, 192
Dahlgren, Naval Weapons Laboratory, 192
Dahlgren Laboratory, Naval Surface Weapons Center, 192
Dale, USS, 74, 85, 142
Dale, John B., 110
Dale, Richard, 25, 98
Dallas, Francis Gregory, 134
Dallas, George Mifflin, 168, 172
Dan Smith, USS, 160
Dana, Homer J., Collection, 200
Danforth, Charles H., 12
Danforth, Herbert L., 48
Daniel, Richard P., 153
Daniels, George H., 134
Daniels, Josephus, 25, 86, 131, 153
Danziesen, Augustus, 174
DAR Americana Collection, 34
Darien Exploring Expedition, 2
Dartmouth College Library, 123
Dash, Privateer, 110
Daughters of the American Revolution, 34
David, John, 90
David W. Taylor Naval Ship Research and Development Center, 89
Davis, Charles Henry (1807–77), 113
Davis, Charles Henry (1845–1921), 113
Davis, Frederic E., 72
Davis, Glenn B., 150
Davis, Herman Stearns, 177
Davis, Louis Poisson, 150
Davisville Construction Battalion Center, 180
Day, Alfred, 168
Day, Joseph S., 25, 166
Dean, Benjamin C., 160
Deane, Silas, 13
DeCamp, John, 134
Decatur, Privateer, 94
Decatur, USS, 136
Decatur, Stephen, 23, 25, 48, 134, 161, 168, 173
Decatur, Stephen, Mrs., 134
Decatur House Papers, 25
Decker, Benton C., 5

Declaration of Independence Autographs, 144
Declaration of London, 1909, 7
Defence, Maryland Navy, 92
Defense Advisory Committee on Women in the Services, 111
Defense Atomic Support Agency, 67
Defiance, HMS, 134
Defoe Shipbuilding Company, 158
DeGolyer Foundation Library, 187
De Grasse, Francois Joseph Paul, Comte, 115, 140
DeHaven, Edwin Jesse, 48, 98
Delafield Papers, 146
Delano, Francis H., 177
Delano, Frederick H., 177
Delaware, USS (ship-of-the-line), 95
Delaware, USS (steamer), 128, 139
Delaware, Historical Society of, 19
De Long, George W., 96
De Monteil, Chevalier, 115
Denby, Edwin, 113–14
Denig, Robert G., 48
Denison Public Library, 187
Dennison, Robert Lee, 120–21
Dent, John H., 48
Department of State, 65
Derby Family Papers, 105
De Revel, Comte, 127
De Rohan, William, 56
D'Estaing, Charles H., Comte, 114, 168, 178
De Steiguer, Louis R., 160
Destouches, Charles Rene Dominique Gochet, 3
Detroit Public Library, 113
Devereaux, Patrick S., 104
Dewey, George, 25, 45, 48, 127, 134, 140, 145–46
DeWolf Family, 179
Dichman, Grattan C., 56
Dickerson, Mahlon, 125, 127, 165
Dickins, Francis Asbury, 154, 195
Dickins, Francis W., 48
Dickinson, Dwight, Jr., 5
Dickinson College Library, 166
Digby, Kenelm, 140
Diggins, Bartholomew, 140
Dillard University, 85
Dillen, Roscoe F., 49
Dillon, William Henry, 149
Diocesan War Councils, 23
District Courts, 102
Division of Naval History, Smithsonian Institution, 60–62
Division of Political History, Smithsonian Institution, 62
Division of Transportation, Maritime Section, Smithsonian Institution, 62
Dixie, USS, 91
Dixon, Thomas Hunter, and Family Papers, 118

Dobbin, James Cochran, 127, 147, 152
Dobbins, Daniel, 130
Dodson, C. Marion, 92
Dolan, Thomas J., 79
Dolan, William, 76
Dolphin, USS, 135
Donaldson, Edward, 92
Dorn, Edward J., 49
Dorsett, Edward Lee, 49
Dorsey, John, 92
Dorton, Henry F., 92
Douglas, James, 114
Dow, Leonard James, 49
Downes, John, 96
Downs, Joseph, Manuscript and Microfilm Collection, 20
Doyle, Peter, 173
Drake, Charles Daniel, 159
Drayton Family, 168
Drayton, Percival, 140, 168
Dreer, Julius Ferdinand, 168
Dreller, Louis, 43
Dribble, Samuel, 183
Drury, Clifford Merrill, 173
Duane, W., 134
DuBarry, Edmund Louis, 145
Dubois, John L., 92
Duc, Henry Archibald, Jr., 147
Duc, Henry Archibald, Sr., 147
Duckworth, John, 78
Duckworth, Thomas, 16
Dudley, James A., 109
Dudley, Thomas Cochrane, 61, 114
Dudley, Thomas Haines, 3
Dudley Knox Library, 8
Dugan, Hammond, 92
Duke University, 147–49
Dulany, Bladen, 49, 92
Duncan, Silas, 25
Duncan, William P. S., 148
Dundas, Henry, First Viscount Melville, 28, 114
Dundas, Robert Saunders, Second Viscount Melville, 3, 28, 114, 148
Dundas, William Oswald, 23
Dungan, William W., 49
Dunn, Herbert O., 56
Dunn, Lucius C., 56
Dunn, Robert Steed, 123
Du Perron, Joachim, Comte de Revel, 127
DuPont, Samuel Francis, 19, 184
Durand, George R., 134
Durgin, Calvin T., 43
Durgin, Edward, 180
DuSimitiere, Pierre Eugene, 171
Duval, Miles P., 23, 43
Dwight D. Eisenhower Library, 83
D'Wolf, James, 135
Dyer, George Leland, 150

E

Eagle, Henry, 25
Earhart, Amelia (Putnam), 39, 57
Earl Gregg Swem Library, College of William and Mary, 191
East Carolina University, 149–51
Eaton, Charles Phillips, 135
Eaton, William, 3, 101, 189
Eberstadt, Ferdinand, Collection, 46
Eccles, Henry E., 181
Edgren, John A., 117
Edison, Charles, 96
Edon, John James, 25
Edson, Merritt A., 27
Edwards, E. Harleston, 184
Eisenhower, Dwight D., Library, 83
Ekstrom, Clarence E., 5
Elbert, Samuel S., 56
Eld, Henry, 15–16, 27
Electric Boat Company, 105
Eleutherian Mills Historical Society, 19
Eliot, George Fielding, 27
Elliott, Edward, 56
Elliott, Jared L., 27
Ellyson, Theodore G., 56, 194
Elseffer, Harry S., 27
Elsey, George M., 120
Ely, Eugene, 56
Emergency Fleet Corporation, World War I, 60, 173
Emery, John, 123, 131
Emmons, George Foster, 10, 16
Emory, William H., 49
Emory University Library, 72–73
English, Robert A. J., 43
Enoch Pratt Free Library, 90
Enterprise, USS (schooner, 1831–44), 55
Enterprise, USS (sloop-of-war), 57, 110
Erben, Henry, 135
Ericsson, John, 27, 135, 165
Erie, USS, 104
Erie County Historical Society, 166
Ernest Hinds, USS, 174
Essex, USS (frigate), 110–11, 132, 141, 169
Essex, USS (steamer), 76
Essex Institute, 105
Etter, Ross A., 176
Ettings, Frank M., 169
Eugene C. Barker Texas History Center, 188–89
Europe, Naval Forces, 41
Evans, Amos, 16, 114, 140
Evans, Robley D., 49, 132

Evans, Samuel, 140
Everett, Edward, 169
Ewell, Benjamin S., 191
Ewell, Thomas, 191
Experimental Ammunition Unit, Washington Navy Yard, 100
Experimental Model Basin, Washington, D.C., 89
Explorers Club, 132
Ex-Soldiers' and Sailors' League of Franklin County, 160

F

Fabbri, Alessandro, 27
Fackenthal Library, Franklin and Marshall College, 167
Fahey, James C., 100
Fahrner, Alvin A., 150
Fahs, Charles T., 27
Fairchild, Charles, 135
Fairfield, USS, 29
Fairfield, John, 27
Falmouth, USS, 110
Farragut, David Glasgow, 3, 19, 27, 49, 56, 77, 96, 105, 135, 140, 145
Faser, Karl E., 150
Fay, Paul B., Jr., 108
Fear, Lyle, 164
Febiger, John C., 135
Federal Archives and Records Centers, 64; *see also* place names
Federal Maritime Commission, 66
Feltus, W. W., 169
Fentress Walter E. H., 49, 127
Ferebee, Gregory, and McPherson Family, 154
Ferebee, Nelson McPherson, 154
Ferguson, Glover T., 56
Ferrell, Thomas J., 131
Field, Thomas Y., 32
Fife, James, Jr., 15
Fillebrown, Thomas S., 49
Finn, Tim, 188
Fisher, Samuel Rhoads, 188–89
Fitch, Aubrey W., 43
Flaccus, William Kimball, 123
Flandera, Frank J., 32
Fleet Operations Division, Office of the Chief of Naval Operations, 41
Fleischman, Henry P., 61
Fleming, Walter L., Collection, 86
Fletcher, Frank Friday, 194
Flint, Henry Sanborne, 179
Flirt, USS, 49
Florida, CSS, 154, 191

Florida, USS (steamer), 136
Florida, USS (BB-30), 176
Florida, Naval Air Stations, 72
Florida State Archives, 69
Florida State University Library, 69
Floyd Family Collection, 132
Fogler, Raymond H., Library, 87
Folsom, Charles, 109
Foltz, Jonathan Messersmith, 167
Fondren Library, 187
Fontana, Paul J., 150
Foote, Andrew Hull, 15, 27, 77, 185
Foote, Percy Wright, 154
Footman, Harold, 140
Forbes, Edwin Fairfield, 148
Forbis, Archibald M., 174
Force, Peter, Collection, 25–26, 29, 30
Foreign Records Seized, 66
Forney, Edward H., 5
Forrest, Douglas F., 154
Forrest, French, 154, 197
Forrest Family Papers, 154
Forrestal, James Vincent, 43, 127, 131
Fort, George H., 150
Fort Delaware, 169
Fort Louisbourg, 116
Fort McHenry National Monument and Historic Shrine, 90
Fort Sumter, 161
Forton Prison, England, 27
Fortune, Privateer, 180
Foskett, James H., 120
Foster, Freeman, Jr., 86
Foulk, George Clayton, 10, 49, 140
Fox, Gustavus Vasa, 3, 62, 77, 135
Fox, John L., 95
Fox, Josiah, 49, 111
Fox, Virginia L. (Mrs.), 135
Foxardo Affair, 27
Frailey, James Madison, 170
Francis, William A., 176
Franklin, USS (brig), 30, 169
Franklin, USS (ship-of-the-line), 10, 142
Franklin, Samuel R., 135, 140
Franklin and Marshall College, 167
Franklin County, Ohio, Ex-Soldiers' and Sailors' League, 160
Franklin D. Roosevelt Library, 132–33
Franklin Institute, 167
Freeman, Miller, 199
French, William J., 150
French Fleet Signal Book, 114
Frolic, USS, 76
Fullam, William F., 49
Fullinwider, Simon P., 61
Fuller, Ben H., 32

Fulton, Robert, 27, 96, 127, 131, 134–36, 140, 169
Furber, Robert S., 117
Furer, Julius A., 49
Furlong, W. R., 61
Furman, Greene C., 49
Furman, Moore, 127
Fyffe, Joseph P., 49

G

G. W. Blunt White Library, 14
Gaillard, Samuel, 184
Gallery, Daniel Vincent, 98
Gallop, Alexander, 135
Gamero, Daniel E., 174
Gamet, Wayne Neal, 5
Ganges, USS, 53
Gantt, Benjamin S., 49
Gardiner Collection, 169
Gardner, Obed, 49
Garrett, John Work, Library, Johns Hopkins University, 91
Gatewood, James Duncan, 95
Gauntt, Charles, 96
Gautier, Thomas Nicholas, 154
Geiger, Roy S., 32
Geisinger, David, 27, 92
Gelston, David, 135
General Archives Division, National Archives, 64
General Board of the Navy, 42
General Grant, USS, 136
General Sullivan, Privateer, 27
George Arents Research Library, Syracuse University, 145
Georgetown University Library, 23
Georgia, CSS, 191
Georgia (mail steamer), 135
Georgia Naval Air Stations, 72
Georgia Department of Archives and History, 73
Georgia Historical Society, 74
Georgia Navy, Adjutant General's Office, 73
Georgia Navy and Army, Register of Commissioned Officers, 73
Germain, George, 114
German Naval Association, 202
German Navy, 43
Germantown, USS, 74, 131, 142, 195
Gibbons, J. H., 188
Gift, George Washington, 154
Gilbert, Charles, 151
Gile, Chester A., 117
Gill, Charles C., 49
Gillespie, Archibald H., 10
Gillespie, John E., 95
Gillett, Simon P., 49
Gilliam, Henry, 74

Gillis, James H., 49, 142
Gillis, John Prichet, 19
Gilmer, Thomas Walker, 191
Gilpin Papers, 170
Gipson, James C., 202
Glazier, James Edward, 3
Gleaves, Albert, 49, 56, 96, 145
Glenn, John H., Jr., 27
Gloucester County Historical Society Library, 125
Glover, Jonathan, 109
Glynco, Naval Air Station, 72
Goddard, Robert Hutchings, 98
Godon, Sylvanus W., 159
Goff, Nathan, 201
Goffe, Phipps D., 135
Goldsborough, Louis M., 27, 140, 148, 157, 169
Goodhue Family Papers, 105
Goodrich, Caspar Frederick, 135
Goodwin Family, 16
Goodwin, Hugh H., 5
Goodwin, Walton, 56
Gordon, Charles, 90
Gove Family, 49
Governor's Island, U.S. Coast Guard, 95
Graham, William Alexander, 148, 152, 154
Grampus, USS, 136
Granger, Lester B., 131
Grant, Albert Weston, 202
Grant Papers, 146
Grattan, John W., 49
Gratz Collection, 169
Graves, Charles Iverson, 154
Graves, Samuel, 109
Gray, Alfred Gilliat, 188
Gray, Edwin Fairfax, 188
Gray, John, 174
Gray Herbarium Library, Harvard University, 106
Great Britain, Admiralty, 27, 51, 91, 180
Great Britain, Royal Marines, 162
Great Britain, Royal Navy, 17, 43, 139, 147, 169, 180
Great Lakes, U.S. Coast Guard Stations, 76
Great Western, SS, 103
Great White Fleet, 56, 138
Green, Ezra, 109
Green, Joseph F., 49
Greene, Albert S., 49
Greene, Benjamin C., 174
Greene, Samuel Dana, 135
Greene, Theodore P., 135
Greene, Wallace M., Jr., 32
Greenfield Village and Henry Ford Museum, 113
Greenland Expedition, *see* Peary, Robert E.
Greenleaf, J., 102
Greenslade, John W., 49, 56
Greenwood, Miles, 159
Greer, Harry W., 56

Grenfell, Elton W., 5
Gregory, Francis, 97
Gregory Family, 105
Grening, Paul C., 56
Griffin, Samuel Palmer, 130
Griffin, Virgil C., Jr., 49
Griffith, Alfred, 163
Griffith, John W., 62
Grimball, John Berkley, 148, 184
Griswold, John A., 61
Grumman Aerospace Archives, 133
Grunwell, A. G., 174
Guam, Advance Headquarters, U.S. Pacific Fleet and Pacific Ocean Areas, 7
Guam, Government of, 2
Guam, Office of the Territories, 2
Guerriere, USS, 81
Guile, Leslie, 174
Gulligan, John J., 160
Gunther, Charles F., 76
Gurley, Jacob B., Collection, 13
Grinnell, Henry, 130
Guthrie, Harry A., 5
Guthrie, John Julius, 152
Guy W. Bailey Library, 190
Gwin, P. M., 174
Gwin, William McKendree, 10
Gwinn, John, 49

H

Habersham, Alexander W., 27
Habersham Family Papers, 27
Haislip, Harvey S., 104
Halas, J. A., 151
Hale, Frederick, 145
Hale, John Parker, 123
Halifax, Nova Scotia, U.S. Prisoners of War at, 170
Hall, Charles Francis, 61
Hall, John L., 191
Hall, Reynold T., 56
Hall of Records Commission of Maryland, 90
Hallock, Isaac, 27
Halsey, William F., 49
Halstead-Maus Family Papers, 177
Hambleton, John N., 92
Hambleton, Samuel, 92
Hambleton Family Papers, 92
Hamden, Continental Ship, 179
Hamersly, Thomas S., 27
Hamilton, Alexander, Jr., 135
Hamilton, Paul, 184
Hamilton, T. J., 69
Hamisch, C. M., 56
Hammond-Harwood House Manuscript Collection, 92

Hamond, Andrew Snape, 148, 194
Hancock, USS, 174
Hancock, John, 91
Hancock, Joy Bright, 74
Hanford, Franklin, 140
Hanlon, Raymond J., 174
Hanson, Malcolm Parker, 202
Harbeck, Charles Thomas, 3
Harden, John F., 97
Harding, Warren G., 160
Hardison, Osborne Bennett, 154
Hardy, Joseph L. C., 184
Hare-Powel, Robert Johnson, 56
Harford and Cecil County Families, 92
Harkness, William, 67, 146
Harlan, Henry Stump, 92
Harlan Family Collection, 92
Harllee, John, 108
Harllee, William Curry, 154
Harmon, George H., 98
Harold B. Lee Library, Brigham Young University, 190
Harrigan, Thomas E., 174
Harrington, Purnell Frederick, 49, 145, 160
Harrington, Sidney, 202
Harris, Field, 32
Harris, George W., 154
Harris, Richard D., 103
Harris, Thomas J., 27
Harrison, George, 169
Harrison, George W., 49
Harrison, Sylvanus T., 203
Harrison, Thomas Locke, 154
Harrison Family, 203
Harrow, Alexander, 113
Harry Ransom Humanities Research Center, University of Texas, 189
Harry S. Truman-Library, 120–21
Hart, Charles A., 13
Hart, Franklin A., 1
Hart, John E., 173
Hart, Thomas C., 43
Hartford, USS, 56, 80, 140
Harvard, USS, 164
Harvard University, 105–07
Harvard University, Naval Radio School, 107
Harvard University, Naval Training School, 107
Harvard University, Navy Supply Corps School, 107
Harvard University, Underwater Sound Laboratory, 107
Harvey Steel Company, 19
Harwood, Andrew Allen, 9
Harwood, Nicholas, 92
Harwood Family, 9
Hassler, Charles A., 95
Haswell, Charles Haynes, 144–45

Hatch, John Porter, 49
Hauber, Charles J., 174
Haverford College Library, 167
Haverhill Public Library, 107
Hawaii State Archives, 75
Hawaiian Islands Collection, 114
Hawker, Jesse Marvin, 83
Hawkins, John T., 140
Hay, John, Library, Brown University, 178
Hayden, Levi, 140
Hayes, Rutherford B., 160
Hayes, Rutherford B., Library, 160–61
Hayes, Walter Sherman, 160
Hayes, Webb Cook II, 160
Hayne, Robert, 184
Healy, Waldo, 76
Heath, Benjamin, Jr., 128
Heinberg, C. J., 71
Hellweg, Julius Frederick, 174
Hemphill, J. N., 56
Henderson, Archibald, 201
Henderson, William R., 138
Henderson-Tomlinson Families, 201
Henley, John Dandridge, 98, 135
Henneberry, James E., 76
Henry, Alexander, 169
Henry, Isaac, 148
Henry E. Huntington Library, 2–4
Hepburn Collection, 173
Herbert, Hilary A., 154
Herbert Hoover Presidential Library, 82
Herndon, William L., 135
Heustis, James Fountain, 154
Hewes, Joseph, 154
Hewitt, Edward L., 27
Hewitt, Henry Kent, 56, 181
Heyl, Erik, 158
Higginson, Samuel, 109
Hiles, Charles C., 205
Hill, Harry W., 43
Hill, John S., 203
Hill, Walter Nickerson, 178
Hill, William P. T., 32
Hinckley, Robert, 96
Hinman, Elisha, 34, 104
Hinton, Addison C., 189
Hirsch, Joseph, 60
Historical Reference (Z) Files, 45
Historical Research Branch, Naval Historical Center, 36
Historical Society of Delaware, 19
Historical Society of Pennsylvania, 168–71
Hitch, John, 104
Hitte, E. A., 174
Hobson, Richard Pearson, 27
Hodgkin, Henry Harrison, 117

Hodgson, Richard, 134
Hoel, William R., 159
Hoes, Roswell Randall, 27
Hog Island, Pa., 172
Hoke, William Alexander, 154
Holcomb, Thomas, 32
Hole, Frank Rufus, 175
Holland, George F., 56, 80
Holland, John P., 15
Hollins, George N., 92
Holloway, James L., Jr., 145
Holmes, Silas, 17
Holy Cross College, 107
Holzhauser, Frederick Henry, 174
Hood, John Mifflin, 92
Hooker, Edward, 17
Hooker Family Papers, 17
Hooper, Stanford C., 49
Hoover, Herbert, Presidential Library, 82
Hoover Institution on War, Revolution, and Peace, 4–7
Hopkins, Esek, 161, 179
Hopkinson, Francis, 91
Horan, Walter F., Collection, 200
Horndahl, Eric William, 177
Horne, Frederick J., 49
Horner, Gustavus Richard Brown, 49, 95, 194–95
Hornet, USS, 136
Horsford, Eben Norton, 144
Hoskins, Anthony Hiley, 114
Hoskins, Emmett A., 5
Hoste, William, 141
Houghton Library, Harvard University, 107
House Armed Services Committee, 159, 183
House Committee on Naval Affairs, 30, 105, 109, 130, 154, 157, 169, 178, 197
House of Representatives, U.S., 66
Houston, Edwin Samuel, 75
Houston, Victor Steuart Kaleoaloha, 75
Howard, Gene Frank, 114
Howard, Sumner, 114
Howard, William L., 56
Howard Ship Yards and Dock Company, 80
Howard-Tilton Memorial Library, 85
Howe, Louis McHenry, 132
Howe Family, 114
Howe, Earl Richard, 3, 114
Howell, Glenn F., 45
Hudson, USS, 91, 140
Hudson, Manley O., 181
Hudson, William Leverreth, 16, 130, 154
Hudson Manuscript Collection, 69
Hughes, Aaron Konkle, 141
Hughes, Benjamin Franklin, 189
Hull, Isaac, 27, 56, 101–02, 110, 135, 173
Hulse, Isaac, 71

Humphreys, A. Y., 81
Humphreys, Joshua, 169, 173
Humphreys, Samuel, 98, 169
Hunley, CSS, 1
Hunley Collection, 1
Hunt, Frederick V., 106
Hunt, Timothy, 15
Hunt, Theodore, 121
Hunt, William Henry, 28
Hunter, HMS, 135
Hunter, Raymond P., 56
Hunter, William M., 135
Hunter, William W., 85
Huntington, Henry E., Library, 2—4
Huntington, Joshua, 109, 169
Huntly, John C., 169
Hurd, Jacob S., 159
Hurst, George, 28
Huse, Samuel, 135
Hutchins, Hamilton, 123
Huyler, Adam, 128
Hyde Windlass Company, 61
Hydrographic Office, U.S., 65

I

Illinois State Historical Library, 77
Imperial, 170
Independence, USS, 49, 56, 58
Inderwick, James, 141
Indiana Historical Society Library, 80
Indiana State Library, 80
Indiana University, 80
Indianhead, Naval Proving Ground, 192
Ingersoll, Jared, Sr., 15
Ingersoll, Royal R., 49, 56
Ingersoll Family Papers, 15
Ingram, Jonas Howard, 80
Inland Rivers Library, 159
International Marine Archives, Inc., 108
Iowa State Historical Department, 82
Iowa State Historical Society, 82
Iris, USS, 10
Iroquois, USS, 57, 80
Irwin, John, 135
Izard, Allen C., 184
Izard, Ralph, 184
Izard, Ralph, Jr., 184

J

Jackson, Alonzo C., 28
Jackson, Samuel, 169
Jacksonville, Naval Air Base, 7

Jacobs, Charles Clark, 119
Jacobs, Fred Clark, 119
Jahncke, Ernest Lee, 86
James, Jules, 150
James Carson Breckenridge Library, 33, 192
James Duncan Phillips Library, 105
Jamestown, USS, 188
Jannotta, Alfred V., 77
Japan, Expedition to (1853—54), 61, 92, 114, 128, 141—42; *see also* Perry, Matthew Calbraith
Japanese Navy, 43
Japanese Print Collection, 61
Jaques, William H., 128
Jarvis, J. W., 96
Jarvis, William, 190
Jay, John, Collection, 131
Jeanette Expedition, 96
Jenkins, Joseph H., 45
Jenkins, Thornton Alexander, 3
Jennings, C. Brooke, 150
Jennings, Curtis H., 175
Jennings, Ralph E., 5
Jennison, William, 169
Jewett, George Frederick, Naval History Collection, 199
John Adams, USS, 14, 74, 104
John C. Pace Library, University of West Florida, 71
John Carter Brown Library, Brown University, 178
John F. Kennedy Library, 108
John Hay Library, Brown University, 178
John M. Olin Library, Cornell University, 131
John Work Garrett Library, Johns Hopkins University, 91
Johns Hopkins University, 43, 91
Johnson, Lyndon B., Space Center, 187
Johnson, Philip C., 49
Johnson, Robert E., 148
Johnson, Roe L., 121
Johnson Family Papers, 197
Johnston, Rufus Z., 154
Joint Army and Navy Board, Navy Secretariat, 42
Joint Army and Navy Boards and Committees, 66
Joint Chiefs of Staff, 66
Jones, Catesby ap Roger, 154
Jones, Charles Lucian, 74
Jones, George, 80
Jones, Hilary P., 50
Jones, James Hemphill, 19
Jones, John Paul, 3, 9, 28, 50, 96—97, 107, 135, 144, 165, 178
Jones, P. A. J. P., 50
Jones, Richard B., 99
Jones, Thomas ap Catesby, 195
Jones, William, 74, 169
Jones, William K., 150
Joseph Regenstein Library, University of Chicago, 78

Joy, Charles T., 5
Judge Advocate General (Navy), 65
Julian, Charles C., 50
Juniata, USS, 200

K

Kaiser, Louis A., 50
Kane, Elisha Kent, 9, 165, 169
Kane, Theodore F., 179
Kansas, USS, 58, 141
Kansas City Federal Archives and Records Center, 120
Kansas State Historical Society, 83
Katz, Mark Jacob, 101
Kearny, Lawrence, 125
Kearny, Thomas, 50
Kearsarge, USS, 14, 111, 141, 161, 177, 185
Keeler, William T., 97
Keep Family Papers, 71
Kell, John McIntosh, 148
Kellogg, Edward N., 50
Kellogg, Edward S., 50
Kempff, Louis, 77
Kennedy, John F., Library, 108
Kennedy, Frank M., 205
Kennedy, John Pendleton, 90, 196
Kenney, W. John, 120
Kennon, Beverly, 135
Kent, E., 104
Kentucky, USS, 128
Kerr, Mark, 181
Kershner, Edward, 148
Key West, Naval Air Station, 72
Keyes, John Shepard, 105
Kilauea, USS, 204
Kimball, Dan A., 120
Kimball, James B., 57
Kimberly, Lewis Ashfield, 50, 76
Kimmel, Husband E., 50, 99, 205
Kincaid, Earl H., 57
King, Ernest J., 43, 50
King, Porter, 57
King, R. H., 135
King, Thomas Butler, 154
Kingsley, Louis A., 50
Kirby, Absalom, 61
Kirk, Alan G., 43, 50, 108
Kirkland, William A., 150
Kirkpatrick, John E., 150–51
Kittery, USS, 117
Kittery, Me., Naval Shipyard, *see* Portsmouth, N.H., Navy Yard
Kittredge, Tracy B., 5, 43
Klyce, Horace Scudder, 28
Knapp, Harry S., 99

Knapp, Myron H., 113
Knowles, Herbert B., 51
Knox, Dudley, Library, 8
Knox, Dudley W., 51
Knox, Franklin, 28, 43
Knox, Robert, Sr., 110
Knox, Samuel R., 108, 111
Kohl, Mrs. Jessie W., 95
Kohler, John T., 120
Konter, Richard W., 51
Korea, U.S. *Charge d'Affaires,* 10
Kramer, Frank N., 175
Kramer, Hugo, 175
Krulak, Victor H., 5
Kupfer, Walter H., 175

L

Lackawanna, USS, 28
Lademan, Joseph U., Jr., 5
Lafayette, Marquis de, 144
Lafot, Edward, and Family Papers, 117
Lafot, Lloyd, 117
La Guayra, American Cousul, 93
Laguna Niguel, Federal Archives and Records Center, 2
Lake, Simon, 15
Lake Champlain, 171
Lake Forest, USS, 176
Lake Torpedo Boat Company, 15
Lakeland Public Library, 69
Lamberton, Benjamin P., 61
Lancaster, USS, 11, 126
Lancey, Thomas C., 10
Land, Emory Scott, 16, 28
Lane, Warren S., 150
Langdon, John, 123
Langdon, Young, Meares Family Papers, 154
Lange, Dorothea, 98
Laning, Caleb Barrett, II, 177
Laning, Harris, 77, 177
Laning, James, 76
Laning Family, 177
Lanman, Joseph, 97
Larimer, Marc Winthrop, 194
Larkin, Thomas Oliver, 10
Latimer, William K., 93
Latrobe, Benjamin, 25
Latrobe, Osmun, 93
Lauerman, Henry C., 150
Laurens, Henry, 183
Lavallette, Elie A. F., 148
Lawrence, USS, 179
Lawrence, Jonathan, 178
League Island, *see* Philadelphia Navy Yard
Leahy, Edward P., 150

220

Leahy, William D., 28, 43, 203
LeBoeuf, Randall J., Jr., 136
Lee, Harold B., Library, Brigham Young University, 190
Lee, Richard Henry, 91
Lee, Samuel Phillips, 51, 127, 152
Lee Collection, 107
Leffingwell, Ernest DeKoven, 175
Leigh, Richard Henry, 69, 119
LeJeune, John A., 28
Lenthall, John, 28, 167
Leonard, John C., 51
Leopard, HMS, 170
Lever, Charles, 28
Levy, Uriah Phillips, 28, 101, 158
Lewis, John R. C., 141
Lewis, Oscar C., 136
Lewis, William, 191
Lexington, USS, 129, 196, 199
Library Company of Philadelphia, 171
Library of Congress, 24–31, 47–54
Lincoln, Abraham, Museum, 185
Lincoln, Abraham, Papers, 77, 121
Lincoln Memorial University, 185
Lining, Charles E., 189, 192
Linnet, HMS, 51
Litchfield Historical Society, 14
Little, Charles G., 51
Little, Louis M., 32
Little, William McCarty, 181
Little America Expedition, 202
Little Creek, Va., *see* Norfolk
Lloyd, James, 107, 109
Lockwood, Charles A., Jr., 5, 51
Lockwood, Samuel, 17
Lodge, Henry C., 57
Logistics Plans Division, Office of the Chief of Naval Operations, 40
London International Naval Conference (1909), 7, 28
London Naval Conference (1930), 111
Long, Andrew Theodore, 154
Long, John Davis, 109, 144
Long, Victor D., 5
Longfellow National Historic Site, 108
Lord, John, 142
Louisiana, USS, 161
Louisiana Historical Association Collection, 85
Louisiana State University Library, 85–86
Louisville, Naval Ordnance Plant, 76
Louttit, Chauncey McKinley, 17
Lovell, William Storrow, 28, 186
Lowe, John, 51, 57
Lowell, Addison H., 176
Lowell, Austin W., 176
Lowry, Robert K., 93
Luce, Stephen B., 51, 136, 181
Lull, Edward P., 51

Lusitania, SS, 4
Lyman, William Cullen, 136
Lyndon B. Johnson Space Center, 187
Lynn, Harold F., 5

Mc, MaC

MacArthur, Douglas, 192
MacArthur Memorial Archives, 192
McBlair, Charles H., 141, 152
McBlair, Thomas P., 141
McBlair, Virginia Myers, 73
McBlair, William, 73
McBlair Family, 141
McCain, John S., 119
McCain Amphibious Warfare Library, 194
McCauley, Edward Yorke, 136
McCleery, Robert W., 51
McClernand, John A., 77
McClure, David, 110
McCook, Anson G., 57
McCormick, Lynde D., 28
McCrea, John L., 132
McCrea, Joubert S., 176
McCreery, Stephen A., 95
McCulloh, George B., 93
McCulloh Family Papers, 93
McCully, Newton Alexander, 51, 156
McCutcheon, Keith B., 32
McDonald, David Lamar, 145
MacDonald, Donald J., 121
MacDonald, Gordon G., 141
Macdonough, Privateer, 179
McDonough, Charles S., 97
MacDonough, Thomas, 10, 19, 28, 190
McElmell, Jackson, 23
MacGill, Charles, 148
McGowan, Samuel, 51, 57, 148, 184
McGregor, Charles, 51
McGrory, John, 175
McIntire, Ross T., 132
McIntosh Family Papers, 197
McKean, Edward, 93
MacKenzie, Alexander Slidell, 136
McKethan, Alfred Augustus, 148
McKinley, Alexander, 19
McKinney, Thomas Freeman, 189
McLane, Allen, 136
MacLaren, Donald, 126
McLaughlin, J. T., 141
McNair, Frederick V., 51, 57
McNeely, Robert Whitehead, 184
NcNeely Family, 155
MacRae, Archibald, 148
MacRae, Hugh, 148

McSherry, Richard, 93
McVay, Charles B., 51

M

Maas, Charles Oscar, 28
Macay and McNeely Family Papers, 155
Macedonian, HMS (later USS), 23, 57, 135, 142, 159
Maclay, Edgar S., 188
Madison, John R., 16
Madrid, U.S. Military Attache, 3
Maffitt, John Newland, 155
Mahan, Alfred Thayer, 28, 51, 145, 147, 181
Maies, William H., 117
Maine, USS, 57, 101
Maine Historical Society, 87
Malcolm, Pulteney, 114
Mallory, Stephen Russell, 112, 155
Malvern, USS, 51
Mangum, Willie Person, 28, 148, 152, 155
Mangum Family Papers, 155
Manila Bay Society, 51
Manitowoc Shipbuilding Corporation, 203
Manley, John, 179
Mann, William, 101
Mann, William Leake, 189
Mannhardt, Charles, 175
Mansfield, Newton D., 160
Manuscript Division, Library of Congress, 24–31, 47–54
Marathon County Historical Society, 202
Marblehead, USS, 44
Marblehead Historical Society, 109
Marchand, John B., 181
Mare Island Depot, 199
Mare Island Naval Shipyard, 11
Maretti, C. J., 176
Marianas, Naval Forces, 41
Marietta, USS, 10
Marine Corps, 31–33, 65
Marine Corps Archives, 31
Marine Corps Art Collection, 33
Marine Corps Aviation Museum, 33, 193
Marine Corps Band, 33, 61
Marine Corps Development and Education Command, Quantico, 33, 192–93
Marine Corps Education Center, Quantico, 192
Marine Corps Historical Center, 31–33
Marine Corps History and Museums Division, 31-33
Marine Corps Library, 31
Marine Corps Military Music Collection, 33
Marine Corps Motion Picture and Television Archives, 33
Marine Corps Museum, 33
Marine Corps Oral History Collection, 31

Marine Corps Reference Section, 31
Marine Corps Still Photographic Archives, 33
Marine Historical Society, 202
Marine Transportation History Collection, Smithsonian Institution, 62
Mariners Museum, 194
Marion, USS, 91, 116
Maritime Administration, U.S., 66
Maritime Commission, U.S., 66
Marmion, Nicholas, 201
Marmion, Robert A., 201
Marmion, William V., 201
Marsh, Charles C., 51
Marshall, William A., 51
Marston, John, 51, 97
Martin, Glenn L., 28
Martin, Harold, 185
Martin, William Francis, 155
Martine, William L., 19
Marvin, Ross, 131
Maryland, First, Naval Battalion, 90
Maryland, Hall of Records Commission, 90
Maryland, Land Office, 92
Maryland, National Guard, 90
Maryland, Naval Brigade, 90
Maryland, Naval Militia, 93
Maryland Historical Society, 91-94
Maryland Military and Naval Papers, 93
Mason, Christopher, 114
Mason, Frank Earl, 203
Mason, John T., 192
Mason, John Young, 156, 196
Mason, Theodorus Bailey Myers, 61, 75
Massa, Samuel B., 145
Massachusetts, Archives Division, 104
Massachusetts, Commissary General, 104
Massachusetts, House of Representatives, 104
Massachusetts, Provincial Congress, 104
Massachusetts, Revolution Rolls, 104
Massachusetts, State Library, 112
Massachusetts, U.S. Marshal, 105
Massachusetts Historical Society, 109
Matthews, Francis P., 120
Matthews, Mitchell D., 43
Matthewson, Arthur, 51
Mattice, Asa M., 131
Maurice Family Papers, 156
Maury Family Collection, 3, 195
Maury, Matthew Fontaine, 3, 28, 148, 156, 191, 195–96
Maxfield, Lewis H., 117
May, James G., Collection, 160
May, William, 93
Mayo, Henry O., 138
Mayo, Isaac, 93
Mayrant, John, 51

Meade, Richard Worsam, III, 136
Means, Edward J., 86
Meigs, John F., 51
Melville, First and Second Viscounts, see Henry Dundas and Robert Saunders Dundas
Melville, George W., 51, 132
Memorial Hall Library, 110
Memphis/Shelby County Public Library and Information Center, 185
Menelaus, HMS, 161
Mentor, HMS, 71
Menzel, Donald H., 107
Merrill, Aaron Stanton, 51, 156
Merrill, Robert T., 57
Merrimack, USS, 128, 138, 141–42, 144, 147; see also *Virginia*, CSS
Merritt, Ernest George, 132
Messenger, L. B., 20
Messersmith, John S., 51
Metacomet, USS, 161
Meyer, George von Lengerke, 28, 109
Meyers, William H., 10
Michelson, Albert Abraham, 99
Michigan, USS, 159
Michigan, Naval Militia, 114
Middlebrush, Frederick A., 121
Middleton, Edward, 156, 184
Midnight, USS, 160
Midvale Steel Collection, 167
Miles, E., 169
Miles, Milton E., 5, 181
Miles, Wilma S. (Mrs. Milton E.), 181
Military Academy Library, 145–46
Military-Naval Club, 133
Miller, Alexander R., 86
Miller, Cyrus R., 51
Miller, Joseph F., 176
Miller, Samuel, 32
Miller, Taulman A., 81
Milwaukee County Historical Society, 202
Mine Force, Atlantic Fleet, 176, 190
Mine Unit, Washington Navy Yard, 100
Minkler, Chester T., 181
Minneapolis, USS, 174
Minnesota, USS, 56
Minnesota Historical Society, 117–18
Minor, Hubbard Taylor, 177
Minor, James Monroe, 195
Minor, Lewis Willis, 195
Minor, Robert Dabney, 177, 196
Minor Family, 196
Mish, Simon Cameron, 172
Mississippi, USS (BB-23), 86
Mississippi (Spanish-American War), 174
Mississippi, USS (steamer), 57-58, 94, 127–28, 141
Mississippi Department of Archives and History, 119
Mississippi State University Library, 119
Missouri Historical Society, 121
Mitchell, Benjamin, 28
Mitchell, John (naval agent), 170
Mitchell, John (naval contractor), 172
Mitchell, John Kirkwood, 196
Mitchell, S. Weir, 140
Mitscher, Marc Andrew, 28, 203
Moale, Edward, Jr., 51
Mobile Public Library, 1
Modern Military Branch, National Archives, 64
Moeller, George Herman, 175
Moffett, William Adger, 60, 99
Mohican, USS, 95
Molly, Maryland Navy, 90
Momsen, Charles B., 43
Monitor, USS, 61, 97, 129, 138, 141–42, 144
Monongahela, USS, 136
Montague, Gilbert Holland, 140
Montross, Lynn J., 145
Moody, William Henry, 28, 107
Moore, Charles J., 181
Moore, Edwin Ward, 188
Moore, John Samuel, 148
Moorhead, William G., 160
Moran, Edward, 96
Moreell, Ben, 5, 7
Moreno, Robert W., 5
Morgan, Adalia (Jacobs), 119
Morgan, James Morris, 51, 184
Morgan, Pierpont, Library, 142
Morison, Samuel Eliot, 40, 107, 204
Moro Castle, 116
Morrill, Samuel Jordan, 136
Morris, Charles, 115, 136
Morris, Gouverneur, Collection, 131
Morris, Richard K., Collection, 15
Morristown National Historical Park, 125
Morrow, James, 184
Morse, Freeman H., 161
Morse, John O., 51
Morse Family Collection, 29
Motion Picture Library, Naval Photographic Center, 58
Mount Vernon, USS, 93, 103
Moyerman Collection, 166
Muckle, John S., 170
Mullan, Dennis W., 136
Mullaney, James R. Madison, 170
Mullen, Isaac S., 124
Munro, D. J., 51
Murray, Alexander (1754–1821), 93
Murray, Alexander (1816–84), 93
Murray, George D., 57
Murray Family Papers, 93
Muse, William S., 93

Muse Family Papers, 93
Museum and Library of Maryland History, 91-94
Museum of Modern Art, 133
Mustin, Henry C., 51, 57
Myers, Leonard, 170
Mystic Seaport, 14

N

Nalle, Thomas B., 148
Nantucket, USS, 117, 128
Narragansett, USS, 110
Nash, Francis Smith, 196
Nashville, CSS, 197
Nast, Charles, 177
Natchez, USS, 91
Natchez, Miss., 86
National Aeronautics and Space Administration, 33, 187
National Air and Space Museum Library, 60
National Archives, 36, 61, 64-67
National Catholic War Council, 23
National Jewish Welfare Board, 101
National Library of Medicine, 95
National Museum of History and Technology, 60-62
National Personnel Records Center, St. Louis, Mo., 64
National Society of the Daughters of the American Revolution, 34
National Watercraft Collection, Smithsonian Institution, 62
Nauman, William H., 61
Naval Academy, Annapolis, Md., 65, 96-100, 117, 121, 147
Naval Academy (at Newport, R.I.), 180
Naval Academy Museum, 96-98
Naval Aides to the President, 83
Naval and Military Order of the Spanish American War, 136
Naval Aviation Museum, 69
Naval Chronicle, 36
Naval Construction Forces, 7
Naval Consulting Board, 97
Naval Districts, 65, 199
  4th, 167
  5th, 167
  6th, 72
  13th, 199
  17th, 199
Naval Facilities Engineering Command Archives, 7
Naval Historical Center, 34-45
Naval Historical Collection, Naval War College, 180-82
Naval Historical Foundation, 46-58
Naval Historical Society, 136
Naval History Division, 34
Naval Institute, 44, 100

Naval Observatory, 54, 65, 67, 158, 177
Naval Order of the United States, 76, 137
Naval Pay Officers School, 23
Naval Photographic Center, 35, 58
Naval Postgraduate School, Monterey, 8
Naval Records Collection of the Office of Naval Records and Library, 65
Naval Research Laboratory, 37, 59
Naval Reserve Officer Training Corps, *see* university or college entries
Naval Ship Research and Development Center, 89-90
Naval Surface Weapons Center, 100, 192
Naval Technical Mission to Europe, 43
Naval Transportation Service Division, Office of the Chief of Naval Operations, 40
Naval Veteran Post 76, Grand Army of the Republic, 93
Naval War College, 42, 54, 180-82
Naval War Records Office, 34
Navy and Old Army Branch, National Archives, 64
Navy Chaplains Collection, 173
Navy Civil Engineer Corps, 7
Navy Department Library, 36-37
Navy League of the U.S., Kansas, 83
Navy League of the U.S., Philadelphia, 29, 170
Navy Memorial Museum, Naval Historical Center, 37
Navy Neutrality Board, 23
Navy Registers, 36
NC-4 Flying Boats, 205
Nebraska, USS, 122
Nebraska State Historical Society, 122
Need, Harry W., 57
Neithercott, Harry A., 175
Nelson, HMS, 181
Nelson, Horatio, 3, 51, 97, 107, 115, 181
Nelson, William, 10
Nepean, Evan, 51
New American Navy (book), 144
New England Historic Genealogical Society, 110
New Hampshire Historical Society, 123
New Haven Colony Historical Society, 15
New Ironsides, USS, 161
New Jersey, Naval Reserve, 128
New Jersey Historical Society, 125
New London, Commissary for Prisoners, 30
New London, Naval Research Station, 132
New London, Naval Submarine Base, 95
New London County Historical Society, 15
New Weapons, Research, and Development Section, Commander in Chief, U.S. Fleet, 41
New York, USS (armored cruiser), 174
New York, USS (BB-34), 177
New York, Navy Enlisters at, 137
New York, Navy Units and Offices, 105
New York, Office of Audit and Control Accounts, 145
New York Historical Society, 133-38

New York Navy Yard, 97
New York Public Library, 139–42
New York Seamen's Retreat Hospital, 95
New York Shipbuilding Corporation, 173
New York State Historical Association, 142
New York State Library, 144
Newark, USS, 175
Newberry, Truman Handy, 113
Newberry Library, 77
Newcomb, Richard, 104
Newcomb, Simon, 29
Newman, Frederick Bernard, 128
Newman, L. Howard, 14
Newman, William B., 14
Newman, William D., 14
Newman Family Papers, 14
Newport, *see also* Naval War College
Newport, Naval Base, 182
Newport, Naval Station, 182
Newport, Naval Torpedo Station, 19, 178, 181
Newport, Naval Training Station, 117
Newport, Naval Underwater Systems Center, 178
Newport, Women's Officer School, 182
Newport Historical Society, 179
Niblack, Albert P., 80
Nicaragua and Isthmian Canal Commission Papers, 84
Nichols, Francis, 20
Nicholson, James, 137
Nicholson, Reginald F., 51
Nicholson, Sommerville, 51
Nicholson, Thomas A., 148
Nicholson, John B., 3
Nields, Henry C., 51
Niles, Nathan Eric, 110
Nimitz, Chester W., 43, 100, 181
Nimitz Library, U.S. Naval Academy, 98–100
Noble, James, Jr., 159
Noland, Callender St. George, 195
Noland Family, 195
Nones, Joseph B., 102
Nonsuch, Privateer, 52, 104
Norfleet, Ernest, 156
Norfleet Family Papers, 156
Norfolk, Naval Air Station, 167
Norfolk, Naval Amphibious School, 194
Norfolk Navy Yard, 167
Norfolk Public Library, 194
Norman, Naval Air Station, 163
North, James Heyward, 156
North Carolina, USS, 19, 125, 150, 156
North Carolina, Naval Militia, 152
North Carolina Battleship Commission, 151
North Carolina Department of Cultural Resources, 151–52
North Carolina Shipbuilding Collection, 150
North Pacific Exploring Expedition (1853–56), 59

Northwest African Waters, Naval Forces, 41, 44
Northwest Ohio-Great Lakes Research Center, 158
Nottingham, Wells B., 204
Nunn, Romulus A., 152
Nye, Haile C. T., 141

O

Oakland Public Library, 9
Oberlin, E. G., 57
O'Brien, Timothy J., 151
Occupation Headquarters, U.S. (World War II), 66
Ocracoke Lifesaving Station, 152
Office of the Deputy Chief of Naval Operations (Air), 22
Office of the Chief of Naval Operations, 7, 39–41, 65
Office of Naval Information, 42
Office of Naval Intelligence, 7
Office of Naval Procurement and Material, 120
Office of Naval Records and Library, 34, 37, 65
Office of Naval Research, 30, 37, 65, 78–79
Office of Public Affairs, Bureau of Medicine and Surgery, 67
Office of Scientific Research and Development, 66
Office of Territories, 2, 66
Officer Biographies Branch, Office of Naval Information, 42
Ofstie, Ralph A., 44
O'Hara, John Francis, 81
Ohio, USS, 48, 110
Ohio, Naval Brigade, 160
Ohio Historical Center, 159–60
Ohio Historical Society, 159–61
Old Dartmouth Historical Society and Whaling Museum, 110
Old Dominion University Archives, 194
Olin, John M., Library, Cornell University, 131
Oliver, Frederick L., 57
Olympia, USS, 3, 57, 164, 176
Omaha, USS, 8
Oneida, USS, 117, 156
O'Neil, Charles F., 52, 57, 160
O'Neil, John, 149
Onis, Luis de, 52
Ontario, USS, 29, 136, 188
Operational Archives, Naval Historical Center, 37–45
Operations Division, Commander in Chief, U.S. Fleet, 41
Operations Evaluation Group, 43
Oral History Office, Columbia University, 44, 131, 180
Oregon, USS, 164, 174
Oregon Historical Society, 164
Organization Research and Policy Division, Office of the Chief of Naval Operations, 40

Osborn, Joseph B., 29
Osborn, Philip R., 57
Ossipee, USS, 10
Osterhaus, Hugo, 57
Otis, Elwell Stephen, 146
Otis, Thomas, 95
Otis Collection, 131
Ottawa, USS, 137
Our Navy Photographic Collections, 100
Outerbridge, William Woodward, 83
Overbaugh, J. C., 176
Ozark, USS, 159

P

P. K. Yonge Library of Florida History, 70
Pace, John C., Library, University of West Florida, 71
Pacific Fleet, 7, 44
Pacific Scientific Information Center, Bernice P. Bishop Museum, 75
Page, Richard Lucian, 156
Page, Thomas Jefferson, 149
Palmer, George M., 175
Palmer, Nathaniel Brown, 29
Palmer, William Pendleton, 161
Palmer-Loper Papers, 29
Panama Canal, 23, 177
Panama City, Naval Coastal Systems Center, 70
Panama City, Navy Mine Countermeasures Station, 70
Panama City, Navy Mine Defense Laboratory, 70
Panay, USS, 97
Parker, Daniel, 168, 170
Parker, James, 129
Parker, James Lawrence, 137, 172
Parker, Jameson, 93
Parker, Richard Leroy, 172
Parker, William A., 10
Parkman, John Eliot, 109
Parks, Gordon, 98
Parrish, Joseph, 57, 141
Parrott, Enoch Greenleafe, 149
Parrott, John Fabyan, 123
Parsons, Lewis B., 77
Parsons, Samuel Holden, 161
Parsons, Usher, 178–79
Parsons, William S., 8, 52
Patterson, Daniel T., 52
Patterson, John E., 149
Patterson, Ralph C., 121
Patterson, Samuel D., 170
Patton, James W., 153
Patuxent, Naval Officer, 93
Paulding, Hiram, 129
Paulding, James K., 141
Paullin, Charles O., 52

Peabody, George, Department of the Enoch Pratt Free Library, 90
Peabody Museum, 110–11
Peacock, USS, 125, 137
Peale, Titian Ramsay, 29
Pearce, Cromwell, Collection, 168
Pearl, John M., 13
Peary, Robert E., 130, 132, 165
Pegram, George Braxton, 131
Pegram, John Combe, 196
Pegram, Robert Baker, 196
Pegram, Johnson, and McIntosh Family Papers, 197
Pelham, William, 52
Pence, Harry L., 11
Pendleton, Joseph H., 33
Penn, William, Memorial Museum and Archives, 172
Pennsylvania, Court of Admiralty, 170
Pennsylvania, Historical Society of, 168–71
Pennsylvania, Records of the Comptroller General, 172
Pennsylvania, Revolutionary Governments, 172
Pennsylvania Historical and Museum Commission, 172
Pennsylvania State University Libraries, 172
Pensacola, USS, 75, 135–36, 140
Pensacola, Navy Airship Pilots School, 205
Pensacola Naval Activities, 69, 71, 205
Peralte, Charlemagne Massena, 52
Percival, John, 109
Perkins, George C., 2
Perkins, George Hamilton, 52, 57, 123
Perkins, Samuel Clarke, 170
Perkins, William, Library, Duke University, 147–49
Perry, USS, 197
Perry, Arthur, 164
Perry, Matthew Calbraith, 18-19, 29, 52, 61, 99, 128, 132, 197; *see also* Japan, Expedition to
Perry, Oliver Hazard, 14, 52, 115, 128, 137, 158
Perry, Raymond H., 29
Peshine, John Henry Hobart, 3
Peterson, Oscar E., 86
Pettengill, George T., 52
Phelon, Henry A., 156
Phelps, Harry, 152
Phelps, S. Ledyard, 121
Phelps, Thomas S., 57
Phelypeaux, Jean-Frederic, 131
Philadelphia, USS, 48, 92, 132
Philadelphia, Naval Agent, 169–70
Philadelphia Federal Archives and Records Center, 167
Philadelphia Marine Hospital, 171
Philadelphia Maritime Museum, 172–73
Philadelphia Naval Home, 171
Philadelphia Navy Yard, 127, 156, 167, 170–71
Philbrick, William M. C., 14
Philip, Woodward, 97

Phillips, Dinwiddie B., 141
Phillips, James Duncan, Library, 105
Phillips, Richard H., 52
Phillips Exeter Academy Library, 124
Phoenix, Lloyd, 52, 99
Photographic Section, Naval Historical Center, 35
Pickering, Charles W., 14, 97, 165
Pickering-Beach Historical Museum, 142
Pierce, Frank H., 141
Pierpont Morgan Library, 142
Pierson, Edward A., 126
Pinkney, Ninian, 52
Piper, Richard S., 151
Pleadwell, Frank L., 68
Plymouth, USS, 104
Pocock, George, 3
Poindexter, Gale Aylett, 195
Point Barrow Refuge Station, 108
Polar and Scientific Archives, National Archives, 64, 67
Polaris Expedition, 59, 61
Polaris Missile Program, 100
Politico-Military Affairs Division, Office of the Chief of Naval Operations, 41
Pollock, Edwin T., 52
Pond, Charles F., 10
Pook Family, 52
Poole, Charles A., 14
Poor, Charles Henry, 3
Pope, John, 112
Porcher, Philip, 184
Porpoise, USS, 110, 127
Port Royal, USS, 136
Porter, USS, 136
Porter, David, 27, 52, 115, 141, 170
Porter, David Dixon, 3, 29, 52, 77, 97, 115, 132, 135, 137, 145–46, 149
Porter, Evelina Anderson, 137
Porter, William David, 104
Porter Collection, 146
Porter Family Papers, 52, 115
Portsmouth, USS, 10, 110, 124, 136
Portsmouth, N. H., Proprietors of, 27
Portsmouth, N. H., Navy Yard, 49, 87, 123–24
Portsmouth, Va., Navy Yard, *see* Norfolk Navy Yard
Post, Lauren Chester, 86
Potomac, USS, 92, 148
Potter, Woodburne, 127
Potts, Robert, 173
Powel, Mary Edith, 52
Powell, Joseph P., 121
Powhatan, USS, 93, 114, 138, 148
Prairie, USS, 175
Pratt, Enoch, Free Library, 90
Pratt, William Veazie, 44, 52, 181
Preble, Edward, 29, 87, 137, 190

Preble, George Henry, 36, 101, 109–10, 123–24
Presbyterian Historical Society, 173
President Lincoln, USS, 54, 57
Presidents, U.S., Autographs, 142–43
Preston, William Ballard, 197
Price, Rodman McCauley, 3, 10
Price, Samuel, 170
Price Family, 170
Princeton University Library, 127
Providence, Continental Ship, 116, 179
Providence, Privateer, 180
Puget, Peter, 75
Puget Sound Navy Yard, 164, 199
Puleston, William D., 44
Purcell, H. G., 57
Puryear, Bennet, Jr., 150
Putnam, Amelia Earhart, 39, 57
Putnam, Paul A., 150
Pyne, Frederick G., 57

Q

Quackenbush, John N., 137, 149–50
Queenstown Association, 57
Quinby, Austin, 111
Quinn, Clifton, 149
Quinnebaug, USS, 56
Quonset Point, Naval Air Station, 179, 181

R

Raborn, William Francis, Jr., 145
Radcliffe College, 111
Radford, William, 52
Rae, Charles W., 52
Rainbow, HMS, 104
Rambler, privateer, 180
Ramsay, Alston, 150
Ramsey, Dewitt Clinton, 44, 60
Ransom, Harry, Humanities Research Center, University of Texas, 189
Rawson, Edward K., 52
Ray, Grace E., Photographic Collection, 163
Rayner, Isidore, 156
Read, Albert C., 57
Read, George Campbell, 141, 170
Reaney, William Henry Ironsides, 81
Red Books (Maryland State Papers), 91
Red River Campaign (Civil War), 85
Redman Collection, 55
Reed and Forde Collection, 170
Reed, John, Jr., 170
Regenstein, Joseph, Library, University of Chicago, 78
Registered Publications Library, Washington, D.C., 43

Reid, George C., 33
Reid, Samuel Chester, 29
Reid, William L., 52
Reid, William Moultrie, Collection, 184
Release, USS, 28
Relief, USS, 18
Remey, Charles Mason, 82, 118, 145
Remey, George Collier, 29, 52, 82, 118, 145, 149, 170
Remey Family, 29, 82, 118
Remick Family Collection, 87
Rensselaer Polytechnic Institute, 144
Republic, USS, 136
Rescue, USS, 130
Reserve Officers Association of the United States, 82
Resolution, Maryland Navy, 90
Reuber, Johannes, 127
Revenge, USS, 14
Revenue Cutter Service, 16, 108; *see also* Coast Guard
Revolution, American, Collection, 101
Revolution, American, Generals Autographs, 142
Revolutionary War Prize Cases, 66
Reynard, Elizabeth, 111
Reynolds, Clark G., 87
Reynolds, John P., 160
Reynolds, Robert Burns, 132
Reynolds, William, 52, 167
Rhode Island, General Assembly, 180
Rhode Island, Maritime Court, 179
Rhode Island, State Archives, 180
Rhode Island Historical Society, 179-80
Rhodes, Hilary H., 149
Rice Institute, 187
Richardson, Henry A., 161
Richardson, Holden C., 52, 57
Richmond, USS, 141, 154, 161
Richmond, Naval Training School, 204
Ridenour, Louis N., 79
Ridgely, Charles G., 52
Ridgely, Frank E., 52
Rigdon, William McKinley, 121, 132
Riggs, Arthur S., 52
Riley, William E., 52
Rio Bravo, USS, 86
Rivers, L. Mendel, 183
Rives, William Cabell, 29, 195
Robbins, Thomas H., Jr., 57
Robert Hudson Tannahill Research Library, 113
Roberts, Carson Abel, 150
Roberts, Charles, Autograph Collection, 167-68
Roberts, Edmund, 29, 124
Robinson, Alexander, 115
Robinson, Arthur G., 5
Robinson, Beverley R., Naval Prints, 96
Robinson, Horatio G., 145
Robinson, Lydia S. M., 29
Robinson, Richard Hallett Meredith, 137

Rochelle, James Henry, 149
Rodgers, Christopher Raymond Perry, 137
Rodgers, John (1773–1838), 23, 52, 137
Rodgers, John (1812–1882), 52, 57, 170
Rodgers, John (1881–1926), 29
Rodgers, John Augustus, 93
Rodgers, Raymond Perry, 149
Rodgers, Robert Smith, 149
Rodgers, William L., 52
Rodgers, William T., 52
Rodgers Family, 29, 52
Rodney, George Brydges, 137
Rodney, Thomas M., 20
Roe, Francis Asbury, 52, 146
Rogers, Henry Huddleston, Ship Models, 96
Rogers, James Lloyd, 93
Rogers, Robert Lyon, 93
Roosevelt, Franklin D., 132
Roosevelt, Franklin D., Library, 132–33
Roosevelt, James, 133
Roosevelt, Theodore, 29, 107, 115, 132, 161
Roosevelt, Theodore, Jr., 160
Rootes, Thomas R., 184
Rorer, David, 82
Rosasco, William S., 69
Rose, Reed A., 204
Rosenbach Collection, 97
Rosenberg Library, 188
Rosendahl, Charles E., 189
Rosenwald, Maurice G., 6
Ross, F., 141
Ross, John, 93, 170
Rottet, Ralph K., 150
Rowan, Stephen C., 52
Royal Marines, *see* Great Britain
Royal Navy, *see* Great Britain
Ruge, Friedrich, 183
Ruhe, William James, 150
Runk, B. F. D., 195
Ruschenberger, William Samuel Waithman, 165
Russell, John H., 52
Rutgers University, 127–29
Rutherford B. Hayes Library, 160–61
Rutledge, Edward, 91
Ryan, George P., 52
Ryan, Paul B., 4
Ryder, William H., Collection, 112

S

Sackville, George, 114
Saco, Me., U.S. Marshal, 87
Safford, Laurence F., 205
St. Louis, USS, 114, 125, 132
St. Paul, USS, 137

Saipan Campaign, 177
Salisbury, Stanton Willard, 173
Salomon, Henry, Jr., 204
Salt Lake City, USS, 57
Salt Wells Pilot Plant, 8
Salter, John, 124
Saltonstall, Dudley, 15
Saltonstall, Edward Hallam, 137
Samar, USS, 57
Samoa, American, 2
San Bruno, Federal Archives and Records Center, 2
San Diego, Naval Electronics Laboratory Center, 8
San Diego, Naval Ocean Systems Center, 8
San Diego, Naval Training Center, 8
San Diego, Naval Undersea Center, 8
San Diego, Navy Personnel Research and Development Center, 9
San Francisco, U.S. Naval Office, 3
San Jacinto, USS, 76, 137
Sanders, Harry E., 58, 83
Sands, Benjamin F., 137
Sands, Joshua R., 97
Sanford, Joseph P., 76
Sanford, Naval Air Station, 72
Santa Rosa County, Fla., Naval Live Oak Reservation, 71
Santee, USS, 25
Santiago, Battle of, 141
Saratoga, USS (sloop-of-war), 136, 142
Saratoga, USS (CV-3), 58
Sargent, Nathan, 52
Saufley, R. Caswell, 156
Saufley, Salley (Rowan), 156
Saunders, Harold E., 89
Saunders, John Loyall, 29
Savannah, USS, 138
Savannah Siege (1779), 178
Savannah Squadron, Confederate States Navy, 73
Sawyer, Herbert, 141
Sawyer, Horace B., 53, 142
Sayer, Daniel, 181
Scales, Alfred Moore, 150
Scales, Archibald H., 150, 156
Scales, Dabney M., 149
Scandlin, William G., 101
Schain, Josephine, 111
Schlesinger, Arthur and Elizabeth, Library of the History of Women in America, 111
Schley, Frederick, 58
Schley, Winfield Scott, 97, 99, 132, 156
Schmidt, Harry, 6
Schoff Civil War Collection, 116
Schoonmaker, Cornelius M., 53
Schreiber, Benjamin, 10

Schriver, Albert S., 149
Schroek, Albert F., 61
Schueler, Frank E., 176
Scott, James Brown, 23
Scott, Winfield, Collection, 97
Seabees (Construction Battalions), 7
Seach, William, 177
Seattle, Naval Training Unit, 199
Seattle, Federal Archives and Records Center, 199
Secretaries of the Navy, 137, 141, 186
Secretary of Defense, Office of, 66
Security Watch Officer and Duty Officer, Office of the Chief of Naval Operations, 41
See, Thomas J. J., 29
Seitz, Frederick, 79
Selden, George L., 29
Selden, Robert R., 29
Selfridge, Thomas O., Jr., 53
Selfridge, Thomas O., Sr., 53, 58, 116
Sellers, David F., 53, 97
Semmes, Alexander A., 53, 142
Semmes, Raphael, 29, 86, 197
Senate, U.S., 65
Senate Committee Investigating the National Defense Program (Truman Committee), 121
Senate Naval Affairs Committee, 1, 2, 10, 24, 27–29, 69–70, 107, 109, 123, 127, 145, 148–49, 152, 155, 168, 172, 183–84, 195
Service Force, Atlantic Fleet, 41
Settle, Thomas, 156
Seventh Fleet, 41
Sever, James, 30
Shafroth, John Franklin, 53, 82
Shaler, Nathaniel, 170
Shaler, William, 170
Shaler Family, 170
Shankland, William F., 30
Sharp, Alexander, Jr., 58
Shaw, John, 53
Shaw, Nathaniel, 15, 17
Shaw, Nathaniel and Thomas, Letters and Papers, 15
Shaw, Thomas, 15, 30
Shaw Manuscripts (Peter Force Collection), 30
Shenandoah, CSS, 191–92
Shenandoah, USS (airship), 160
Shepard, Burritt, 129
Sherman, Forrest P., 44
Sherman, Frederic, 156
Sherman, William T., 53
Shields, William F., 119
Shilling, Charles W., 95
Ship Material Readiness Division, Office of the Chief of Naval Operations, 41
Ship Movement Report Center, Office of the Chief of Naval Operations, 41
Shipbuilding Labor Adjustment Board, 78–79

Shipbuilding Stabilization Committee, 66
Shippen, Edward, 170
Shipping Board, U.S., 60, 65, 173
Ships' History Branch, Naval Historical Center, 45
Shoemaker, Ferris, 132
Shoup, David M., 6
Shovell, Cloudisley, 3
Shovell-Rooke Papers, 3
Shubrick, Irvine, 19
Shubrick, William Branford, 137
Shufeldt, Robert Wilson, 53, 141, 165
Siboney, USS, 58
Sicard, Montgomery, 53, 58, 132
Sicilian Navy, 56
Siegmazer, William, 175
Sigsbee, Charles Dwight, 144, 179
Silver Lake, USS, 173
Silver Spring, Naval Ordnance Laboratory, 100
Silver Spring, Naval Surface Weapons Center, 100
Simmers, Clayton M., 53
Simpson, Edward, 8, 94
Simpson, John, 161
Sims, William S., 53, 58
Sipps, George N., 176
Sisson, Charles A., 119
Slack, William B., 62
Slayback, George P., Jr., 58
Sloat, John D., 2
Smith, Augustus William, 178
Smith, Daniel A., 53
Smith, Erastus Washington, 100
Smith, Frank, 131
Smith, Franklin E., 149
Smith, Holland M., 1, 33, 177
Smith, Horace J., 204
Smith, Howard, 95
Smith, James L., 77
Smith, Julian C., 33
Smith, Lloyd W., Collection, 125
Smith, P. B., 204
Smith, Ralph, 177
Smith, Richard, 90
Smith, Robert, 30, 94, 138
Smith, Roy C., 181
Smith, Samuel, 90
Smith, Stuart F., 53
Smith, Sophia, Collection, 111
Smith, Uselma C., Collection, 169
Smith, W. B., 134
Smith, William H. (CSN), 184
Smith, William H. (Acting Third Assistant Engineer), 86
Smith, William H. (enlisted, Spanish American War), 176
Smith College, 111
Smith Naval Collection, 116

Smithsonian Archives, 59
Smithsonian Institution, 59–62
Smyth, Henry, 165
Snow, Elliot, 53
Society of the Cincinnati, 63
Sofranoff, Michael, 62
Solomon Islands Campaign (1942–43), 7
Solomons Island, Md., Navy Mine Warfare Test Station, 70
Somers, Richard, 125, 138
Sonntag Family Papers, 177
Sonntag, George, 177
Sonoma, USS, 13
Sousa, John Philip, 33, 61
South Carolina, Commissioners of the Navy, 183
South Carolina Department of Archives and History, 183
South Carolina Historical Society, 183
South Caroliniana Library, University of South Carolina, 184
South Pacific, Army Command, 44
Southard, Samuel Lewis, 30, 105, 127, 141
Southerland, William H., 188
Southern Historical Collection, University of North Carolina, 153–57
Southern Rights, CSS, 116
Southwest Pacific Area (World War II), 44
Spafford, Samuel, 94
Spafford Family Papers, 94
Spalding, Lyman Greenleaf, 101, 149
Spalding Family, 101
Spanish American War Naval Veterans, 174
Sparks and Lee Collections, 107
Spears, William O., 156
Speiden, Edgar, 62
Speiden, William, 62
Speiden Family Papers, 62
Spence, Keith, 3
Spence, Robert T., 53, 93
Spence-Lowell Collection, 3
Sperry, Charles Stillman, 30, 53
Spires, James O., 176
Sproston, John Glendy, 30
Spruance, Raymond A., 6, 44, 181
Sprunt, James L., 151
Stallings, Edith Langdale, 74
Standley, William Harrison, 11, 53, 58
Stanfell, Francis, 141
Stanford, Alfred B., 83
Stanford University Libraries, 9
Stanton, Oscar F., 14
Staples, Harold H., 86
Starr, Floyd T., 170
State Historical Society of Wisconsin, 202–04
Staton, Adolphus, 156
Steamship Historical Society Library, 95

Stearns, Simeon A., 141
Steedman, Charles, 149
Steele, Guy, 94
Steele, John, 171
Steele, Thomas B., 94
Steichen, Edward J., 6, 98, 133
Stelljes, Milbern Frank, 151
Stellwagen, Daniel S., 53
Stellwagen, Henry S., 97, 173
Sterling Memorial Library, Yale University, 16–18
Stetson, William Mitchell, 144
Stevens' Battery (ironclad steamer), 142
Stevens, Henry K., 184
Stevens, Thomas Holdup (1795–1841), 53
Stevens, Thomas Holdup (1819–1896), 53, 137–38, 149, 184, 188
Stevens, Thomas Holdup (1848–1914), 53
Stevens Family, 53
Stevens Family (naval contractors), 129
Stevens Institute of Technology, 129
Stevenson, Harry C., 6
Stevenson, J. T., 151
Stewart, Charles, 53, 100, 125, 170
Stewart, Charles Samuel, 142
Stewart, David R., 53
Stewart, Joseph Lester, 1
Stiles, Ezra, 15
Still, William N., Jr., 150
Still Photo Library, Naval Photographic Center, 58
Stillman, George, 53
Stiner, William H., 138
Stinnett, Robert B., 7
Stockton, Francis Barton, 77, 129
Stockton, Gilchrist B., 7
Stockton, Robert Field, 127
Stockton Family Collection, 127
Stoddert, Benjamin, 30, 173
Stone, George, 142
Stone, Raymond, 58
Stonewall, CSS, 192
Storer, Horatio R., 181
Storer, Malcolm, Naval Medals, 96
Storrs, Henry Randolph, 130
Stowell, Ellery C., 7
Strategic Bombing Survey, U.S., 42, 66
Strategic Plans Division, Office of the Chief of Naval Operations, 40
Stratton, Richard A., 7
Strauss, Joseph, 53, 58
Strauss, Lewis L., 7
Strawberry Banke, Inc., 124
Strength Statistics and Casualty Branches, Bureau of Naval Personnel, 42
Stricker, John, 94
Strobel, Lee, 176
Strong, Augustus R., 159

Strott, G. G., 151
Stryker, Joe W., 150–51
Stuart, Gilbert, 96
Submarine Force Library and Museum, 15
Submarine Patrol Reports, Word War II, 16, 39
Submarine Squadron Fifty, 44
Submarine Warfare Division, Office of the Chief of Naval Operations, 41
Submarines, Pacific Fleet, 44
Submarines, Seventh Fleet, 41
Sugg, H. A. I., 150
Sullivan, John L., 121
Sully, Thomas, 96
Sumner, George W., 58
Supreme Court, U.S., 66
Susquehanna, USS, 53
Sutton, John, 166
Suzzallo, Henry, 199
Suzzallo Library, University of Washington, 199
Swanson, Claude Augustus, 149, 195
Swem, Earl Gregg, Library, College of William and Mary, 191
Swift Papers, 145
Symington, Powers, 53
Syracuse University, 145

T

Tagus, HMS, 141
Tait, Charles, 1
Talbot, Paul H., 7
Talbot, Silas, 14, 180
Talcott, Andrew, 197
Tannahill, Robert Hudson, Research Library, 113
Tarbell, John F., 53
Task Force 122 (Normandy Landings), 44
Taussig, Edward D., 53
Taussig, Joseph K., 53
Taylor, David W., Naval Ship Research and Development Center, 89–90
Taylor, George William, 116
Taylor, Henry C., 53
Taylor, Ignatius, 90
Taylor, John, 94
Taylor, Montgomery M., 53
Taylor, Robert, 94
Taylor, William V., 179
Tecumseh, USS, 62
Tennessee, CSS, 191
Tennessee State Library and Archives, 185
Tenth Fleet, 41
Terret, Colville, 53
Texas Navy, 179, 188–89
Texas State Library, 188–89
Thatcher, Henry Knox, 53, 145–46
Thayer Papers, 145

Theaters of War, U.S., (World War II), 66
Theobald, Robert A., 7
Third Amphibious Force, 44
Third Fleet, 44
Thomas, Charles M., 53, 58
Thomas, Gardner, 53
Thomas, Lewin W., 58
Thomason, John William, Jr., 189
Thompson, Charles C. B., 30, 81
Thompson, Charles P., 181
Thompson, Richard Wigginton, 80–81, 138, 160–61
Thompson, Smith, 138
Thorne, Herman, 30
Thornton, Thomas Gilbert, 87
Ticknor, Benajah, 17
Tillman, Benjamin Ryan, 183–84
Tilton, McLane, 33
Tingey, Thomas, 53
Titus, Robert, 204
Titus, William O., 204
Tod, John Grant, 188–89
Tolley, Kemp, 94, 151
Tomb, James H., 156
Tomb, William V., 156
Tonawanda, USS, 204
Top Secret Control Office, Commander in Chief, U.S. Fleet, 41
Top Secret Control Office, Office of the Chief of Naval Operations, 41
Toucey, Isaac, 13
Townsend, Robert, 15
Tracy, Benjamin Franklin, 30
Training Division, U.S. Navy, 7
Trammell, Park, 69–70
Transit of Venus Expedition, 67
Trenholm Family Papers, 156
Trenholme, William M., 121
Trenton, USS, 104
Trevett, Samuel Russel, Jr., 30
Trinity College, 16
Tripoli, U.S. Consul, 99
Tripolitan War Collection, 101
Trotter, Thomas K., 181
True, Rowland S., 173
Truman, Harry S., Library, 120–21
Trumbull, Continental Ship, 15
Truxtun-Decatur Naval Museum, 46
Truxtun, Thomas, 3, 30, 54, 97, 171
Tuber, John W., 151
Tucker, USS, 16
Tucker, Samuel, 30, 107
Tucker-Coleman Papers, 191
Tufts College Library, 112
Tulane University, 85
Turk, William, 126
Turner, John H., 151

Turner, Peter, 162
Turner, Richmond Kelly, 44
Turner, Thomas, 54, 138, 140, 142
Tuscarora, USS, 188
Tuve, Merle, 30
Twiggs, Levi, 33
Twining, Nathan Crook, 204
Tyler, USS, 159
Tyler Papers, 191

U

Ullman, Edward L., 199
Ultor, Privateer, 94
Underwood, Joseph A., 16
United States, USS, 104, 110, 169, 173
United States Army, *see* Army, War Department, Military Academy entries
United States Coast Guard, *see* Coast Guard
United States Exploring Expedition (Wilkes Expedition), 16, 18, 29, 59, 62, 92, 108, 128, 144, 165, 167; *see also* Wilkes, Charles
United States Fleet, Commander in Chief, 41, 44
United States Marine Corps, *see* Marine Corps
United States Navy and Naval, *see* Navy, Naval, and place name entries
University of Baltimore Library, 95
University of California, Berkeley, 9
University of California, Los Angeles, 10
University of California, San Diego, 11
University of Chicago, 78
University of Florida, 70
University of Georgia, 74
University of Hawaii, 75
University of Illinois, Naval Reserve Officers Training School, 79
University of Illinois, Navy Diesel School, 79
University of Illinois, Navy Signal School, 79
University of Illinois, V-12 School, 79
University of Illinois at Urbana-Champaign, 79
University of Maine, 87
University of Michigan, 113–16
University of Missouri, 121
University of Missouri, Naval Diesel Training School, 121
University of Missouri, Naval Reserve Officers Training Corps, 121
University of North Carolina, 153–57
University of Notre Dame, 81
University of Oklahoma, 163
University of Oregon, 164
University of Pittsburgh, 177
University of Rochester, 146
University of the South, 186
University of South Carolina, 184
University of Southern California, Los Angeles, 11

University of the State of New York, 144
University of Texas at Austin, 188–89
University of Texas at Dallas, 189
University of Vermont, 190
University of Virginia, 194–95
University of Washington, 199
University of Washington, Naval Training Unit, 199
University of West Florida, 71
University of Wyoming, 99, 205
Upham, Oscar C., 33
Upshur, Abel P., 141, 191
Upshur, William Peterkin, 156
Usher, Nathaniel R., 80
Utley, Harold H., 33

V

V-12 School, 79
Vallejo Naval and Historic Museum, 11
Van Benthuysen, Alfred C., 85
Van Buskirk, Philip C., 199
Van Cleaf, William W., 129
Vandalia, USS, 142
Van Duzer, George, 138
Van Duzer, John B., 138
Van Gieson, Ransford E., 30
Van Hook, Clifford E., 7
Van Keuren, Alexander H., 7
Van Metre, T. J., 151
Van Noppen, Leonard Charles, 156
Vauclain, James L., 173
Vera Cruz, Mexico, 148
Vernon, Edward, 30
Vernon, William, 179
Vicksburg, USS, 80
Victory, HMS, 107
Victory, USS, 203
Victory At Sea (motion picture), 204
Viking, USS, 138
Vincennes, USS, 16, 18, 48, 95, 104–05, 110, 136, 142, 197
Vining, R. E., 7
Virginia, CSS, 128, 148; see also *Merrimack*, USS
Virginia Historical Society, 195–96
Virginia State Library, 197
Vogel, Clayton B., 33
Voorhees, Charles H., 128
Voorhees, George V. W., 127
Vroom, Guysbert B., 54
VT Fuze, 30, 43, 89

W

Wabash, USS, 138

Waddell, James Iredell, 100, 152
Wadsworth, Alexander, 87
Wadsworth, Henry, 87, 108
Wager, Charles, 30
Wagner, Frank D., 60
Wainwright, Richard (1817–62), 54
Wainwright, Richard (1849–1926), 54, 58
Wainwright, William, 14
Wainwright Family, 54
Walker, John Grimes, 54, 84, 97
Walker, Richard C., 151
Wallace-Dickey Papers, 77
Walker, William M., 20
Waller, Littleton W. T., 33
Wallin, Homer N., 44
Walsh, David I., 107, 109
Walsh, John Henry, 200
Wanamaker, John, 171
War Crimes Records, World War II, 66
War Department Collection, 65
War Diaries of Naval Commands (World War II), 39
War of 1812 Collection, 94, 116
War Plans Division, Office of the Chief of Naval Operations, 40
War Shipping Administration, 66
Ward, A. G., 151
Ward Family Papers, 105
Ware, Catherine Ann, 86
Ware, Eleanor Percy, 86
Warminster, Air Material Center, 171
Warminster, Naval Air Development Center, 171
Warminster, Naval Air Modification Unit, 171
Warner, Andrew, 138
Warner and Swasey Company, 158
Warren, Continental Ship, 179
Warren, USS, 125, 127, 129
Warren, Peter, 116, 138
Warren, Robert H., 182
Warren, R. I., 137
Washington, USS, 14, 91, 126
Washington, George, 91, 97, 102
Washington Conference on Arms Limitation (1921–22), 190
Washington National Records Center, Suitland, 31, 59, 64
Washington Navy Yard, 89, 93, 100, 142
Washington State University, 199
Washington's Headquarters State Historic Site, 146
Wasp, USS, 27
Water Witch, USS, 58
Waterman, Alan T., 30
Waterman, George, 95
Waterman, Zuriel, 95, 180
Waters, Joseph, 111
Watkins, William A., 151
Watmough, James H., 10

Watmough, Pendleton G., 58
Watson, Adolph Eugene, 23
Watson, Adolphus E., 58
Watson, John C., 54
WAVES, 100, 111, 204
Weakley, Charles E., 7
Weaver, Aaron Ward, 142
Weaver, William H., 138
Webb, G. Creighton, 138
Webster, Harrie, 54
Wederstrandt, P. C., 29
Weems, Philip Van Horn, 62, 185
Weems System of Navigation, 185
Welch, George E., 100
Welles, Gideon, 4, 11, 13, 30, 56, 77, 86, 121, 142, 173, 197
Welles, Roger, 54
Wells, Tom Henderson, 54
Welsh, Charles W., 152
Welsh, George P., 54
Welsh, George S., 54, 58
Wensinger, Walter W., 33
West Elasco, USS, 164
West Virginia University, 201
Western Naval Task Force, Normandy Landings, 44
Western Reserve Historical Society, 161–62
Weston, Edward, 98
Whaling and Marine Manuscript Archives, 108
Wharton-Willing Collection, 171
Wheeler, William K., 138
Whipple, Abraham, 116, 180
Whipple, James Aldrich, 116
Whipple, William, 91
Whistler, Charles W., 58
White, Beverly W., 151
White, G. W. Blunt, Library, 14
White, John, 204
White, John M. Butler, 161
White, Kenneth, 204
White Fleet, *see* Great White Fleet
White Oak Laboratory, Naval Surface Weapons Center, 100
Whiting, Charles J., 7
Whiting, William H., 54
Whitney, William, 30
Whittaker, James, 173
Whittle, John S., 195
Whittle, Lewis Neale, 156
Whittle, William Conway, 156, 194–95
Whittle Family Papers, 191, 195
Wholesaler of Naval Stores, 129
Wichita State University, 84
Wichman, Frederick W., 164
Wieser, Paul A., 151
Wilbur, Curtis Dwight, 9, 30
Wilkes, Charles, 30, 59, 83, 106, 142, 165, 204; *see also* United States Exploring Expedition

Wilkes, John, 83
Wilkinson, Robert, 129
Wilkinson, Theodore S., 54, 58
William L. Clements Library, University of Michigan, 16, 113–16
William and Mary, College of, 191
William Penn, SS, 171
William Penn Memorial Museum and Archives, 172
William Perkins Library, Duke University, 147–49
Williams, Charles E., 54
Williams, Henry, 54, 176
Williams, Otho Holland, 94
Williams, S. C., Library, Stevens Institute of Technology, 129
Williams, Samuel May, 188
Williams, Samuel Wells, 18
Williams Family, 18
Williamson, Thom, 194
Willink, Henry Frederick, 73
Willis, Frank B., 160
Wilson, Eugene E., 182
Wilson, George G., 182
Wilson, John, 10
Wilson, John C., 54
Wilson, Samuel L., 54
Winder Family Papers, 92
Winnipec, USS, 56
Winona, USS, 118
Winslow, Cameron McRae, 138, 182
Winslow, Francis, 54, 58
Winslow, John Ancrum, 54, 138
Winston, George Tayloe, 157
Winston, Hollis T., 157
Winston, Robert Watson, 153
Winterthur Museum, 20
Winthrop, Privateer, 104
Wirt Family Papers, 157
Wirtz, John B., 11
Wisconsin State Historical Society, 202–03
Wise, Henry A., 30
Wise, Henry Alexander, 105, 157, 197
Wise, Henry Augustus, 54, 77, 138
Wise, John Cropper, 197
Wister, Owen J., 171
Wister Family Collection, 171
Wizard, USS, 129
Women, Assistant Chief of Staff for, Bureau of Naval Personnel, 42
Women Accepted for Volunteer Emergency Service, *see* WAVES
Women Officers School, Newport, 182
Wood, Chester C., 182
Wood, John Taylor, 157
Wood, Spencer S., 45
Wood, Thomas Newton, 54
Wood, William M., 10
Wood, William W., 54

Wood Family, 54
Woodbury, Levi, 30, 123–24, 141
Woodhouse, Samuel, 100, 171
Woodhouse, Samuel W., Collection, 168
Woodhouse Family, 171
Woods, George W., 199
Woods, Louis E., 33
Woodward, Clark Howell, 30
Woodworth, Selim Edwin, 4, 54
Woolsey, Melancthon Brooks, 113
Woolsey, Melancthon Taylor, 113
Worden, John L., 54, 185
Workman, Robert Dubois, 173
World Cruise of American Fleet (1907–09), see Great White Fleet
World War I Naval Veterans, 176
World War II Battle Evaluation Group, Naval War College, 42
World War II Letters Collection, 121
Wormeley, Ralph Randolph, 109
Wotherspoon, Alexander S., 31, 177
Wotherspoon Family Papers, 31, 177
Woyshner, Paul, 33
Wright, Theodore P., 205
Wyckoff, Ambrose B., 199
Wyckoff, Edward Guild, 132
Wyoming, USS, 197

Y

Yale University, 16–18
Yale University, Aviation Unit, 16
Yale University, Cross Cultural Survey, 7
Yale University, Naval Reserve Officers Training Corps, 102
Yancy, Benjamin Cudworth, 157
Yancey, Charles K., 97
Yankee, Privateer, 179, 182
Yankee, USS, 140
Yankee Lass, Privateer, 179
Yantic, USS, 47
Yard, Edward M., 54
Yarnell, Harry E., 31, 44
Yeatman, Phillip W., 45
Yeatman, Thomas Henry, 159
Yonge, P. K., Library of Florida History, 70–71
Yonge Family Papers, 71
Yorke, Joseph, 144
Yorktown, USS, 174
Yorktown Siege (1781), 144
Yosemite, USS, 101, 116
Youd Papers, 71
Young, Golson C., 176
Yulee, David Levy, 71

Z

Zabriskie, Christian A., Collection, 97–98
Zavala, Texas Navy, 189
Zebulon B. Vance, SS, 150
Zederman, George, 176

www.ingramcontent.com/pod-product-compliance
Lightning Source LLC
Chambersburg PA
CBHW082115230426
43671CB00015B/2706